THE ELEMENTS OF MORAL PHILOSOPHY

NATURAL LAW AND
ENLIGHTENMENT CLASSICS

Knud Haakonssen
General Editor

Front view of old Marischal College

NATURAL LAW AND
ENLIGHTENMENT CLASSICS

The Elements of Moral
Philosophy, in Three Books

with
A Brief Account of the Nature,
Progress, and Origin of Philosophy

David Fordyce

Edited and with an Introduction by
Thomas Kennedy

LIBERTY FUND
Indianapolis

This book is published by Liberty Fund, Inc., a foundation established to encourage study of the ideal of a society of free and responsible individuals.

𒀀𒆪 𒂼𒄄

The cuneiform inscription that serves as our logo and as the design motif for our endpapers is the earliest-known written appearance of the word "freedom" (*amagi*), or "liberty." It is taken from a clay document written about 2300 B.C. in the Sumerian city-state of Lagash.

07 06 05 04 03 C 5 4 3 2 1
07 06 05 04 03 P 5 4 3 2 1

Library of Congress Cataloging-in-Publication Data
Fordyce, David, 1711–1751.
The elements of moral philosophy in three books with a brief account
of the nature, progress, and origin of philosophy/David Fordyce;
edited with an introduction by Thomas Kennedy.
p.   cm. — (Natural law and enlightenment classics)
Includes bibliographical references and index.
ISBN 0-86597-389-X (alk. paper) — ISBN 0-86597-390-3 (pbk.: alk. paper)
1. Ethics.   2. Duty.   3. Conduct of life.   4. Philosophy—History.
I. Kennedy, Thomas D., 1955–
II. Title.   III. Series.

B1373.F673   E55   2003

170—dc21   2002034133

LIBERTY FUND, INC.
8335 Allison Pointe Trail, Suite 300
Indianapolis, Indiana 46250-1684

CONTENTS

THE ELEMENTS OF MORAL PHILOSOPHY

INTRODUCTION

David Fordyce stands among the foremost of those philosophers who achieve a not always deserved resting place in darkest obscurity despite having been influential and highly regarded shortly after their deaths. Indeed, Benjamin Franklin's proclivity to attribute Fordyce's works to Francis Hutcheson[1] may be said to have foreshadowed Fordyce's historical fate of being dismissed as a lesser Francis Hutcheson. Despite his confusion, Franklin thought highly of Fordyce's works, purchasing the second volume of Fordyce's anonymously authored *Dialogues Concerning Education* (London, 1745 and 1748) soon after it became available, and identifying the *Dialogues* as among the works most influential upon his own *Proposals Relating to the Education of Youth in Pennsilvania* (October 1749).

Franklin was by no means alone among Americans in his admiration for Fordyce's thought. Dr. Samuel Johnson, President of King's College (now Columbia University), was likewise impressed.[2] Nor was it only the earlier work of Fordyce that received high praise. Fordyce's *The Elements of Moral Philosophy* circulated widely as a unit of Robert Dods-

1. Franklin, in a letter to William Smith, 3 May 1753, *Papers of Benjamin Franklin*, ed. L. W. Labaree (New Haven, Conn.: Yale University Press, 1961), vol. 4, 79, cited in Peter Jones, "The Polite Academy and the Presbyterians, 1720–1770," in J. Dwyer et al., eds., *New Perspectives on the Politics and Culture of Early Modern Scotland* (Edinburgh: John Donald, 1982), 177.

2. Peter Jones quotes Johnson as describing the *Dialogues* as "the prettyest thing in its kind, and the best System both in physical, metaphysical and moral philosophy as well as the conduct of life that I have seen." Ibid., 167.

ley's *The Preceptor* (London, 1748)[3] both in Britain and in America. Soon after its separate publication, Fordyce's *The Elements of Moral Philosophy* (London, 1754) was introduced into the curriculum of the American universities, where it became a standard text at Harvard University and one of the most widely used texts in American universities in the second half of the eighteenth century.[4] *The Elements of Moral Philosophy* was successful not only in America but in Europe as well. Within three years of its publication, it had been translated into French and German, and only six years after his death Fordyce was described in Germany as a "celebrated" author.[5] Fordyce's celebrity status, however quickly achieved, was likewise quickly lost.

David Fordyce was born at Broadford, near Aberdeen, Scotland, in 1711, the second son of George Fordyce, a frequent provost of Aberdeen, and Elizabeth Brown Fordyce. David Fordyce was one of their twenty children, among whom were the touted pulpiteer, James (famously attacked by Mary Wollstonecraft in *A Vindication of the Rights of Women*), the highly esteemed physician, William, and the infamous rogue banker, Alexander. Elizabeth Fordyce was a relative, probably the niece, of Thomas Blackwell, the elder, minister and principal of Marischal College, Aberdeen. Blackwell left his church in Paisley in 1700 to pastor a congregation in Aberdeen. In 1711 he was selected for the chair of divinity at Marischal College. Following a purge of Jacobite sympathizers on the faculty in 1717, Blackwell became principal of the college as well, a position he held from 1717 to 1728, during which time David Fordyce was himself a student at Marischal.

David Fordyce entered Marischal College in 1724 and received his

---

3. Dale Randall discusses the reception of *The Preceptor* at Rutgers University in "Dodsley's Preceptor—A Window into the Eighteenth Century," *Journal of the Rutgers University Library* 22 (December 1958): 10–22.

4. See Norman Fiering, *Moral Philosophy at Seventeenth-Century Harvard* (Chapel Hill, N.C.: University of North Carolina Press, 1981), 51; and David W. Robson, *Educating Republicans: The College in the Era of the American Revolution 1750–1800* (Westport, Conn.: Greenwood Press, 1985).

5. T. E. Jessop, *A Bibliography of David Hume and of Scottish Philosophy from Francis Hutcheson to Lord Balfour* (New York: Russell & Russell, 1966), viii.

master of arts degree in 1728, after which he studied divinity with James Chalmers, who had succeeded Blackwell in the chair of divinity. Fordyce was then licensed to preach; however, he was unable to secure a patron and thus received no call to serve a congregation, a lifelong disappointment for him. The next several years of his life are something of a mystery. His father died in 1733, and Fordyce was then home for a time to comfort his mother.[6]

In the mid-1730s David Fordyce spent some time in Glasgow, where he heard Francis Hutcheson lecture and where he developed a friendship with William Craig, then a student at Glasgow University and later a Moderate minister of the Wynd Church, Glasgow. Back in Aberdeen, and writing to Craig in August of 1735 from his mother's home in Eggie, Fordyce complained of intellectual loneliness: "I have none here with whom I can enter into the Depths of Philosophy or from whom by a friendly Communication of Sentiments I can receive or strike out new Lights."[7] But if stimulating conversation was not to be had in Aberdeen, he could at least engage Craig in the philosophical dialogue he was missing. Thus, Fordyce suggested to Craig that his mentor, Francis Hutcheson, had failed to attend sufficiently to "the Authority and Dignity of Conscience," a far greater defect of Hutcheson's moral theory than of the theory of Lord Shaftesbury, Fordyce argued. Their philosophical "conversations" continued at least another four months, with Fordyce writing a lengthy missive to Craig in December of 1735 objecting that Craig overplayed the role of benevolence and un-

6. The most detailed information available about David Fordyce's life appears in Alexander Chalmers, *The General Biographical Dictionary containing an historical and critical account of the lives and writings of the most eminent persons in every nation, particularly the British and Irish, from the earliest accounts to the present time,* new edition, revised and enlarged (London: J. Nichols & Son, 1812–17), vol. 14, 468–70. Chalmers professes to be drawing upon material from a sixth and unpublished volume of Andrew Kippis's *Biographia Britannica* (London: C. Bathurst, 1778–93).

7. David Fordyce to William Craig, 24 August 1735, National Library of Scotland, MS 584, 971. To say that there were none in Aberdeen with whom he might have entered into the "depths of philosophy" was clearly a mistake. Thomas Reid, one year older than Fordyce, was at the time of this letter the librarian at Marischal College.

derplayed "other Principles in our Nature which must be taken into our account of moral Approbation," for example, trust, gratitude, and piety, traits of character themselves worthy of respect, independent of their relation to benevolence.[8]

By the late 1730s Fordyce had established connections with Philip Doddridge, preacher and master of the dissenting academy at Northampton, England, and John Aiken, Doddridge's young protégé. Aiken, Doddridge's first student in his academy at Kibworth, had received his master of arts degree from King's College, Aberdeen, in 1737 and then moved to Northampton to assist Doddridge. Doddridge himself had been awarded the doctor of divinity degree from the Aberdeen colleges in 1736, so by the mid-1730s there was a warm relationship between Doddridge and the English dissenters and the Aberdeen colleges. Fordyce was a welcome visitor to Doddridge's community.

It is unclear how much time Fordyce spent with Doddridge in Northampton, but Fordyce did visit him and observe his teaching and the workings of the academy in Northampton during a sojourn in England in the mid- to late 1730s. Philip Doddridge was impressed with and supportive of Fordyce, in a letter describing him as "an excellent Scholar" and professing that he had never met a young person who had made "deeper and juster Reflections of Human Nature."[9] He made generous introductions of Fordyce to his friends in London, including the Anglican cleric William Warburton, whose first volume of *The Divine Legation of Moses* (London, 1738) had recently been published, and the nonconformist minister at St. Albans, the Reverend Samuel Clark. Warburton was initially quite taken with Fordyce, assuring Doddridge, "Young Fordyce has great merit, and will make a figure in the world, & do honor to Professor Blackwell, whom I have a great esteem for."[10] However, Warburton, never the easiest of men to get along with,

8. David Fordyce to William Craig, 23 December 1735, National Library of Scotland, MS 2670, f. 158.

9. Philip Doddridge to Samuel Clark, 27 February 1738, Dr. Williams' Library, LNC MS L1/10/47.

10. William Warburton to Philip Doddridge, 12 February 1738, Dr. Williams' Library, LW MS 24.180.

was later to complain to Doddridge that he had been abused by Fordyce, after which Doddridge quickly intervened to allay the ill will that
had arisen between the two.[11] The young Fordyce enjoyed his time in
London, listening to the debates in Parliament and mixing with the
coffee-shop society.

As a result of Doddridge's influence, Fordyce served from September
of 1738 to November of 1739 as something of an interim minister at
Newport Pagnell, Buckinghamshire, after which he became the private
tutor and chaplain for the family of John Hopkins of Bretons, near
Romford, Essex. Fordyce lived with the Hopkins family for about a
year and a half.

The spring of 1741 brought another change of circumstances for Fordyce. Leaving his position with the Hopkins family, he traveled to
France, returning to Scotland at the end of June for rambles in the
south and north of his homeland. By early fall of 1741 he was in place
as an assistant minister to George Wishart at the Tron Kirk, High
Street, Edinburgh, and was pleased with his place. Fordyce assessed
Wishart, brother of the principal of the University of Edinburgh, William Wishart, as "one of the most eloquent preachers and worthiest
men we have in this country."[12] This position, too, lasted for little more
than a season. In June of 1742 Fordyce returned to Aberdeen, and in
September of that year he took up his position as regent at Marischal
College.

At Marischal College Fordyce had the usual duties of a regent; during the 1742/43 school year, his responsibilities were for the tertians, or
third-year students, with lectures on natural philosophy. Fordyce saw
this group of students through their final year, 1743/44, with lectures on
moral philosophy. His complete rotation with a class of students began
in the 1744/45 school year with the semis, or second-year students,

---

11. Geoffrey F. Nuttall, *The Calendar and Correspondence of Philip Doddridge, DD
(1702–1751)*, Historical Manuscripts Commission, Joint Publications Series 26 (London: Her Majesty's Stationery Office, 1979), 615–16.

12. David Fordyce to Philip Doddridge, 22 August 1741, Dr. Williams' Library,
London, LNC MS L1/5/170.

when he lectured on civil and natural history. This class he would see through their final three years of education at Marischal.

Fordyce did not find his teaching labors light or entirely to his liking. In June of 1743 he wrote to Doddridge, reaffirming his desire to serve as minister and commenting on his duties as regent:

> I wish the Business was confined as you seem to think it is to the teaching of moral philosophy; since that Province would sute my Taste most; but the Professors of Philosophy in our University have a larger sphere assigned them, being obliged to go the Round of all the Sciences, Logics, Metaphysics, Pneumatics, Ethics strictly so called & the Principles of the Law of Nature and Nations with natural and experimental Philosophy which last is to be my task next Winter. I had last winter besides my public class a private one to which I read Lectures on Morals, Politics & History upon that Plan of which I showed you a small Part when in England. I believe I shall have a great deal of Pleasure in inspiring the minds of the Youth with just & manly Principles of Religion & Virtue, & doubt not but I shall reap Advantage myself by the practice of Teaching.[13]

Fordyce remained at Marischal as a regent until his death in September of 1751. In 1750 he had secured a leave of absence from the college in order to travel in France, Italy, and other parts of Europe. In February of 1751 he wrote playfully to his mother that he had been enjoying Carnival and while in Rome had seen the Pretender as well as the Pope, although he had not yet had the opportunity to kiss the Pope's hand. He closed his letter, "Pray keep warm, drink heartily & keep merry till I come home & we shall laugh till our sides crack."[14] But that reunion was not to be. In September of 1751 Fordyce set sail from Amsterdam on his voyage home aboard the *Hopewell* of Leith. When a storm overtook the ship, David Fordyce was one of the passengers lost at sea.

Fordyce's eight years as a regent at Marischal were prosperous, at

---

13. David Fordyce to Philip Doddridge, 6 June 1743, Dr. Williams' Library, London, LNC MS L1/5/171.

14. David Fordyce to Elizabeth Fordyce, 16 February 1750/51, National Library of Scotland, Edinburgh, NLS MS 1707, f. 33.

least in literary terms. The first volume of his *Dialogues Concerning Education,* anonymously authored, was published in London in 1745. A second volume, also anonymous, followed in 1748. Fordyce had begun work on the *Dialogues* perhaps as early as 1739. In October of that year he sent to Doddridge an "essay on Human Nature," of which he said:

> I believe you will find some of the passions considered in a light that is not quite so common, & connexions in human nature seized that I have not seen traced elsewhere; some difficulties attempted to be explained that have not before been, as I know of, at all considered, an endeavour to distinguish some powers of the mind that have been confounded, & to explain some beautiful allegories and maxims of antiquity particularly the grand rule of the heathen moralists, that of living according to Nature. It was the work of some years; therefore you may expect a difference in the style & compositions, several repetitions, a deal of rubbish, an intolerable luxury of fancy & language.[15]

Fordyce went on to suggest that he could probably reduce the essay by as much as one-third, an assessment with which many readers of the *Dialogues* would have no quarrel.

With the success of the first volume of his *Dialogues Concerning Education,* Fordyce made ready his second volume. About this same time, the London poet and bookseller Robert Dodsley, sensing a need for a text that would equip young men to ably and virtuously fulfill the duties of their respective "stations of life," began collecting material for a new textbook, *The Preceptor.* Perhaps due to the success in England of Fordyce's own *Dialogues,* Dodsley contracted with Fordyce to write the essay on moral philosophy for his textbook. Fordyce presented Dodsley with "The Elements of Moral Philosophy," which was published as section 9 of *The Preceptor.*

The Preceptor met with great success, for Dodsley had secured tal-

---

15. David Fordyce to Philip Doddridge, 3 October 1739, Dr. Williams' Library, London, MS L1/5/167.

ented authors for his project, including Dr. Samuel Johnson.[16] One of those impressed by Dodsley's *Preceptor* was William Smellie, editor and compiler of the first edition of the *Encyclopaedia Britannica* (Edinburgh, 1771), who used a generous selection of Fordyce's *Preceptor* work on moral philosophy as the article "Moral philosophy, or Morals" for the encyclopedia. Fordyce's essay remained a major entry in the encyclopedia well into the nineteenth century.

Smellie's judgment of the value of Fordyce's essay was anticipated shortly after its publication by a review of the *Elements* in the *Monthly Review* of May 1754. There, William Rose described the essay as "the most entertaining and useful compendium of moral philosophy in our own, or perhaps in any other, language."[17]

Fordyce's *The Elements of Moral Philosophy* was thus available in three forms in the third quarter of the eighteenth century—as section 9 of Dodsley's *Preceptor,* as a treatise published posthumously by Robert and John Dodsley in 1754, and as an article in the *Encyclopaedia Britannica.* Few essays of eighteenth-century moral philosophy can be said to have circulated so widely.

Several other works written by Fordyce were published posthumously, chief among them his *Theodorus: A Dialogue Concerning the Art of Preaching* (London, 1752) and *The Temple of Virtue* (London, 1757), both edited by his brother James.

---

16. In his *Life of Samuel Johnson, LL.D.,* James Boswell wrote of *The Preceptor:*

Mr. Dodsley this year brought out his PRECEPTOR, one of the most valuable books for the improvement of young minds that has appeared in any language; and to this meritorious work Johnson furnished "The Preface," containing a general sketch of the book, with a short and perspicuous recommendation of each article; as also, "The Vision of Theodore, the Hermit, found in his Cell," a most beautiful allegory of human life, under the figure of ascending the mountain of Existence. The Bishop of Dromore heard Dr. Johnson say, that he thought this was the best thing he ever wrote. (*Boswell's Life of Johnson,* 2 vols. [New York: Oxford University Press, 1933], vol. 1, 129).

17. William Rose in *Monthly Review* 10 (May 1754): 394.

Note on the Texts

This edition of *The Elements of Moral Philosophy* is based on the 1754 edition of Robert and John Dodsley, the first publication of *The Elements* as an independent work. Few alterations have been made to the text and those only to correct printer's errors. In addition, notes have been added to clarify Fordyce's references. Fordyce followed the not uncommon eighteenth-century practice of providing emphasis by placing material in quotation marks; we have not altered that practice.

We also include *A brief Account of the Nature, Progress, and Origin of Philosophy delivered by the late Mr. David Fordyce, P. P. Marish. Col: Ab^{dn} to his Scholars, before they begun their Philosophical course. Anno 1743/4* with *A Few advices of the late M^r Da. Fordyce to his Scholars at the end of the Session Concerning Reading,* available here in print for the first time. This manuscript is held by the Aberdeen University Library, MS.M 184, fol. 28, and is likely the prolegomenon to the lectures on moral philosophy that Fordyce delivered to his magistrands, or senior students, during the 1743/44 school year. Minor changes have been made in the text in order to facilitate comprehensibility. Most frequently these changes consist of the removal of commas or the addition of some other punctuation. More significant interventions in the text are indicated by angle brackets, i.e., ⟨ ⟩. Notes of correction and amplification have been added to both texts as well, identifying the sources upon which Fordyce drew and the figures he esteemed most highly. Fordyce's own notes, as in the original, are indicated by the symbols * and †. The editor's annotations of Fordyce's notes appear in square brackets, i.e., [ ].

Thomas Kennedy

ACKNOWLEDGMENTS

Many are the debts I have incurred over my years of working on David Fordyce; only a few of those debts can here be acknowledged. The Eighteenth-Century Scottish Studies Society and Richard B. Sher have provided genial and encouraging venues for my explorations. Norman Fiering, who initially sparked my interest in Fordyce, assisted me on this project with some difficult references, as did Edward V. George. Gilbert Meilaender puzzled with me over Fordyce's handwriting, as well as some Greek and Latin phrases.

Above all, I am grateful for the interest that M. A. Stewart has shown in my work on Fordyce, and the errors from which he has rescued me, and to the general editor of this series, Knud Haakonssen, whose vast knowledge is equaled by his attentiveness and generosity.

Finally, appreciation is extended to Colin A. McLaren, former head of Special Collections at the Aberdeen University Library, who first guided my examination of manuscripts in Aberdeen, and to the University of Aberdeen for permission to print the Fordyce manuscript in this volume.

THE
ELEMENTS
OF
Moral Philosophy

IN THREE BOOKS

1. Of Man, and his Connexions. Of Duty or Moral Obligation—Various Hypotheses—Final Causes of our Moral Faculties of Perception and Affection.

2. The principal Distinction of Duty or Virtue. Man's Duties to
Himself—To Society—To God.

3. Of Practical Ethics, or the Culture of the Mind. Motives to
Virtue from Personal Happiness—From the Being and Providence of God—From the Immortality of the Soul.

The Result, or Conclusion.

By the late Rev. Mr. D A V I D   F O R D Y C E

Professor of Moral Philosophy, and Author of the
Art of Preaching, *inscribed to his Grace*
the Archbishop of CANTERBURY

L O N D O N:

Printed for R. and J. DODSLEY in *Pallmall*
MDCCLIV

I

Book I

[Μ]άλιστα ἐπιμελητέον ὅπως ἕκαστος ἡμῶν τῶν ἄλλων μα-
θημάτων ἀμελήσας τούτου τοῦ μαθήματος καὶ ζητητὴς καὶ
μαθητὴς ἔσται, ἐάν ποθεν οἷός τ᾽ ᾖ μαθεῖν καὶ ἐξευρεῖν, τίς
αὐτὸν ποιήσει δυνατὸν καὶ ἐπιστήμονα, βίον καὶ χρηστὸν
καὶ πονηρὸν διαγιγνώσκοντα, τὸν βελτίω ἐκ τῶν δυνατῶν
ἀεὶ πανταχοῦ αἱρεῖσθαι, [καὶ] ἀναλογιζόμενον πάντα τὰ νῦν
δὴ ῥηθέντα, ξυντιθέμενα ἀλλήλοις καὶ διαιρούμενα πρὸς ἀρ-
ετὴν βίου πῶς ἔχει, εἰδέναι, τί κάλλος πενίᾳ ἢ πλούτῳ κρα-
θὲν καὶ μετὰ ποίας τινὸς ψυχῆς ἕξεως κακὸν ἢ ἀγαθὸν ἐργάζεται, [καὶ τί εὐγένειαι καὶ δυσγένειαι καὶ ἰδιωτεῖαι καὶ
αρχαὶ καὶ ἰσχύες καὶ ἀσθένειαι καὶ εὐμάθειαι καὶ δυσμά-
θειαι]* καὶ πάντα τὰ τοιαῦτα τῶν φύσει περὶ ψυχὴν ὄντων
καὶ τῶν ἐπικτήτων τί ξυγκεραννύμενα πρὸς ἄλληλα
ἐργάζεται, ὥστε ἐξ ἁπάντων αὐτῶν δυνατὸν εἶναι
συλλογισάμενον αἱρεῖσθαι, πρὸς τὴν τῆς ψυχῆς φύσιν ἀποβ-
λέποντα, τόν τε χείρω καὶ τὸν ἀμείνω βίον.¹

—*Plat.* de *Repub.* Lib. 10.

*The bracketed material was omitted in the original.
1. Plato, *The Republic.* X.618c–d.

Every single one of us has to give his undivided attention—to the detriment
of all other areas of study—to trying to track down and discover whether there
is anyone he can discover and unearth anywhere who can give him the compe-
tence and knowledge to distinguish a good life from a bad one, and to choose a
better life from among all the possibilities that surround him at any given moment. He has to weigh up all the things we've been talking about, so as to know
what bearing they have, in combination and in isolation, on living a good life.
What are the good or bad results of mixing good looks with poverty or with

Human KNOWLEDGE has been distributed by Philosophers into different Branches, and into more or fewer Divisions, according to the more or less extensive Views, which they have taken of the various Subjects of *Human* Enquiry.

Partition of Knowledge

A great Philosopher* has laid it out into three general Provinces, HISTORY, POETRY, and PHILOSOPHY; which he refers to three several Powers of the Mind, MEMORY, IMAGINATION, and REASON. *Memory* stores up Facts, or Ideas, which are the Materials of Knowledge. *Imagination* ranges and combines them into different Assemblages or Pictures. *Reason* observes their Differences, Connections, and mutual Relations, and argues concerning them.

Philosophy in general

The *last* is the proper Business of PHILOSOPHY, which has been defined, the "*Knowledge of whatever exists,*"[2] or the "*Science of Things Human and Divine.*"[3] According to this Definition, its Object comprehends the *Universe* or *Whole of Things.* It traces whatever can be known by Man concerning the *Deity* and his *Works,* their Natures, Powers, Operations, and Connections.

----

wealth, in conjunction with such-and-such a mental condition? What are the effects of the various combinations of innate and acquired characteristics such as high and low birth [involvement and lack of involvement in politics, physical strength and frailty, cleverness and stupidity, and so on]? He has to be able to take into consideration the nature of the mind and so make a rational choice, from among all the alternatives, between a better and a worse life." Plato, *Republic,* trans. Robin Waterfield (Oxford: Oxford University Press, 1993), 376.

In the preceding extract, the square brackets signify words that were omitted by Fordyce.

* *Vid. Bacon. Aug. Scient. Lib. II. cap. 1.* [Francis Bacon, Lord Verulam (1561–1626), was an English philosopher, statesman, and scientist, one of whose projects was the reform of education. His *De dignitate et augmentis scientiarum* (1623) is a translation and elaboration of his *The Advancement of Learning* (1605). For Fordyce's admiration of Bacon see his fulsome praise in *A Brief Account,* paragraph 33.]

2. In his *A Brief Account,* Fordyce attributes this view to Pythagoras. See paragraph 1.

3. "Wisdom, moreover, as the word has been defined by the philosophers of old, is 'the knowledge of things human and divine and of the causes by which those things are controlled.'" Cicero, *De Officiis,* Loeb Classical Library, p. 173.

Therefore to give our Definition more Precision, PHILOSOPHY may be defined, the Knowledge of the Universe, or of Nature, and of its Powers, Operations and Connections, with just Reasonings deduced from thence. *Natural Philosophy* investigates the Properties and Operations of *Body* or *Matter*. *Moral Philosophy* contemplates *Human Nature*, its *Moral Powers* and *Connections*, and from these deduces the Laws of Action; and is defined more strictly the "*Science of* MANNERS or DUTY, which it traces from Man's Nature and Condition, and shews to terminate in his Happiness." Therefore it is called *Ethics, Disciplina Morum*. In fewer Words, it is the "*Knowledge of our* DUTY *and* FELICITY, or the *Art of being virtuous and happy.*"

Division of Philosophy

Natural

Moral

It is denominated an ART, as it contains a System of Rules for becoming *virtuous* and *happy*. Whoever practises these Rules, by so doing, attains an habitual Power and Facility of becoming *virtuous* and *happy*. It is likewise called a SCIENCE, as it deduces those Rules from the Principles and Connections of our Nature, and proves that the Observance of them is productive of our Happiness.

How an Art

How a Science

It is an *Art,* and a *Science* of the highest Dignity, Importance, and Use. Its *Object* is Man's Duty, or his Conduct in the several Moral Capacities and Connections which he sustains. Its *Office* is to direct that Conduct, to shew whence our Obligations arise and where they terminate. Its *Use,* or *End,* is the Attainment of Happiness; and the *Means* it employs are Rules for the right Conduct of our *Moral Powers.*

Its Object

Its Office

Its End

Its Means

As every Art and Science is more or less valuable, as it contributes more or less to our Happiness, this *Moral Art* or *Science* which unfolds our Duty and Happiness, must be a proper Canon or Standard, by which the Dignity and Importance of every other Art or Science are to be ascertain'd. It is therefore pre-eminent above all others; it is that *Master-Art,* that *Master-Science,* which weighs their respective Merits, adjusts their Rank in the Scale of Science, prescribes their Measures, and superintends their Efficacy and Application in Human Life. Therefore *Moral Philosophy* has been honoured with the glorious Epithets of the

The Standard of other Arts and Sciences

Directress of Life, the *Mistress of Manners,* the *Inventress of Laws and Culture,* the *Guide to Virtue and Happiness,* without some degree of which Man were a Savage, and his Life a Scene of Barbarity and Wretchedness.

Having thus settled the *Subject* and *End* of the Science, the Elements of which we are attempting to discover, and sufficiently distinguished it from all others, it seems proper next to fix the *Method* of prosecuting it. *Moral Philosophy* has this in common with *Natural Philosophy,* that it appeals to *Nature* or *Fact;* depends on Observation, and builds its Reasonings on plain uncontroverted Experiments, or upon the fullest Induction of Particulars of which the Subject will admit. We must observe, in both these Sciences, *Quid faciat & ferat Natura;* how Nature is affected, and what her Conduct is in such and such Circumstances. Or in other words, we must collect the *Phaenomena,* or *Appearances of Nature* in any given Instance; trace these to some *General Principles,* or *Laws of Operation;* and then apply these *Principles* or *Laws* to the explaining of other *Phaenomena.*

The Method

Therefore Moral Philosophy enquires, not how Man *might have been,* but how he *is constituted;* not into what *Principles,* or *Dispositions* his Actions *may be artfully* resolved, but from what Principles and Dispositions they *actually* flow; not what he *may,* by Education, Habit, or foreign Influence, come to *be,* or *do,* but what by his *Nature,* or *Original Constituent Principles* he is *formed* to *be* and *do.* We discover the *Office, Use* or *Destination* of any Work, whether *natural* or *artificial,* by observing its Structure, the Parts of which it consists, their Connection or joint Action. It is thus we understand the *Office* and *Use* of a Watch, a Plant, an Eye, or Hand. It is the same with a *Living Creature,* of the *Rational,* or *Brute Kind.* Therefore to determine the *Office, Duty,* or *Destination* of *Man,* or in other words what his *Business* is, or what *Conduct* he is *obliged* to pursue, we must inspect his *Constitution,* take every Part to pieces, examine their *mutual Relations* one to the other, and the common Effort or Tendency of the Whole.

Of Man and His Connections

In giving a rude Sketch or History in Miniature of *Man,* we must remember that he rises from small Beginnings, unfolds his Faculties and Dispositions by degrees, as the Purposes of Life require their Appearance, advances slowly thro' different Stages to Maturity, and when he has reached it, gradually declines till he sinks into the Grave. Let us accompany him in his Progress through these successive Stages, and mark the *Principles* which actuate, and the *Fortunes* which attend him in each, that we may have a full View of him in each.

Man is born a weak, helpless, delicate Creature, unprovided with Food, Cloathing, and whatever else is necessary for Subsistence, or Defence. And yet, exposed as the Infant is to numberless Wants and Dangers, he is utterly incapable of supplying the *former,* or securing himself against the *latter.* But though thus feeble and exposed, he finds immediate and sure Resources in the *Affection* and *Care* of his Parents, who refuse no Labours, and forego no Dangers, to nurse and rear up the tender Babe. By these powerful Instincts, as by some mighty Chain, does Nature link the *Parent* to the *Child,* and form the strongest *Moral Connection* on his Part, before the Child has the least Apprehension of it. *Hunger* and *Thirst,* with all the Sensations that accompany or are connected with them, explain themselves by a Language strongly expressive, and irresistibly moving. As the several Senses bring in Notices and Informations of surrounding Objects, we may perceive in the young Spectator, early Signs of a growing *Wonder* and *Admiration.* Bright Objects and striking Sounds are beheld and heard with a sort of Commotion and

Man's Infant State

Surprize. But without resting on any, he eagerly passes on from Object to Object, still pleased with whatever is most new. Thus the *Love* of *Novelty* is formed, and the Passion of *Wonder* kept awake. By degrees he becomes acquainted with the most familiar Objects, his Parents, his Brethren, and those of the Family who are most conversant with him. He contracts a *Fondness* for them, is uneasy when they are gone, and charmed to see them again. Those Feelings become the Foundation of a *Moral Attachment* on his Side, and by this reciprocal Sympathy he forms the Domestic Alliance with his Parents, Brethren, and other Members of the Family. Hence he becomes interested in their Concerns, and feels *Joy,* or *Grief, Hope,* or *Fear* on their Account, as well as his own. As his Affections now point beyond himself to others, he is denominated a *good* or *ill* Creature, as he stands *well* or *ill affected* to them. These then are the first Links of the *Moral Chain,* the early Rudiments, or Out-lines of his Character, his first rude Essays towards Agency, Freedom, Manhood.

His Childhood   When he begins to make Excursions from the Nursery, and extend his Acquaintance abroad, he forms a little Circle of Companions, engages with them in Play, or in quest of Adventures; and leads, or is led by them, as his Genius is more or less aspiring. Though this is properly the Season in which *Appetite* and *Passion* have the *Ascendant,* yet his *Imagination* and *Intellectual* Powers open apace; and as the various Images of Things pass before the Mental Eye, he forms a Variety of Tastes; relishes some things and dislikes others, as his Parents, Companions, and a thousand other Circumstances lead him to combine agreeable, or disagreeable Sets of Ideas, or represent to him Objects in alluring or odious Lights.

As his Views are enlarged, his *Active* and *Social* Powers expand themselves in proportion; the *Love of Action,* of *Imitation,* and of *Praise, Emulation, Docility,* a *Passion for Command,* and *Fondness of Change.* His Passions are quick, variable, and pliant to every Impression, his Attachments and Disgusts quickly succeed each other. He compares Things, distinguishes Actions, judges of Characters, and loves or hates them, as they appear well or ill affected to himself, or to those he holds dear.

Mean while he soon grows sensible of the Consequences of his own Actions, as they attract Applause, or bring Contempt; he triumphs in the former, and is ashamed of the latter; wants to hide them, and blushes when they are discovered. By means of these Powers he becomes a fit Subject of Culture, the Moral Tie is drawn closer, he feels that he is accountable for his Conduct to others as well as to himself, and thus is gradually ripening for Society and Action.

As Man advances from *Childhood* to *Youth*, his Passions as well as Perceptions take a more extensive Range. New Senses of Pleasure invite him to new Pursuits; he grows sensible to the Attractions of Beauty, feels a peculiar Sympathy with the Sex, and forms a more tender kind of Attachment than he has yet experienced. This becomes the Cement of a *new Moral Relation,* and gives a softer Turn to his Passions and Behaviour. In this turbulent Period he enters more deeply into a *Relish of Friendship, Company, Exercises* and *Diversions;* the *Love of Truth,* of *Imitation* and of *Design* grows upon him; and as his Connections spread among his Neighbours, Fellow-Citizens and Countrymen, his *Thirst of Praise, Emulation,* and *Social Affections* grow more intense and active. Mean while, it is impossible for him to have lived thus long without having become sensible of those more august Signatures of Order, Wisdom, and Goodness, which are stamped on the visible Creation; and of those strong Suggestions within himself of a Parent-Mind, the Source of all Intelligence and Beauty; and Object as well as Source of that Activity, and those Aspirations which sometimes rouze his inmost Frame, and carry him out of himself to an all-mighty and all-governing Power: Hence arise those Sentiments of *Reverence,* and those Affections of *Gratitude, Resignation,* and *Love,* which link the Soul with the Author of Nature, and form that most sublime and god-like of all Connections. His Youth

Man having now reached his Prime, either new Passions succeed, or the old Set are wound up to an higher Pitch. For, growing more sensible of his Connection with the Public, and that particular Community to which he more immediately belongs; and taking withal a larger Prospect of Human Life, and its various Wants and Enjoyments, he forms His Manhood more intimate Friendships, grasps at Power, courts Honour, lays down cooler Plans of Interest, and becomes more attentive to the Concerns of Society; he enters into Family-Connections, and indulges those Charities which arise from thence. The *reigning* Passions of this Period, powerfully prompt him to provide for the Decays of Life; and in it *Compassion* and *Gratitude* exert their Influence in urging the *Man,* now in full Vigour, to requite the Affection and Care of his Parents, by supplying their Wants and alleviating their Infirmities.

Old Age   At length human Life verges downwards, and *Old Age* creeps on apace with its *Anxiety, Love of Ease, Interestedness, Fearfulness, Foresight,* and *Love of Offspring.* The Experience of the Aged is formed to direct, and their Coolness to temper the Heat of Youth; the former teaches them to look back on past Follies, and the latter to look forward into the Consequences of Things, and provide against the worst.* Thus every Age has its peculiar Genius and Set of Passions, corresponding to that Period, and most conducive to the Prosperity of the rest. And thus are the *Wants* of one Period supplied by the *Capacities* of another, and the *Weaknesses* of one Age tally to the *Passions* of another.

Passions of   Besides these, there are other Passions and Affections of a less *ambula-*
every Age   *tory* Nature, not peculiar to one Period, but belonging to every Age, and acting more or less in every Breast throughout Life. Such are, *Self-Love, Benevolence, Love of Life, Honour, Shame, Hope, Fear, Desire, Aversion, Joy, Sorrow, Anger,* and the like. The two first are Affections of a cooler Strain, one pointing to the Good of the Individual, the other to that of the Species; *Joy* and *Sorrow, Hope* and *Fear,* seem to be only Modifications, or Exertions of the same *Original* Affections of *Love* and *Hatred, Desire* and *Aversion,* arising from the different Circumstances or Posi-

---

* See *Hor. de Art. Poet.* [In *Ars Poetica,* c. 20 B.C., the Roman poet Quintus Horatius Flaccus, or Horace (65–8 B.C.), advises poets to "note the characteristics of each stage of life and . . . grant what is appropriate to changing natures and ages." See lines 153–78, translated by Leon Golden in O. B. Hardison Jr. and Leon Golden, *Horace for Students of Literature: The Ars Poetica and Its Tradition* (Gainesville: University Press of Florida, 1995), 12.]

tion of the Object desired or abhorred, as it is present or absent. From these likewise arise other *Secondary,* or *Occasional* Passions, which depend, as to their Existence and several Degrees, upon the Original Affections being gratified or disappointed, as *Anger, Complacence, Confidence, Jealousy, Love, Hatred, Dejection, Exultation, Contentment, Disgust,* which do not form *Leading* Passions, but rather hold of them.

By these simple, but powerful Springs, whether *periodical* or *fixed,* the Life of Man, weak and indigent as he is, is preserved and secured, and the Creature is prompted to a constant Round of Action, even to supply his own numerous and ever-returning *Wants,* and to guard against the various *Dangers* and *Evils* to which he is obnoxious. By these Links, Men are connected with each other, formed into Families, drawn into particular Communities, and all united, as by a common League, into one System or Body, whose Members feel and sympathize one with another. By this admirable Adjustment of the Constitution of *Man* to his *State,* and the gradual Evolution of his Powers, Order is maintained, Society upheld, and Human Life filled with that Variety of Passion and Action, which at once enliven and diversify it.

Their joint Effects

This is a short Sketch of the *Principal Movements* of the Human Mind. Yet, these Movements are not the Whole of Man; they impel to Action, but do not direct it; they need a *Regulator* to guide their Motions, to measure and apply their Forces. And accordingly they have one that naturally *superintends* and *directs* their Action. We are conscious of a *Principle* within us, which examines, compares and weighs Things, notes the Differences, observes the Forces, and foresees the Consequences of Affections and Actions. By this Power we look back on past Times, and forward into Futurity, gather Experiences, estimate the real and comparative Value of Objects, lay out Schemes, contrive Means to execute them, and settle the whole Order and Oeconomy of Life. This Power we commonly distinguish by the Name of REASON, or REFLECTION, the Business of which is not to suggest any original Notices or Sensations, but to canvass, range, and make Deductions from them.

The Directing Power

The judging or approving Powers We are intimately conscious of another Principle within us, which approves of certain *Sentiments, Passions* and *Actions,* and disapproves of their Contraries. In consequence of the Decisions of this inward Judge, we denominate some Actions and Principles of Conduct, *right, honest, good,* and others *wrong, dishonest, ill.* The former excite our *Esteem, Moral Complacence,* and *Affection,* immediately and originally of themselves, without regard to their Consequences, and whether they affect our Interest or not. The latter do as naturally and necessarily call forth our *Contempt, Scorn,* and *Aversion.* That Power, by which we perceive this Difference in Affections and Actions, and feel a consequent Relish or Dislike, is commonly called CONSCIENCE, or the MORAL SENSE. Whether such a Power belongs to human Nature or not, must be referred to every one's Experience of what passes within himself.

These Powers different from Affections These two Powers of *Reason* and *Conscience,* are evidently Principles different in *Nature* and *Kind* from the Passions and Affections. For the Passions are mere *Force* or *Power, blind Impulses,* acting violently and without Choice, and ultimately tending each to their respective Objects, without regard to the Interest of others, or of the whole System. Whereas the *Directing* and *Judging* Powers distinguish and ascertain the different Forces, mutual Proportions and Relations, which the Passions bear to each other and to the Whole; recognize their several Degrees of Merit, and judge of the whole Temper and Conduct, as they respect either the Individual or the Species; and are capable of directing or restraining the blind Impulses of Passion in a due Consistency one with the other, and a regular Subordination to the Whole System.—Let this Difference be remembered.

Division of the Passions This is some Account of the *Constituent Principles* of our Nature, which, according to their different Mixtures, Degrees, and Proportions, mould our Character and sway our Conduct in Life. In reviewing that large Train of Affections which fill up the different Stages of Human Life, we perceive this obvious Distinction among them; that some of them respect the *Good* of the *Individual,* and others carry us beyond Ourselves to the *Good* of the *Species,* or *Kind.* The former have therefore been called *Private,* and the latter *Public* Affections. Of the first Sort are *Love of Life,* of *Pleasure,* of *Power,* and the like. Of the last are *Compassion, Gratitude, Friendship, Natural Affection,* and the like. Of the *Private* Passions,* some respect merely the *Security* and *Defence* of the Creature, such as *Resentment,* and *Fear;* whereas others aim at some *Positive* Advantage or Good, as *Wealth, Ease, Fame.* The former sort therefore, because of this Difference of Objects, may be termed *Defen-sive* Passions. These answer to our *Dangers,* and prompt us to avoid them if we can, or boldly to encounter them when we cannot.

Defensive Passions

The other Classes of *Private* Passions, which pursue *private positive* Good, may be called *Appetitive.* However we shall still retain the Name of *Private,* in Contradistinction to the *Defensive* Passions. Man has a great Variety of Wants to supply, and is capable of many Enjoyments, according to the several Periods of his Life, and the different Situations in which he is placed. To these therefore, a suitable Train of *Private* Passions correspond, which engage him in the Pursuit of whatever is necessary for his Subsistence, or Welfare.

Private or Appetitive Passions

Our *Public* or *Social* Affections are adapted to the several *Social Connections* and *Relations* which we bear to others, by making us sensible of their Dangers, and interesting us in their Wants, and so prompting us to secure them against one, and supply the other.

Public Passions

Whether this historic Draught of *Man,* and of that Groupe of Figures and Connections with which he is environed be just or not, is a Matter, not so much of Reasoning, as common Sense and common Experience. Therefore let every one consult his Experience of what he feels within, and his Knowledge of what is transacted abroad, in the *little,* or the *great* World in which he lives; and by that Experience, and that Knowledge, let the Picture be acknowledged *Just,* or pronounced the *Contrary.*

The Appeal

---

* *Here we use* Passions *and* Affections *without Distinction. Their Difference will be marked afterwards.*

For to that Experience, and to that Knowledge, and to these alone, the Designer appeals.

This is the first Step then to discover the *Duty* and *Destination* of Man, the having analyzed the Principles of which he is composed. It is necessary, in the next place, to consider in what *Order, Proportion,* and *Measure* of those inward Principles, *Virtue,* or a sound Moral Temper, and right Conduct consists; that we may discover whence *Moral Obligation* arises.

Of Duty, or Moral Obligation

It is by the *End* or *Design* of any *Power* or *Movement,* that we must di-rect its *Motions,* and estimate the *Degree* of Force necessary to its just Action. If it want the Force requisite for the obtaining its End, we call it *defective;* if it has too much, so as to be carried beyond *it,* we say it is *overcharged;* and in either Case it is imperfect, and ill-contrived. If it has just enough to reach the Scope, we esteem it *right,* and as it should be. Let us apply this Reasoning to the Passions. _{The Measure of Powers}

The *Defence* and *Security* of the Individual being the *Aim* of the *defen-sive Passions,* that *Security* and *Defence* must be the *Measure* of their *Strength* or *Indulgence.* If they are so *weak* as to prove insufficient for that End, or if they *carry us beyond it,* i.e. raise unnecessary Commo-tions, or continue longer than is needful, they are unfit to answer their original Design, and therefore are in an unsound and unnatural State. The Exercise of *Fear* or of *Resentment,* has nothing desirable in it, nor can we give way to either without painful Sensations. Without a certain Degree of them we are naked and exposed. With too high a Proportion of them we are miserable, and often injurious to others. Thus *Coward-ice* or *Timidity,* which is the Excess of Fear, instead of saving us in Dan-ger, gives it too formidable an Appearance, makes us incapable of at-tending to the best Means of Preservation, and disarms us of *Courage,* our natural Armour. *Fool-hardiness,* which is a Want of a due measure of *Fear,* leads us heedlessly into Danger, and lulls us into a pernicious Security. *Revenge,* i.e. *excessive Resentment,* by the Violence of its Com- _{Measure of the defensive Passions}

motion, robs us of that *Presence of Mind* which is often the best Guard against Injury, and inclines us to pursue the Aggressor with more Severity than Self-defence requires. *Pusillanimity,* or the Want of a just Indignation against Wrong, leaves us quite unguarded, and sinks the Mind into a passive enervating Tameness. Therefore, "*to keep the defensive Passions duly proportion'd to our Dangers,* is their *natural* Pitch and Tenour."

Measure of the private Passions

The *private* Passions lead us to pursue some *positive* Species of *private* Good. That *Good* therefore, which is the Object and End of each, must be the *Measure* of their respective Force, and direct their Operation. If they are too *weak* or *sluggish* to engage us in the Pursuit of their several Objects, they are evidently *deficient;* but if they defeat their End by their *Impetuosity,* then are they strained beyond the just Tone of Nature. Thus *Vanity,* or an *excessive Passion for Applause,* betrays into such Meannesses and such little Arts of Popularity, as makes us forfeit the Honour we so anxiously court. On the other hand, a *total Indifference about the Esteem of Mankind,* removes a strong Guard and Spur to Virtue, and lays the Mind open to the most abandoned Prosecutions. Therefore, "*to keep our private Passions and Desires proportioned to our* WANTS, *is the just Measure and Pitch of this Class of Affections.*"

Comparative Force

The *defensive* and *private* Passions do all agree in general, in their Tendency or Conduciveness to the Interest or Good of the Individual. Therefore when there is a Collision of Interest, as may sometimes happen, that *Aggregate of Good* or *Happiness,* which is composed of the particular Goods to which they respectively tend, must be the common Standard by which their *comparative Degrees* of Strength are to be measured. That is to say, if any of them in the Degree in which they prevail, are incompatible with the greatest Aggregate of Good, or most extensive Interest of the Individual, then are they unequal and disproportionate. For, in judging of a particular *System* or *Constitution* of Powers, we call that the *supreme* or *principal* End, in which the Aims of the several Parts or Powers coincide, and to which they are subordinate, and reckon them in due Proportion to each other, and right with regard to the Whole, when they maintain that Subordination or Subserviency. Therefore, "to proportion our defensive and private Passions in such measure to our Dangers and Wants, as best to secure the Individual, and obtain the greatest Aggregate of private Good or Happiness, is their just Balance, or comparative Standard in case of Competition."

In like manner, as the *public* or *social* Affections point at the Good of others, that *Good* must be the Measure of their Force. When a particular *social* Affection, as *Gratitude* or *Friendship,* which belongs to a particular *social Connection, viz.* that of a *Benefactor* or of a *Friend,* is too feeble to make us act the *grateful* or *friendly* Part, that Affection being insufficient to answer its End, is *defective* and *unsound.* If, on the other hand, a particular Passion of this Class counteract or defeat the Interest it is designed to promote, by its Violence or Disproportion, then is that Passion *excessive* and *irregular.* Thus *natural Affection,* if it degenerates into a *passionate* Fondness, not only hinders the Parents from judging coolly of the Interest of their Offspring, but often leads them into a most partial and pernicious Indulgence.

Measure of the public Affections

As every kind Affection points at the Good of its particular Object, it is possible there may be a Collision of Interests or Goods. Thus the Regard due to a *Friend* may interfere with that which we owe to a *Community.* In such a Competition of Interests, it is evident, that the *greatest* is to be chosen; and that is the greatest Interest, which contains the greatest Sum or Aggregate of public Good, greatest in *Quantity* as well as *Duration.* This then is the *common Standard,* by which the respective Forces and Subordinations of the social Affections must be adjusted. *Therefore* we conclude, that "this Class of Affections are sound and regular, when they prompt us to pursue the *Interest* of *Individuals* in an entire Consistency with the *public Good,*" or, in other words, "when they are duly proportioned to the *Dangers* and *Wants* of others, and to the various *Relations* in which we stand to *Individuals,* or to *Society.*"

Collision of social Affections

Thus we have found by an Induction of Particulars, the *natural Pitch* or *Tenour* of the *different Orders of Affection,* considered apart by themselves. Now as the *Virtue* or *Perfection* of every Creature lies in following its Nature, or acting suitably to the just Proportion and Harmony of its several Powers; therefore, "the VIRTUE of a Creature endow'd with such Affections as *Man,* must consist in observing, or acting agreeably to their *natural Pitch and Tenour.*" Let this suffice at least for its first rude Sketch.

Balance of Affection But, as there are no independent Affections in the Fabric of the Mind, no Passion that stands by itself, without some Relation to the rest, we cannot pronounce of any one considered APART, that it is either *too strong,* or *too weak.* Its Strength and just Proportion must be measured, not only by its Subserviency to its own immediate End, but by the Respect it bears to the whole System of Affection. Therefore, we say a Passion is *too strong,* not only when it defeats its own End, but when it impairs the Force of other Passions, which are equally necessary to form a *Temper of Mind,* suited to a certain *Oeconomy,* or *State;* and *too weak,* not merely on account of its Insufficiency to answer its End, but because it cannot sustain its *Part* or *Office,* in the Balance of the whole System. Thus the *Love of Life* may be *too strong,* when it takes from the *Regard* due to one's Country, and will not allow one bravely to encounter Dangers, or even Death on its Account. Again, the *Love of Fame* may be *too weak,* when it throws down the Fences which render Virtue more secure, or weakens the Incentives which make it more active and public-spirited.

Limits of private Affections If it be asked, "How far may the Affections towards private Good or Happiness be indulged?" One Limit was before fixed for the particular Indulgences of each, *viz.* their Subordination to the common Aggregate of Good to the private System. In these therefore, a due Regard is always supposed to be had to *Health, Reputation, Fortune,* the *Freedom of Action,* the *unimpair'd Exercise of Reason,* the *calm Enjoyment of one's self,* which are all private Goods. Another Limit now results from the Balance of Affection just named, *viz.* "*The Security and Happiness of others,*" or to express it more generally, "a *private* Affection may be safely indulged, when, by that Indulgence, we do not violate the Obligations which result from our higher Relations, or public Connections." A just

Respect therefore being had to these Boundaries, which Nature has fixed in the Breast of every Man, what should limit our Pursuits of private Happiness? Is Nature sullen and penurious? Or does the God of Nature envy the Happiness of his Offspring?

Whether there is ever a real Collision of Interests between the *public* and *private* System of Affections, or the *Ends* which each Class has in view, will be afterwards considered; but where there is no Collision, there is little or no danger of carrying either, but especially the *public,* Affections to Excess, provided both Kinds are kept subordinate to a discreet and cool *Self-love,* and to a calm and universal *Benevolence,* which Principles stand as Guards at the Head of each System.

Collision of Interests

This then is the Conduct of the Passions, considered as *particular* and *separate* Forces, carrying us out to their respective Ends; and this is their Balance or Oeconomy, considered as *compound* Powers, or Powers mutually related, acting in conjunction towards a *common End,* and consequently as forming a *System* or *Whole.*

Result

Now, whatever adjusts or maintains this *Balance,* whatever in the human Constitution is formed for *directing* the Passions, so as to keep them from defeating their own End, or interfering with each other, must be a Principle of a *superior* Nature to them, and *ought* to direct their Measures, and govern their Proportions. But it was found that REASON or Reflection is such a Principle, which points out the Tendency of our Passions, weighs their Influence upon private and public Happiness, and shews the best Means of attaining either. It having been likewise found, that there is another directing or controuling Principle, which we call CONSCIENCE, or the MORAL SENSE, which, by a native kind of Authority, judges of Affections and Actions, pronouncing some *just* and *good,* and others *unjust* and *ill;* it follows that the Passions, which are mere Impulses, or blind Forces, are Principles inferior and subordinate to this *judging* Faculty. THEREFORE, if we would follow the Order of Nature, *i.e.* observe the mutual Respects and the Subordination which the different Parts of the human Constitution bear to

Subordination of Powers

one another, the Passions ought to be subjected to the Direction and
Authority of the *leading* or *controuling* Principles.

In what it
consists

We conclude therefore from this *Induction*, that "The *Constitution* or
just Oeconomy of *human Nature*, consists in a regular *Subordination* of
the *Passions* and *Affections* to the AUTHORITY of CONSCIENCE, and the
DIRECTION of REASON."

Oeconomy of
Nature, or
right Temper

That *Subordination* is *regular,* when the Proportion formerly mentioned is maintained; that is to say, "When the DEFENSIVE Passions
are kept proportioned to our DANGERS; when the PRIVATE Passions
are proportioned to our WANTS; and, when the PUBLIC Affections are
adapted to our PUBLIC CONNECTIONS, and proportioned to the
Wants and Dangers of others." This last Branch is expressed somewhat
differently from the two former, in order to include that most important Relation in which we stand, and those indispensible Laws of Duty
which we owe to the great Author of our Nature, who, being supremely
perfect and happy, has no Wants to supply, and is obnoxious to no Pos-
sibility of Change.

Human Virtue
and Perfection

But the *natural State,* or the *sound* and *vigorous Constitution* of any
Creature, or the *just Oeconomy* of its Powers, we call its *Health* and *Per-
fection;* and the acting agreeably to these, its VIRTUE or GOODNESS.
THEREFORE, "the HEALTH and PERFECTION of Man must lie in the
aforesaid SUPREMACY of CONSCIENCE and REASON, and in the SUB-
ORDINATION of the Passions to their AUTHORITY and DIRECTION.
And *his* VIRTUE or GOODNESS must consist in *acting agreeably* to that
ORDER or OECONOMY."

How conform-
able to Reason

That such an Oeconomy of the Mind, and such a Conduct of its Powers and Passions will stand the Test of *Reason,* cannot admit of any Dispute. For, upon a fair Examination into the Consequences of Things,
or the Relations and Aptitudes of *Means* to *Ends, Reason* evidently dem-
onstrates, and *Experience* confirms it, that "To have our *defensive Passions* duly proportioned to our *Dangers,* is the surest way to avoid or get

clear of them, and obtain the Security we seek after."—"To proportion our *private Passions* to our *Wants,* is the best Means to supply them;— and, to adapt our *public Affections* to our *social Relations,* and the *Good* of others, is the most effectual Method of fulfilling *one,* and procuring the *other.*" In this Sense therefore, *Virtue* may be said to be a "*Conduct* conformable to *Reason,*" as Reason discovers an apparent *Aptitude* in such an *Order* and *Oeconomy* of Powers and Passions, to answer the End for which they are *naturally* formed.

If the Idea of *Moral Obligation* is to be deduced merely from this *Aptitude* or *Connection* between certain Passions, or a certain Order and Balance of Passions, and certain Ends obtained, or to be obtained by them, then is *Reason* or *Reflection,* which perceives that Aptitude or Connection, the proper Judge of *Moral Obligation;* and on this Supposition it may be defined, as hath been done by some, the Connection between the *Action* and the *Motive;* for the *End* is the *Motive,* or the *final Cause,* and the *Affection* is the *Action,* or its immediate, natural Cause. A Man, from mere Self-love, may be induced to fulfil that Obligation, which is founded on the Connection between the *defensive* Passions and their *Ends,* or the *private* Passions and their *Ends;* because in that Case his own Interest will prompt him to indulge them in the due Proportion required. But if he has no Affections which point beyond himself, no Principle but *Self-love,* or some subtle Modification of it, what shall interest him in the Happiness of others, where there is no Connection between it and his own; or what Sense can he have of *Moral Obligation* to promote it? Upon this Scheme therefore, without public or social Affection there could be no *Motive,* and consequently no Moral Obligation to a beneficent, disinterested Conduct.

Connection between Affections and Ends, not the Idea of Moral Obligation

But if the mere Connection between certain Passions, or a certain Order of Passions, and certain Ends, are what constitutes, or gives us the Idea of *Moral Obligation,* then why may not the Appositeness of any Temper or Conduct, nay, of any Piece of Machinery to obtain its End, form an equally strict *Moral Obligation?* For the Connection and Aptitude are as strong and invariable in the latter Instances as in the former. But as this is confounding the most obvious Differences of

things, we must trace the Idea of *Moral Obligation* to another and a
more natural Source.

Idea of it from **Experience** Let us appeal therefore to our inmost Sense and Experience, "How we
stand affected to those different Sets of Passions, in the just Measure
and Balance of which we found a right Temper to consist." For this is
entirely a Matter of Experience, in which we must examine as in any
other natural Enquiry, "What are the genuine Feelings and Operations
of Nature, and what Affections or Symptoms of them appear in the
given Instance."

Why the **defensive Passions approv'd** The DEFENSIVE Passions, as *Anger* and *Fear,* give us rather Pain than
Pleasure, yet we cannot help feeling them when provoked by Injury, or
exposed to Harm. We account the Creature imperfect that wants them,
because they are necessary to his Defence. Nay we should in some measure condemn ourselves, did we want the necessary Degree of *Resentment* and *Caution.* But if our *Resentment* exceeds the Wrong received,
or our Caution the Evil dreaded, we then *blame* ourselves for having
over-acted our Part. Therefore, while we are in Danger, to be totally
destitute of them we reckon a *blameable Defect,* and to feel them in a
just, *i.e.* necessary Measure, we *approve,* as suited to the Nature and
Condition of such a Creature as Man. But our Security obtained, to
continue to indulge them, we not only *disapprove as hurtful,* but *condemn* as *unmanly, unbecoming,* and *mean-spirited:* Nor will such a Conduct afford any self-approving Joy, when we coolly reflect upon it.

Why the **private** With regard to the PRIVATE Passions, such as *Love of Life, Pleasure,
Ease,* and the like, as these aim at private Good, and are necessary to the
Perfection and Happiness of the Individual, we should reckon any
Creature *defective,* and even *blameable,* that was destitute of them.
Thus, we condemn the Man who imprudently ruins his Fortune, impairs his Health, or exposes his Life; we not only pity him as an unfortunate Creature, but feel a kind of *Moral Indignation* and Contempt of
him, for having made himself such. On the other hand, though a discreet Self-regard does not attract our Esteem and Veneration, yet we *ap-*

prove of it in some Degree, in an higher and different Degree from what we would regard a well-contrived Machine, as necessary to form a finish'd Creature, nay to complete the virtuous Character, and as exactly suited to our present indigent State. There are some Passions respecting private Good, towards which we feel higher Degrees of Approbation, as the *Love of Knowledge*, of *Action*, of *Honour*, and the like. We esteem them as Marks of an ingenuous Mind, and cannot help thinking the Character in which they are wanting, remarkably stupid, and in some degree *immoral.*

With regard to the SOCIAL Affections, as *Compassion, natural Affection, Friendship, Benevolence,* and the like, we approve, admire, and love them in ourselves, and in all in whom we discover them, with an Esteem and Approbation, if not different in kind, yet surely far superior in degree to what we feel towards the other Passions. These we reckon necessary, just, and excellently fitted to our Structure and State; and the Creature which wants them we call defective, ill constituted, a kind of Abortion. But the *public* Affections we esteem as self-worthy, originally and eternally amiable. We approve and congratulate ourselves in proportion as we indulge them, and reckon those deserving of our Esteem and Friendship who do so.

Why the public

But among the *social* Affections, we make an obvious and constant Distinction, *viz.* between those particular Passions, which urge us with a sudden Violence, and uneasy kind of Sensation, to pursue the Good of their respective Objects, as *Pity, natural Affection,* and the like; and those calm dispassionate Affections and Desires, which prompt us more steddily and uniformly, to promote the Happiness of others. The former we generally call *Passions,* to distinguish them from the other Sort, which go more commonly by the Name of *Affections,* or *calm Desires.* The *first* kind we approve indeed and delight in; but we feel still higher Degrees of Approbation and moral Complacence towards the *last,* and towards all Limitations of the particular Instincts, by the Principle of *universal Benevolence.* The more Objects the calm Affections take in, and the worthier these are, their Dignity rises in proportion, and with

Distinction between vehement and calm Affections

this our Approbation keeps an exact Pace. A Character, on the other hand, which is quite divested of these public Affections, which feels no Love for the Species, but instead of it, entertains Malice, Rancour and Ill-will, we reckon totally immoral and unnatural.

Such then are the Sentiments and Dispositions we feel, when these several Orders of Affections pass before the mental Eye.

Moral Obligation

Therefore, "that State in which we feel ourselves moved, in the manner above described, towards those Affections and Passions, as they come under the Mind's Review, and in which we are instantaneously and independently of our Choice or Volition, prompted to a *correspondent* Conduct, we call a State of MORAL OBLIGATION." Let us suppose, for instance, a Parent, a Friend, a Benefactor, reduced to a Condition of the utmost Indigence and Distress, and that it is in our Power to give them immediate Relief. To what Conduct are we *obliged?* What *Duty* does Nature dictate and require in such a Case? Attend to Nature, and Nature will tell, will tell with a Voice irresistibly audible and commanding to the *human Heart,* with an Authority which no Man can silence without being self-condemned, and which no Man can elude but at his Peril; "That immediate Relief OUGHT to be given." Again, let a Friend, a Neighbour, or even a Stranger, have lodged a *Deposit* in our Hands, and after some time reclaim it, no sooner do these Ideas of the Confidence reposed in us, and of Property not *transferred,* but *deposited,* occur, than we immediately and unavoidably feel, and recognize the OBLIGATION to restore it. In both these Cases, we should condemn and even loath ourselves, if we acted otherwise, as having done, or omitted doing what we *ought* not, as having acted beneath the Dignity of our Nature;—contrary to our most intimate Sense of *Right* and *Wrong;*—we should accuse ourselves as guilty of Ingratitude, Injustice, and Inhumanity;—and be conscious of deserving the Censure, and therefore dread the Resentment of all rational Beings.—But in complying with the *Obligation,* we feel Joy and Self-approbation,—are conscious of an inviolable Harmony between our Nature and Duty,—and think ourselves entitled to the Applause of every impartial Spectator of our Conduct.

To *describe* therefore what we cannot perhaps *define,* a *State* of MORAL
OBLIGATION, is "that State in which a Creature, endued with such
Senses, Powers, and *Affections* as *Man,* would condemn himself, and
think he deserved the Condemnation of all others, should he refuse to
fulfil it; but would approve himself, and expect the Approbation of all
others, upon complying with it."

Moral
Obligation

And we call him a MORAL AGENT, who is in such a *State,* or is subject
to *Moral Obligation.* Therefore as Man's *Structure* and *Connections* often subject him to such a State of *Moral Obligation,* we conclude that
he is a MORAL AGENT. But as Man may sometimes act without *know-*
ing what he does, as in Cases of *Frenzy* or *Disease,* or in many *natural*
Functions; or knowing what he does, he may act without *Choice* or *Af-*
fection, as in Cases of *Necessity* or *Compulsion,* therefore to denominate
an Action *Moral,* i.e. *approveable,* or *blameable,* it must be done *know-*
ingly and *willingly,* or *from Affection* and *Choice.* "A *morally good Action*
then is to fulfil a *Moral Obligation* knowingly and willingly." And a
morally bad Action, or an *immoral Action,* is "to violate a *Moral Obli-*
gation knowingly and willingly." The proposed Brevity of the Enquiry
will not admit of entering into the minuter Distinctions of Actions.

Moral Agent

Moral Action
good and bad

As not an *Action,* but a *Series of Actions* constitute a CHARACTER; as not
an *Affection,* but a *Series of Affections* constitute a Temper, and as we denominate things by the gross, *a fortiori,* or by the Qualities which
chiefly prevail in them, therefore we call that a "*morally good Character,*
in which a *Series of morally good Actions* prevail"; and that a "*morally*
good Temper, in which a *Series of morally good Affections* have the Ascendant." A bad Character and bad Temper are the Reverse. But where the
above-mentioned *Order* or *Proportion* of Passions is maintained, there
a *Series* of *morally good Affections and Actions* will prevail. THEREFORE,
"to maintain that Order and Proportion, is to have a *morally good Tem-*
per and Character." But a "*morally good Temper and Character,*" is
MORAL RECTITUDE, INTEGRITY, VIRTUE, or the COMPLETION OF
DUTY."

Moral
Character and
Temper good
and bad

How we come by the Idea of Moral Obligation

If it be asked after all, "How we come by the Idea of *Moral Obligation* or *Duty?*" We may answer, that we come by it in the same way as by our other *original* and *primary* Perceptions. We receive them all from Nature, or the great Author of Nature. For this Idea of *Moral Obligation* is not a Creature of the Mind, or dependent on any previous Act of Volition, but arises on certain Occasions, or when certain other Ideas are presented to the Mind, as necessarily, instantaneously, and unavoidably, as *Pain* does upon too near an Approach to the Fire, or *Pleasure* from the Fruition of any Good. It does not, for instance, depend on our Choice, whether we shall feel the *Obligation* to succour a distressed Parent, or to restore a Deposit entrusted to us, when it is recalled. We cannot call this a COMPOUND Idea made up of one or more simple Ideas. We may indeed, nay we must, have some Ideas antecedent to it, *e.g.* that of a Parent—in Distress—of a Child,—able to relieve,—of the Relation of one to the other,—of a Trust,—of Right, *&c.* But none of these Ideas constitute the Perception of *Obligation.* This is an Idea quite distinct from, and something superadded to, the Ideas of the Correlatives, or the Relation subsisting between them. These indeed, by a Law of our Nature, are the Occasion of suggesting it, but they are as totally different from it, as Colours are from Sounds. By Sense or Reflection we perceive the Correlatives, our Memory recals the Favours or Deposit we received, the various Circumstances of the Case are Matters of Fact or Experience; but some delicate inward *Organ* or *Power,* or call it what we please, does, by a certain instantaneous Sympathy, antecedent to the cool Deductions of Reason, and independent of previous Instruction, Art, or Volition, *perceive* the *Moral Harmony,* the *living, irresistible Charms of Moral Obligation,* which immediately interests the correspondent Passions, and prompts us to fulfil its awful Dictates.

The Use of Reason in Moral Cases

We need not apprehend any Danger from the Quickness of its Decisions, nor be frightened, because it looks like *Instinct,* and has been called so. Would we approve one for deliberating long, or reasoning the Matter much at leisure, whether he should relieve a distress'd Parent, feed a starving Neighbour, or restore the Trust committed to him? Should we not suspect the Reasoner of Knavery, or of very weak Affections to Virtue? We employ *Reason,* and worthily employ it in examining the Condition, Relations, and other Circumstances of the Agent or Patient, or of those with whom either of them are connected, or, in other words, the *State of the Case:* And in complicated Cases, where the Circumstances are many, it may require no small Attention to find the true State of the Case; but when the Relations of the Agent or Patient, and the Circumstances of the Action are obvious, or come out such after a fair Trial, we should scarce approve him who demurs on the Obligation to that Conduct which the Case suggests. Thus, suppose one to deposit with us a Sword, which he comes afterwards to reclaim, but in such Circumstances, suppose of Frenzy or Melancholy, as gives us good ground to suspect that he will use it to the Hurt of others, or of himself. In such a Case it belongs to *Reason* or *Prudence,* coolly to weigh every Circumstance, the Condition of the Proprietor, the Consequences of restoring the Deposit, and the like; nor should we on this Supposition, condemn the hesitating about the restoring it; but let the Proprietor return to himself, the Obligation to Restitution being now apparent, we should justly suspect the Demurrer of something criminal or knavish.

As to that Objection against this original Perception of *Moral Obligation,* taken from its being an Instinct or necessary Determination of our Nature; are not the Perceptions or Determinations of Reason equally necessary? Does not every intuitive Perception or Judgment necessarily extort our Assent, when the Agreement or Disagreement of the Ideas which are compared is perceived? *Instinct* indeed has been considered, as something relative merely to bodily *Sense* and *Appetite,* a mere brutal Sensation or Impulse, in which the Mind, or our sublimer Powers have no Part; and therefore it is a Term that has been thought obnoxious to great Exceptions in Morals; but is a moral Power of Perception, or a moral Determination the worse for being interwoven with the very Frame, and Constitution of our Nature, for being instantaneous, uniform and steddy in its Operations or Decision? Why should such a Divine Instinct be thought less rational, less suitable to the Dignity of the Mind, than those intuitive Perceptions which are conversant about ab-

Instinct considered

stract Truths, and arise necessarily and instantaneously from the obvious Relations of Things? And if Reason with all its Sagacity may sometimes err, nay often does, why should any other Power of Perception be
thought infallible, or be condemned as brutal and irrational if it is not?

Pleasure, not   From what has been said it is evident, that it is not the Pleasures, or
the Idea of   agreeable Sensations which accompany the Exercise of the several Af-
Obligation   fections, nor those consequent to the Actions that constitute MORAL
OBLIGATION, or excite in us the Idea of it. That Pleasure is posterior
to the Idea of Obligation, and frequently we are obliged, and acknowledge ourselves under an Obligation, to such Affections and Actions as
are attended with Pain; as in the Trials of Virtue, where we are obliged
to sacrifice private to public Good, or a present Pleasure to a future Interest. We have Pleasure in serving an aged Parent, but it is neither the
Perception nor Prospect of that Pleasure, which gives us the Idea of Obligation to that Conduct.

Therefore, when we use these Terms, *Obligation, Duty, Ought,* and
the like, they stand for a simple Idea, an original uncompounded Feeling or Perception of the human Mind, as much as any Idea whatsoever,
and can no more be defined than any other simple Idea; and this Perception is not a Creature of the Mind, but a Ray emanating directly
from the Father of Lights, a fair genuine Stamp of his Hand, who impressed every vital and original Energy on the Mind, or if we chuse
rather to say, who ordained those Laws of Perception, by which moral
Forms attract and charm us with an irresistible Power.

But because the learned Dexterity of human Wit has so marvellously
puzzled a plain and obvious Subject, we shall consider some of those
ingenious Theories by which Moralists have deduced and explained
Moral Obligation.

Various Hypotheses Concerning Moral Obligation

From the Induction which has been made, we shall be able to judge with more Advantage of the different Hypotheses which have been contrived to deduce the Origin of *Moral Obligation.*

Hobbes, who saw Mankind in an unfavourable Attitude, involved in all the Distraction and Misery of a civil War, seems to have taken too narrow and partial a View of our Nature, and has therefore drawn it in a very odious and uncomfortable Light. Next to the Desire of Self-preservation, he makes the *governing* Passions in Man, the *Love of Glory,* and of *Power;* and from these, by an arbitrary, unnatural, and unsupported Hypothesis, contrary to common Experience, and common Language, he attempts to deduce all the other Passions which inflame the Minds, and influence the Manners of Men. All Men, says he, are by Nature equal, that is to say, according to his own Explanation, the weakest can do as much Mischief as the strongest; all desire, and have an equal Right to the same Things, and want to excel each other in *Power* and *Honour;* but as it is impossible for all to possess the same Things, or to obtain a Pre-eminence in Power and Honour, hence must arise mutual Contests, a natural Passion to invade the Property, and level the Power and Character of each other, and to raise and secure

The Scheme of *Hobbes*

29

themselves against the Attempts of others.* This State of Things, in which every Man having a Right to every Thing, has likewise a Right to prevent his Neighbour by Force or Fraud; he tells us, must naturally produce a State of War and mutual Carnage. In such a State, he adds, nothing can be called unjust or unlawful; for he who has a Right to the End, has also a Right to the only Means of obtaining or securing it, which, according to him, are Force or Fraud. And this State he calls the State of Nature.—But our shrewd Philosopher subjoins, that Men being aware that such a State must terminate in their own Destruction, agreed to surrender their private unlimited Right into the Hands of the Majority, or such as the Majority should appoint, and to subject themselves for the future to common Laws, or to common Judges or Magistrates. In consequence of this Surrender, and of this mutual Compact or Agreement, they are secured against mutual Hostilities, and *bound* or *obliged* to a peaceable and good Behaviour; so that it is no longer lawful or just (the good Man means safe or prudent) to invade and encroach on another. For this would be contrary to Compact, and a Violation of his Promise and Faith.—Therefore as there could be no Injustice previous to this Compact, so the Compact, and it alone, must be the Origin of *Justice*, the Foundation of *Duty* and *Moral Obligation*. This is our subtle Philosopher's Scheme!

But one may ask him, What Obligation is a Man under to keep his Promise, or stand to his Compact, if there be no Obligation, no moral Tie distinct from that Promise, and that Compact, independent of and previous to both? If there is none, they must prove a mere Rope of Sand, and Men are left as loose and unsociable as ever, as much Barbarians and Wolves as before their Union. But if there is a distinct and previous Obligation to Fidelity, Honour, and a Regard to one's Engagements, then Right and Wrong, Justice and Injustice, are antecedent to

---

* *Vid.* Hob. *de Cive,* cap. i, ii, &*c. and Leviath.* c. xvii, &*c.* [Thomas Hobbes's *De Cive* was first published in Paris in 1642 and became available in an English translation as *The Citizen* in 1651, the year of the publication of his better-known *Leviathan.*]

Compact.—Perhaps he will tell us that the Necessity of the Case, or a Regard to our own Safety, which is included in that of the Public, obliges us to adhere to our Engagements. We may be compelled or punished for Breach of Faith by those, to whom we transfer our Rights. *Force,* or *superior Strength* of the Majority to controul or punish the Refractory, is, no doubt, the true Origin of the Obligation, if he will speak out, and *Self-love* is its only *Judge* and *Measure.* And if this be all, then what Obligation is a Man under to Gratitude, Charity, Friendship, and all those Duties of Humanity, which fall not under the Cognizance or Controul of Law? What Obligations to private Veracity, Honesty and Fidelity, when a Man may be a Knave with Safety? That Scheme, therefore, which sets us loose from such Obligations, and involves us in such Absurdities, must be itself both absurd and wicked. That State of Nature which it supposes as its Foundation, is a mere Chimera, a Vision of his own Brain, which, from the Condition and Nature of the Creature, the Growth of a Family, the Rise of a Tribe or Clan, we have no Reason to believe ever subsisted; therefore the Superstructure which he has raised on that Foundation, is fictitious and chimerical. *Hobbes* took it for granted, that all Men were Knaves or Fools, and wanted to dress up a System of Government, agreeable to the corrupt Taste of the reigning Powers, and to the Genius of a most dissolute Court, a Government contrived to make a small Part of Mankind Tyrants, and all the rest Slaves. He measured *Virtue* by *mere Utility,* and while he pretends to be the first that discovered this Connection, and gave the only true Reason for the Practice of Honesty, he seems to have misunderstood, or wilfully overlooked its true Nature, and its inseparable Connection with the Perfection and Happiness of the Individual.

Another Set of Moralists establish Morals upon the Will or positive Appointment of the Deity, and call *Virtue* a Conformity to that Will, or Appointment. All *Obligation,* they say, supposes one who *obliges,* or who has a *Right* to prescribe, and can reward the Obedient, and punish the Disobedient. This can be none but our *Creator.* His *Will* therefore is our *Law,* which we are *bound* to obey. And this they tell us is only

Scheme of Conformity to the Divine Will

sufficient to bind, or oblige such imperfect and corrupt Creatures as we are, who are but feebly moved with a Sense of the Beauty and Excellency of Virtue, and strongly swayed by Passion, or Views of Interest.

That *Virtue,* or such a Conduct of the Passions as hath been above described, is agreeable to the *Will* of *God,* is evident beyond Dispute, as that Conduct, or Scheme of Duty, is pointed out to us by our Inward Structure, and as that Inward Structure is the Effect of the Will or Appointment of the Deity. Whatever therefore is agreeable, or correspondent to our Inward Structure, must likewise be agreeable, or correspond to the Will of God. So that all the *Indications,* or *Sanctions* of our Duty, which are declared, or enforced by our Structure, are, and may be, considered as *Indications,* or *Sanctions* of the Will of our Creator. If these Indications, through Inattention to, or Abuse of the Structure, prove insufficient to declare; or if these Sanctions, through the Weakness or Wickedness of Men, prove insufficient to enforce Obedience to the Divine Will, and the Deity is pleased to superadd new Indications, or new Sanctions; these additional Indications and Sanctions cannot, and are not supposed by the Assertors of this Scheme, to add any new Duty, or any new Moral Obligation; but only a new and clearer Promulgation of our Duty, or a new and stronger Sanction or Motive from Interest, to perform that Duty, and to fulfil that Obligation to which we were bound before. It makes no Difference, as to the Matter of Obligation, after what mannar the Will of our Creator is enforced, or declared to us, whether by Word or Writ, or by certain inward Notices and Determinations of our own Minds, arising according to a necessary Law of our Nature.—By whichever of these Ways we suppose the Divine Will intimated to us, the first Question that naturally occurs to us is, "Why we are obliged to obey the Divine Will?" If it be answered, that he is our *Superior,* and can reward, or punish us, as we are obedient or refractory; this is resting *Obligation* upon the foot of *Interest.* If we say that he is our *Creator,* and *Benefactor,* and we *ought* to *obey* our *Creator* and be *grateful* to our *Benefactor,* this refers the Obligation to an inward Sense, or Perception, that *Obedience* is due to one's *Creator, Gratitude* to one's *Benefactor.* Upon what other Principle but this, can we connect those *Relations,* and that Obedience and Gratitude, unless we recur to the Principle of Self-interest just now mentioned? If the Scheme of Duty and *Moral* Obligation be thought to rest on too slight a Foundation, when built on Moral Perception, and the Affections of our Nature, because these are found insufficient to bind, or rather compel Men to their Duty, we fear the same Objection will militate against this Scheme, since all the Declarations and Sanctions of the Divine Will have not hitherto had their due Effect in producing a thorough and universal Reformation.

When some speak of the *Will of God,* as the *Rule of Duty,* they do not certainly mean a blind, arbitrary Principle of Action, but such a Principle as is directed by Reason, and governed by Wisdom, or a Regard to certain Ends in Preference to others. Unless we suppose some Principle in the Deity analogous to our *Sense* of the *Obligation,* some antecedent Affection, or Determination of his Nature, to prefer some Ends before others, we cannot assign any sufficient, or indeed any possible Reason, why he should will one thing more than another, or have any Election at all. Whatever therefore is the Ground of his Choice, or Will, must be the Ground of *Obligation,* and not the Choice, or Will itself.— That this is so, appears plainly from the common Distinction which Divines and Philosophers make between *Moral* and *Positive* Commands and Duties. The *former* they think *obligatory,* antecedent to Will, or at least to any Declaration of it; the *latter* obligatory only in consequence of a positive Appointment of the Divine Will. But what Foundation can there be for this Distinction, if all Duty and all Obligation be equally the Result of mere Will?

A more refined Tribe of Philosophers have attempted to lay the Foundation of Morals much deeper, and on a more large and firm Bottom, *viz.* the *Natures* and *Reasons,* the *Truth* and *Fitnesses of Things.* Senses and *Affections,* they tell us, are vague and precarious; and though they are not, yet irrational Principles of Action, and consequently very improper Foundations, on which to rest the *eternal* and *immutable* Obligations of Morality. Therefore they talk much of the abstract Natures and Reasons of Things, of eternal Differences, unalterable Relations, Fitnesses and Unfitnesses resulting from those Relations; and from

Scheme of Truth, of the Natures and Reasons of Things

these eternal Reasons, Differences, Relations, and their consequent Fitnesses, they suppose *Moral Obligation* to arise. A Conduct agreeable to
them, or, in other words, "*A Conformity to Truth* they call *Virtue,* and
the Reverse they call *Vice.*"*

We perceive the Nature of Things by different Organs, or Senses,
and our Reason acts upon them when so perceived, and investigates
those Relations which subsist between them, or traces what is true,
what is false, what may be affirmed, and what denied concerning them.
Thus by Sense or Experience we perceive the Nature or Character of a
Benefactor, and of a *Beneficiary* (if one may so express it) and upon comparing them together, a third Idea is suggested to us, which we call the
Relation between the Benefactor and Beneficiary; we likewise perceive
the Foundation of that Relation, some Benefit received. But are any of
these Ideas that which we understand by the *Moral Duty* or *Obligation,*
the Idea of *Gratitude* due to the *Benefactor* from the *Beneficiary?* This is
evidently a distinct Perception, obvious to some *Sense, Organ,* or *Power*
of Perception, but not the Result of *Reasoning.* Suppose farther, the
Benefactor in Prison for a small Debt, and the *Beneficiary* in Affluence,
Reason may suggest to the *latter,* that a little Share of his Wealth be-

---

*See Dr. *Clarke, Woolaston,* and other eminent Writers. [Samuel Clarke
(1675–1729) was rector of St. James Church, Westminster. His Boyle lectures, *A Discourse concerning the Being and Attributes of God* (London, 1705), vol. 1, and *A Discourse concerning the Unchangeable Obligations of Natural Religion and the Truth and
Certainty of the Christian Revelation* (London, 1706), vol. 2, are referred to here.
Clarke traced moral obligation to "eternal and necessary differences of things" or
moral fitness and unfitness. "There is . . . such a thing as fitness and unfitness, eternally, necessarily, and unchangeably, in the Nature and Reason of Things." Vol. 1,
571. Close to Clarke was the independent scholar William Wollaston (1660–1724),
who privately published *The Religion of Nature Delineated* in 1722, correcting the
work for wider distribution in 1724. Wollaston believed that morally evil actions are
actions that are "incompatible" with eternal moral truths. Thus, for example, "Every
Act . . . , and all those omissions, which interfere with truth (i.e. deny any proposition to be true, which is true; or suppose any thing not to be what it is, in any regard)
are morally evil, in some degree or other: the forbearing such acts, and the acting in
opposition to such omissions are morally good: and when any thing may be either
done, or not done, equally without the violation of truth, that thing is indifferent."
(20)]

stowed on the *former,* will make a considerable Change in his State to the better; but will Reason, mere Reason, without some degree of Affection, prompt him to such a well-placed Charity? Or will the Perception of his Relation to his *Benefactor* and of the *Benefit* received, lead him to *approve* such a Conduct, unless we suppose a Sense or Feeling quite different from that Perception of the intervening Relation, and of the Ground of that Relation? We might, therefore, perceive all the possible Reasons, Relations, and Differences of Things, and yet be totally indifferent to this or that Conduct, unless we were endued with some Sense or Affection, by which we approved and loved *one,* or disapproved and disliked the *other* Conduct. *Reason* may perceive a *Fitness,* or *Aptitude* to a certain *End,* but without some *Sense* or *Affection* we cannot propose, or indeed have any Idea of an *End,* and without an *End* we cannot conceive any *Inducement* to Action.—Therefore before we can understand the Natures, Reasons, and Fitnesses of Things, which are said to be the Foundation of Morals, we must know what Natures are meant, to what Ends they are fitted, and from what Principles or Affections they are prompted to act, otherwise we cannot judge of the Duty required, or of the Conduct becoming that Being whom we suppose under *Moral Obligation.* But let the Natures be once given, and the Relations which subsist among them be ascertained, we can then determine what Conduct will be obligatory to such Natures, and adapted to their Condition and Oeconomy. And to the same Natures placed in the same Relations, the same Conduct will be eternally, and invariably proper and obligatory.

To call *Morality* a *Conformity* to *Truth,* gives no Idea, no Characteristic of it, but what seems equally applicable to *Vice.* For whatever Propositions are predicable of *Virtue,* as, that it flows from good Affection, or is agreeable to the Order of our Nature,—tends to produce Happiness,—is beheld with Approbation, and the like, the contrary Propositions are equally true, and may be equally predicated of Vice. What is Truth, but the Conformity of Propositions to the Nature or Existence and Reality of Things? And has not *Vice* its Nature, its Existence, its Adjuncts and Consequences, as much as *Virtue?* And are not Propositions conformable to them *true* Propositions? And therefore is not a

Conduct suited to, or significative of such true Propositions, a *true* Conduct, or a Conduct conformable to Truth? Could we understand a Watchmaker, a Painter, or a Statuary, talking of their respective Arts, should they tell us, that a Watch, a Picture, or Statue, were good when they were *true,* or done according to Truth, and that their Art lay in adjusting them to Truth? Would they not speak more intelligibly, and more to the Purpose, if they should explain to us their End or Use, and in order to that, shew us their Parts both together and separately, the Bearings and Proportions of those Parts, and their Reference to that End? Is not such a Detail likewise necessary to understand Human Nature, its Duty, and End? Will the Truth, the abstract Natures and Reasons, the eternal Relations and Fitnesses of Things, form such a Detail? But suppose it could, yet what *Degrees* of Virtue, or Vice, does Truth admit? *Truth* is a simple, uniform, invariable Thing, incapable of Intension or Remission. But *Virtue* and *Vice* admit of almost infinite Degrees and Variations, and therefore cannot consist of, or be founded upon, a Thing which admits of none. For such as is the Foundation, such must the Superstructure be.

Objection against the Scheme in Section 2 But it is said, that, to deduce *Moral Obligation* from the Constitution of our Nature, and an Inward Sense, is to render it exceedingly precarious and mutable, because Man might have been differently constituted, so as to approve of Treachery, Malice, Cruelty, and then another, or a quite contrary Train of Duties would have been required, or *obligatory.*

The Answer That Human Nature might have been otherwise constituted than it is, is perhaps true, but that it could have been better constituted, considering its present State and Circumstances, may be justly questioned under his Government, who does every thing in Number, Weight, and Measure, and who has poured Wisdom and Beauty over all his Works. The little Sketch that hath been given of our Nature, shews that it is admirably adapted to our present Condition, and the various Connections we sustain. We could not have subsisted, or at least not have subsisted so well, in such a Condition, nor maintained such Connections, without that successive Train of Powers and Passions with which we are endued. Without them, or with a contrary Set, we must have been miserable. And he who ordained the Condition and settled the Connections, must likewise have ordained that Conduct of Powers, and that Balance of Passions which is exactly proportioned to that Condition and to those Connections. Such an Order of Creatures being supposed, and such a Condition with such Connections being given, such a Conduct as has been traced out, must be eternally and invariably *obligatory* to such Creature so placed and so connected. Had Man been a different Creature, and placed in different Circumstances, a Spider for instance, or an Hound, a different Set of Duties would have then become him; the Web, the Vigilance, the rapacious Conduct of the *former;* the Sagacity, the Love of Game, and Swiftness of the *latter,* and the Satisfaction of Appetite, the Propagation and Love of Offspring common to both, would have fulfilled the Destinations of his Nature, and been his proper Business and Oeconomy. But as *Man* is not only a *Sensible,* an *Active,* and a *Social,* but a *Rational,* a *Political,* and a *Religious* Creature, he has a nobler Part to act, and more numerous and more important Obligations to fulfil. And if afterwards, in any future Period of his Duration, he shall be advanced to a superior Station, and take in wider Connections, the Sphere of his Duty, and the Number and Weight of his Obligations, must increase in proportion. Had a Creature, therefore, situated and connected as *Man,* been formed with Dispositions to approve of Treachery, Malice, or Cruelty, such a Temper or Constitution would have been evidently destructive of his Happiness. Now if we imagine the Deity prefers some Ends to others, suppose the Happiness of his Creatures to their Misery, he must likewise prefer the Means most adapted to those Ends. *Therefore,* supposing the Deity necessarily Wise and Good, he could not have implanted in us such Dispositions, or, in other words, could not have annexed Feelings of Approbation to a Conduct so incongruous to our State, and so subversive of our Happiness. Consequently amidst the infinite Variety of possible Constitutions, Vice could never have been *approveable,* and of course, not *obligatory.*—THEREFORE, "The Scheme of Human Nature above proposed, rests on the same Foundation as the Divine Wisdom and Goodness, and the Scheme of *Moral* Obligation erected upon it, must be equally immutable and immortal." And that the Deity is wise and good, supremely and universally so, Nature cries aloud through all her Works.

But it is farther objected against this Scheme, that Mankind differ strangely in their *Moral* Sentiments, some approving *Treachery, Revenge,* and *Cruelty,* nay whole Nations *Theft,* the *Exposition of Infants,* and many other Crimes of as black a Dye: therefore the *Moral* Sense, recommended as the Judge of Morals, is either not universal, or a very uncertain and fallacious Rule.

As to that Diversity of Opinion, or rather of Practice, concerning *Moral* Obligation, we can no more conclude from thence, that the internal *Perception,* or *Moral Sense* of *Right* and *Wrong,* is not an Universal, or Certain Standard or Rule of judging in Morals, than we can infer from the different Opinions concerning the Merit of the same Performances, that there is no Standard in Painting, no certain and uncontroverted Principle of the Art. In the last, Men appeal from particular Tastes, Manners, and Customs, to Nature, as the supreme Standard, and acknowledge that the Perfection of the Art lies in the just Imitation of it; but from a Diversity in Organs, in Capacity, in Education, from Favour, Prejudice, and a thousand other Circumstances, they differ in applying the Rule to particular Instances. The same thing holds in Morals; Men admit the *Rule in general,* and appeal to our *common Nature* and to *common Sense,* nay seldom differ or judge wrong in impartial Cases. When at any time they misapply, or deviate from the received Standard, a fair and satisfying Account may be given of their Variations.

We have heard of States which have allowed Theft, and the Exposition of lame or deformed Children. But in those States there was hardly any Property, all things were common, and to train up a hardy, shifting, sagacious Youth, was thought far preferable to the Security of any private Property. The Exposition of their Children was esteemed the Sacrifice of private Social Affection to the Love of the Public. We need not doubt but they loved their Children; but as such Children were accounted useless, and even hurtful to a Commonwealth, formed entirely upon a warlike Plan, they reckoned it gallant to prefer the *public,* to the strongest and most endearing *private* Interest. So that their Mistake lay in supposing a real Competition between those Interests, not in disavowing, or divesting themselves of parental Affection; a Mistake into which they would not have fallen had they enjoyed a more natural, refined, and extensive System of Policy. In some Countries they put their aged decrepit Parents to Death, but is it because they condemn, or want natural Affection? No; but they think it the best Proof of their Affection to deliver them from the Miseries of old Age, which they do not believe can be counter-balanced by all its Enjoyments. In short, neither Cruelty, nor Ingratitude, nor any Action under an immoral Form, are ever approved. Men *reason wrong only* about the Tendency, the Consequences, Materials, and other Circumstances of the Action. It may appear in different Lights or with different Sides, according to the different Views and Opinions of the Consequences which the Moral Spectator or Actor has, or according to his Passions, Habits, and other Circumstances; but still the general Rule is recognized, the Moral Quality or Species is admired, and the Deviation from the Rule condemned and disliked. Thus, Inhumanity is condemned by all, yet Persecution for the sake of religious Opinions is approved, and even practised by some under the Notion of Compassion to the *Souls* of the Sufferers, or to those of others who, they think, can only *be thus secured* against the Infection of Heresy; or under the Form of Zeal for the Honour of God, a *Divine* Principle, to which they are persuaded whatever is *Human* ought to stoop: though to every large and well-informed Mind such a Conduct must appear most barbarous and inhuman, with how pious a Name soever it may be sanctified.—No Man approves *Malice;* but to hate a wicked Character, or to resent an Injury, are deemed equally conducive to Private Security, and to Public Good, and appear to the Actors, even in their most outrageous Sallies, a noble Contempt of Vice, or a generous Indignation against Wrong. The Highwayman condemns Injustice, and resents the pilfering Knavery of a Brother of the Trade; but to excuse himself he says, Necessity has no Law, an honest Fellow must not starve, he has tried the Way of Industry, but in vain; the prime Law of Self-preservation must be obeyed.—From these, and the like

Topics, it appears no hard Matter to account for the Diversity of Opinions concerning *Moral Obligation, viz.* from Mistakes about the Tendency of Actions, the Nature of Happiness, or of public or private Good, from the partial Connections Men have formed, from false Opinions of Religions and the Will of God, and from violent Passions, which make them misapply the Rule, or not attend to the Moral Quality as they ought. Therefore by separating what is foreign, and appealing to the true Standard of Nature, as ascertained above, and by observing the Reasons of those Variations which we find sometimes among Individuals, we plainly recognize the Stability of the Rule of Moral Obligation, and discern the Universality of the Sense; and the Variations, instead of being Exceptions against either, rather concur in confirming *one,* and demonstrating the *other.*

Conclusion From the whole, we may conclude, that the Nature, the Reasons, and the Relations of things would never have suggested to us this simple Idea of *Moral Obligation* without a proper Sense susceptible of it. It is interwoven with the very Frame and Constitution of our Nature, and by it *We* are in the strictest Sense a LAW to Ourselves. Nor is it left to us to trace out this Law by the cool or slow Deductions of *Reason;* far less is this Law the Result of subtile and metaphysical Enquiries into the abstract Natures and Relations of Things; we need not ascend to Heaven to bring it down from thence, nor descend into the Depths to seek it there; it is *within* us, ever present with us, ever active and incumbent on the Mind, and engraven on the Heart in the fair and large Signatures of *Conscience, Natural Affection, Compassion, Gratitude,* and *universal Benevolence.*

The Final Causes of Our Moral Faculties of Perception and Affection

We have now taken a *General* Prospect of MAN, and of his MORAL POWERS and CONNECTIONS, and on these erected a Scheme of DUTY, or MORAL OBLIGATION, which seems to be confirmed by *Experience,* consonant to *Reason,* and approved by his most inward, and most sacred *Senses.* It may be proper in the next place to take a more *particular* View of the *Final Causes* of those delicate *Springs* by which he is *impelled* to Action, and of those *Clogs* by which he is restrained from it.— By this Detail we shall be able to judge of their Aptitude to answer their End, in a Creature endued with his *Capacities,* subject to his *Wants,* exposed to his *Dangers,* and susceptible of his *Enjoyments;* and from thence we shall be in a Condition to pronounce concerning the *End* of his *whole Structure,* its *Harmony* with his *State,* and, consequently, its Subserviency to answer the great and benevolent Intentions of its Author.

The Survey proposed

In the *Anatomy* of this inward and more elaborate *Subject,* it will not be necessary to pursue every little Fibre, nor to mark the nicer Complications and various Branchings of the more minute Parts. It shall suffice to lay open the larger Vessels and stronger Muscling of this Divine Piece of Workmanship, and to trace their Office and Use in the Disposition of the Whole.

Inward Anatomy of the System of the Mind

The Supreme Being has seen fit to blend in the whole of Things a prodigious Variety of discordant and contrary Principles; *Light* and

Darkness, Pleasure and *Pain, Good* and *Evil.* There are multifarious Natures, *higher* and *lower,* and many intermediate ones between the wide-distant Extremes. These are differently situated, variously adjusted, and subjected to each other, and all of them subordinate to the Order and Perfection of the Whole. We may suppose *Man,* placed as in a Center amidst those innumerable Orders of Beings, by his *Outward* Frame drawn to the *Material* System, and by his *Inward* connected with the INTELLECTUAL, or *Moral,* and of course affected by the Laws which govern both, or affected by that Good and that Ill which result from those Laws. In this infinite Variety of *Relations* with which he is surrounded, and of *Contingencies* to which he is liable, he feels strong Attractions to the *Good,* and violent Repulsions or Aversions to the *Ill.* But as Good and Ill are often blended, and wonderfully complicated one with the other; as they sometimes immediately produce and run up into each other, and at other times lie at great Distances, yet by means of intervening Links, introduce one another; and as these Effects are often brought about in consequence of hidden Relations, and general Laws, of the Energy of which he is an incompetent Judge, it is easy for him to mistake *Good* for *Evil,* and *Evil* for *Good,* and consequently he may be frequently attracted by such things as are destructive, or repelled by such as are salutary. Thus, by the tender and complicated Frame of his Body, he is subjected to a great Variety of Ills, to *Sickness, Cold, Heat, Fatigue,* and innumerable *Wants.* Yet his Knowledge is so narrow withal, and his Reason so weak, that in many Cases he cannot judge, in the way of Investigation, or Reasoning, of the Connections of those Effects with their respective Causes, or of the various latent Energies of Natural Things. He is therefore informed of this Connection by the Experience of certain *Senses,* or *Organs of Perception,* which, by a mechanical instantaneous Motion, feel the *Good* and the *Ill,* receiving Pleasure from *one,* and Pain from the *other.* By these, without any Reasoning, he is taught to attract, or chuse what tends to his Welfare, and to repel and avoid what tends to his Ruin. Thus, by his Senses of *Taste* and *Smell,* or by the *Pleasure* he receives from certain kinds of Food, he is admonished which agree with his Constitution, and by an opposite Sense of *Pain,* he is informed which sorts disagree, or are destructive of it; but is

not by means of these instructed in the inward Natures and Constitutions of Things.

Some of those Senses are armed with strong Degrees of *Uneasiness* or
Pain, in order to urge him to seek after such Objects as are suited to
them. And these respect his more immediate and pressing *Wants;* as the
Sense of *Hunger, Thirst, Cold,* and the like; which, by their painful Importunities, compel him to provide *Food, Drink, Raiment, Shelter.*
Those Instincts by which we are thus prompted with some kind of
Commotion or Violence to attract and pursue *Good,* or to repel and
avoid *Ill,* we call *Appetites* and *Passions.* By our Senses then we are informed of what is *good* or *ill* to the *Private System,* or the *Individual;*
and by our *Private Appetites* and *Passions* we are impelled to one, and
restrained from the other.

In consequence of this Machinery, and the great Train of Wants to
which our Nature subjects us, we are engaged in a continued Series of
Occupations, which often require much Application of Thought, or
great bodily Labour, or both. The Necessaries of Life, Food, Cloaths,
Shelter, and the like, must be provided; Conveniencies must be acquired to render Life still more easy and comfortable. In order to obtain
these, Arts, Industry, Manufactures, and Trade, are necessary. And to
secure to us the peaceable Enjoyment of their Fruits, Civil Government, Policy and Laws must be contrived, and the various Business of
public Life carried on. Thus while Man is concerned and busied in
making Provision, or obtaining Security for himself, he is by Degrees
engaged in Connections with a Family, Friends, Neighbours, a Community, or a Commonwealth. Hence arise new Wants, new Interests,
new Cares, and new Employments. The Passions of one Man interfere
with those of another. Interests are opposed. Competitions arise, contrary Courses are taken. Disappointments happen, Distinctions are
made, and Parties formed. This opens a vast Scene of Distraction and
Embarrassment, and introduces a mighty Train of Good and Ill, both
Public and Private. Yet amidst all this Confusion and Hurry, Plans of
Action must be laid, Consequences foreseen, or guarded against, Incon-

Use of
Appetites and
Passions

Man's outward
State

veniencies provided for; and frequently particular Resolutions must be taken, and Schemes executed, without Reasoning or Delay.

Provisions for it | Now what Provision has the Author of our Nature made for this necessitous Condition? How has he fitted the Actor, Man, for playing his Part in this perplexed and busy Scene? He has admonished the Individual of *private Good* and *private Ill* by peculiar *Senses,* and urged him by keen *Instincts* to pursue the former and repel the latter. But what Provision, what Security has the Deity made for the Community, the Public? Who, or what shall answer for his good Behaviour to it?

By public Senses and Passions | Our Supreme Parent, watchful for the Whole, has not left himself without a Witness here neither, and hath made nothing imperfect, but all things are double one against another. He has not left Man to be informed, only by the cool Notices of Reason, of *Good* or *Ill,* the *Happiness* or *Misery* of his Fellow-Creatures. He has made him sensible of their Good and Happiness, but especially of their Ill and Misery, by an immediate Sympathy, or quick *Feeling* of *Pleasure* and of *Pain.*

Pity | The latter we call PITY or COMPASSION. For the former, though every one, who is not quite divested of Humanity, feels it, in some degree, we Congratulation | have not got a Name, unless we call it CONGRATULATION, or *joyful* SYMPATHY, or that *Good-humour,* which arises on seeing others pleased or happy. Both these Feelings have been called in general the PUBLIC or COMMON SENSE, *Κ ιν νοημο κυνη,*[4] by which we feel for others and are interested in their Concerns as really, though perhaps less sensibly than in our own.

Resentment | When we see our Fellow-Creatures unhappy, through the Fault or In-

---

4. Fordyce's Greek (or the printer's reading of it) is puzzling here. If "*Κ ιν*" is taken as a shortened form of "*κοινον,*" and the ending of "*νοημο*" is changed, thus, "*κοινον νοημα,*" then we have "common sense," although "*κοινονοημοσυνη*" is more common. (See, for example, Francis Hutcheson, *An Essay on the Nature and Conduct of the Passions and Affections with Illustrations on the Moral Sense,* 3d ed., 1742, 5.) "*κυνη,*" however, remains a mystery in this context.

jury of others, we feel RESENTMENT or INDIGNATION against the *unjust* Causers of that Misery. If we are conscious that *it* has happened through our Fault, or *injurious* Conduct, we feel SHAME; and both these Classes of *Senses* and *Passions,* regarding *Misery* and *Wrong,* are armed with such sharp Sensations of *Pain,* as not only prove a powerful Guard and Security to the *Species* or *Public System* against those Ills, it may but serve also to lessen or remove those Ills it does suffer. *Compassion* draws us out of ourselves to bear a part of the Misfortunes of others, powerfully solicits us in their Favour, melts us at a Sight of their Distress, and makes us in some degree unhappy till they are relieved from it. It is peculiarly well adapted to the Condition of Human Life, because, as an eminent Moralist* observes, it is much more, and oftener in our Power to do Mischief than Good, and to prevent or lessen Misery than to communicate positive Happiness; and therefore it is an admirable Restraint upon the more *selfish* Passions, or those violent Impulses that carry us to the Hurt of others.

There are other particular *Instincts* or *Passions,* which interest us in the Concerns of others, even while we are most busy about our own, and which are strongly attractive of *Good,* and repulsive of *Ill* to them. Such are *Natural Affection, Friendship, Love, Gratitude, Desire of Fame, Love of Society,* of *one's Country,* and others that might be named. Now as the *Private* Appetites and Passions were found to be armed with strong Sensations of Desire and Uneasiness, to prompt Man the more effectually to sustain Labours, and encounter Dangers in pursuit of those Goods that are necessary to the Preservation and Welfare of the Individual, and to avoid those Ills which tend to his Destruction; in like manner it was necessary, that this *other* Class of Desires and Affections should be prompted with as quick Sensations of Pain, not only to counteract the Strength of their Antagonists, but to engage us in a virtuous Activity for

Public Affections

---

* *Vid.* Butler's *Serm. on Compassion.* [Joseph Butler (1692–1752), preacher at the Rolls Chapel, London, and subsequently Bishop of Durham. In 1726 he published *Fifteen Sermons* (London), the fifth and sixth under the headings "Upon Compassion."]

our Relations, Families, Friends, Neighbours, Country. Indeed our *Sense* of *Right* and *Wrong* will admonish us that it is our *Duty,* and *Reason* and *Experience* farther assure us, that it is both our *Interest* and best *Security,* to promote the Happiness of others; but that *Sense,* that *Reason,* and that *Experience,* would frequently prove but weak and ineffectual Prompters to such a Conduct, especially in Cases of Danger and Hardship, and amidst all the Importunities of Nature, and that constant Hurry in which the *Private* Passions involve us, without the Aid of those particular *kind* Affections, which mark out to us particular Spheres of Duty, and with an agreeable Violence engage and fix us down to them.

Contrast or Balance of Passions It is evident therefore, that these two Classes of Affection, the *Private* and *Public,* are set one against the other, and designed to controul and limit each other's Influence, and thereby to produce a just Balance in the Whole.* In general, the violent Sensations of Pain or Uneasiness which accompany Hunger, Thirst, and the other private Appetites, or too great Fatigue of Mind as well as of Body, prevent the Individual from running to great Excesses in the Exercise of the higher Functions of the Mind, as too intense Thought in the Search of Truth, violent Application to Business of any kind, and different Degrees of Romantic Heroism. On the other hand, the *finer Senses* of *Perception,* and those *generous Desires* and *Affections* which are connected with them, the *Love of Action,* of *Imitation,* of *Truth, Honour, Public Virtue,* and the like, are wisely placed in the opposite Scale, in order to prevent us from sinking into the Dregs of the *Animal* Life, and debasing the Dignity of Man below the Condition of Brutes. So that by the mutual Reaction of those opposite Powers, the bad Effects are prevented that would naturally result from their acting singly and apart, and the good Effects are produced which each are severally formed to produce.

* *Vid.* Hutch. *Conduct of the Passions, Treat.* 1. §. 2. [Francis Hutcheson (1694–1746) held the Chair of Moral Philosophy at Glasgow University. His *An Essay on the Nature and Conduct of the Passions and Affections with Illustrations on the Moral Sense* was first published in 1728 (London and Dublin).]

The same wholesome Opposition appears likewise in the particular Counterworkings of the *Private* and *Public* Affections one against the other. Thus *Compassion* is adapted to counterpoise the *Love of Ease,* of *Pleasure,* and of *Life,* and to disarm, or to set Bounds to *Resentment;* and *Resentment* of Injury done to ourselves, or to our Friends, who are dearer than ourselves, prevents an effeminate *Compassion* or *Consternation,* and gives us a noble Contempt of Labour, Pain, and Death. *Natural Affection, Friendship, Love of one's Country,* nay, *Zeal* for any particular Virtue, are frequently more than a Match for the whole Train of *Selfish* Passions. On the other hand, without that intimate over-ruling Passion of *Self love,* and those private Desires which are connected with it, the *social* and *tender Instincts* of the Human Heart would degenerate into the wildest Dotage, the most torturing Anxiety, and downright Frenzy.

Contrast or Balance of Public and Private Passions

But not only are the different Orders or Classes of Affection Checks one upon another, but Passions of the same Classes are mutual Clogs. Thus, how many are withheld from the violent Outrages of *Resentment* by *Fear?* And how easily is *Fear* controuled in its turn, while mighty Wrongs awaken a mighty *Resentment?* The *Private* Passions often interfere, and therefore moderate the Violence of each other; and a calm SELF-LOVE is placed at their Head, to direct, influence, and controul their particular Attractions and Repulsions. The *Public* Affections restrain one the other; and all of them are put under the Controul of a calm dispassionate BENEVOLENCE, which ought in like manner to direct and limit their particular Motions.—Thus, most part, if not all the Passions have a twofold Aspect, and serve a twofold End. In *one* View they may be considered as POWERS, impelling Mankind to a certain Course, with a *Force* proportioned to the *apprehended Moment* of the *Good* they aim at. In *another* View they appear as WEIGHTS balancing the Action of the *Powers,* and controuling the Violence of their Impulses. By means of these *Powers* and *Weights* a natural POISE is settled in the Human Breast by its all-wise Author, by which the Creature is kept tolerably steady and regular in his Course, amidst that Variety of Stages through which he must pass.

Contrasts among those of the same Classes

But this is not all the Provision which God has made for the Hurry and Perplexity of the Scene in which Man is destined to act. Amidst those infinite Attractions and Repulsions towards private and public Good and Ill, Mankind either cannot often foresee the *Consequences* or *Tendencies* of all their Actions towards one or other of these, especially where those Tendencies are intricate and point different ways, or those Consequences remote and complicated; or though, by careful and cool Enquiry and a due Improvement of their rational Powers, they might find them out, yet distracted as they are with Business, amused with Trifles, dissipated by Pleasure, and disturbed by Passion, they either have, or can find, no leisure to attend to those Consequences, or to examine how far this or that Conduct is productive of private or public Good on the whole. Therefore were it left entirely to the slow and sober Deductions of Reason to trace those Tendencies, and make out those Consequences, it is evident that, in many particular Instances, the Business of Life must stand still, and many important Occasions of Action be lost, or perhaps the grossest Blunders be committed. On this account the Deity, besides that general Approbation which we bestow on every degree of *kind* Affection, has moreover implanted in Man many particular *Perceptions,* or *Determinations,* to approve of certain *Qualities* or *Actions,* which, in effect, tend to the Advantage of Society, and are connected with private Good, though he does not always see that Tendency, nor mind that Connection. And these *Perceptions,* or *Determinations* do without Reasoning point out, and antecedent to Views of Interest, prompt to a Conduct beneficial to the *Public,* and useful to the *Private* System. Such is that *Sense of Candour* and *Veracity,* that *Abhorrence of Fraud and Falshood,* that *Sense of Fidelity, Justice, Gratitude, Greatness of Mind, Fortitude, Clemency, Decorum;* and that *Disapprobation of Knavery, Injustice, Ingratitude, Meanness of Spirit, Cowardice, Cruelty,* and *Indecorum,* which are natural to the Human Mind. The *former* of those Dispositions, and the Actions flowing from them, are approved, and those of the latter kind disapproved by us, even abstracted from the View of their Tendency, or Conduciveness to the Happiness or Misery of others, or of ourselves. In one we discern a *Beauty,* a *superior Excellency,* a *Congruity* to the *Dignity* of Man; in the other a *Deformity,* a *Littleness,* a *Debasement* of Human Nature.

There are other Principles also, connected with the Good of Society, or the Happiness and Perfection of the Individual, though that Connection is not immediately apparent, which we behold with real Complacency and Approbation, though perhaps inferior in Degree, if not in Kind, such as *Gravity, Modesty, Simplicity of Deportment, Temperance, prudent Oeconomy;* and we feel some degree of Contempt and Dislike where they are wanting, or where the opposite Qualities prevail. These and the like *Perceptions* or *Feelings* are either different *Modifications* of the *Moral Sense,* or *subordinate* to it, and plainly serve the same important Purpose, being expeditious *Monitors* in the several Emergencies of a various and distracted Life, of what is *right,* what is *wrong,* what is to be *pursued,* and what *avoided;* and, by the pleasant, or painful Consciousness which attends them, exerting their Influence, as powerful *Prompters* to a suitable Conduct.

Others of an inferior Order

From a slight Inspection of the above-named Principles, it is evident they all carry a friendly Aspect to *Society,* and the *Individual,* and have a more immediate, or a more remote Tendency to promote the *Perfection* or *Good* of both. This Tendency cannot be always foreseen, and would be often mistaken, or seldom attended, by a weak, busy, shortsighted Creature, like Man, both rash and variable in his Opinions, a Dupe to his own Passions, or to the Designs of others, liable to Sickness, to Want, and to Error. Principles therefore which are so nearly linked with *private Security* and *public Good,* by directing him, without operose Reasoning, where to find *one,* and how to promote the *other,* and by prompting him to a Conduct conducive to both, are admirably adapted to the Exigencies of his present State, and wisely calculated to obtain the Ends of universal Benevolence.

Their general Tendencies

It were easy, by considering the Subject in another Light, to shew, in a curious Detail of Particulars, how wonderfully the Inside of Man, or that astonishing Train of *Moral Powers* and *Affections* with which he is endued, is fitted to the several Stages of that *progressive* and *probationary* State, through which he is destined to pass. As our Faculties are narrow and limited, and rise from very small and imperfect Beginnings, they must be improved by Exercise, by Attention, and repeated Trials. And

Passions fitted to a State of Trial

this holds true, not only of our *Intellectual,* but of our *Moral* and *Active* Powers. The former are liable to Errors in Speculation, the latter to Blunders in Practice, and both often terminate in Misfortunes and Pains. And those Errors and Blunders are generally owing to our Passions, or to our too forward and warm *Admiration* of those partial *Goods* they naturally pursue, or to our *Fear* of those partial *Ills* they naturally repel. Those Misfortunes therefore lead us back to consider where our Misconduct lay, and whence our Errors flowed, and consequently are salutary Pieces of Trial, which tend to enlarge our Views, to *correct* and *refine* our Passions, and consequently improve both our *Intellectual* and *Moral* Powers.—Our Passions then are the rude Materials of our Virtue, which Heaven has given us to work up, to refine and polish into an harmonious and divine Piece of Workmanship. They furnish out the whole Machinery, the Calms and Storms, the Lights and Shades of Human Life. They shew Mankind in every Attitude and Variety of Character, and give *Virtue* both its Struggles and its Triumphs. To conduct them well in every State, is *Merit;* to abuse or misapply them, is *Demerit.* By them we prove what we are, and by the Habits to which they give Birth, we take our Form and Character for the successive Stages of our Life, or any future Period of our Existence.

To a Progressive State The different Sets of *Senses, Powers,* and *Passions,* which unfold themselves in those successive Stages, are both necessary and adapted to that *rising* and *progressive* State. Enlarging Views and growing Connections require new Passions and new Habits; and thus the Mind, by these continually expanding and finding a progressive Exercise, rises to higher Improvements, and pushes forward to Maturity and Perfection.—But on this we cannot insist.

Harmony of our Structure and State In this beautiful Oeconomy and Harmony of our Structure, both outward and inward, with that State, we may at once discern the great Lines of our Duty traced out in the fairest and brightest Characters, and contemplate with Admiration a more august and marvellous Scene of Divine Wisdom and Goodness laid in the Human Breast, than we shall perhaps find in the whole Compass of Nature.

"What a Piece of Work is Man! How noble in Reason! How infinite in Faculties! In Form and Moving how express and admirable! In Action how like an Angel! In Apprehension how like a God! The Beauty of the World! The Paragon of Animals!"

Result

From this Detail it appears, that MAN, by his Original Frame, is made for a *temperate, compassionate, benevolent, active,* and *progressive* State. He is strongly *attractive* of the *Good,* and *repulsive* of the *Ills,* which befall others as well as himself. He feels the highest *Approbation* and *Moral Complacence* in those Affections, and in those Actions which immediately and directly respect the *Good* of others, and the highest *Disapprobation* and *Abhorrence* of the contrary. Besides these, he has many particular *Perceptions* or *Instincts* of *Approbation,* which though perhaps not of the same kind with the others, yet are accompanied with correspondent Degrees of Affection, proportioned to their respective Tendencies to the *Public Good.* THEREFORE, by acting agreeably to these Principles, *Man* acts agreeably to his Structure, and fulfils the benevolent Intentions of its Author. But we call a Thing GOOD, when it answers its *End;* and a Creature GOOD, when he acts in a *Conformity* to his *Constitution.* Consequently, *Man* must be denominated GOOD or VIRTUOUS when he acts suitably to the *Principles* and *Destination* of his Nature. And where his VIRTUE lies, there also is his RECTITUDE, his DIGNITY, and PERFECTION to be found. And this coincides with the Account of *Virtue* formerly given, but presents it in another Attitude, or sets it in a Light something different.

In what Oeconomy Virtue consists

Book II

The Principal Distinctions of Duty
or Virtue

We have now considered the *Constitution* and *Connections* of *Man,* and on these erected a general System of DUTY, or MORAL OBLIGATION, consonant to *Reason,* approved by his most sacred and intimate *Sense,* suitable to his *mixed Condition,* and confirmed by the *Experience* of Mankind. We have also traced the FINAL CAUSES of his *Moral Faculties* and *Affections* to those noble Purposes they answer both with regard to the *private* and the *public System.*

From this Induction it is evident, that there is *one* Order or Class of Duties which *Man* owes to HIMSELF. *Another* to *Society.* And a *third* to GOD.

General Division of Duty

The Duties he owes to HIMSELF are founded chiefly on the DEFENSIVE and PRIVATE Passions, which prompt him to pursue whatever tends to *private Good* or *Happiness,* and to avoid, or ward off whatever tends to *private Ill* or *Misery.* Among the various Goods which allure and solicit him, and the various Ills which attack or threaten him, "To be intelligent and accurate in selecting *one,* and rejecting the *other,* or in preferring the most *excellent Goods,* and avoiding the most *terrible Ills,* when there is a Competition among either, and to be discreet in using the best Means to attain the *Goods* and avoid the *Ills,* is what we call PRU-

Duties to one's self

53

DENCE." This, in our *inward* Frame, corresponds to *Sagacity,* or a *Quickness of Sense* in our *outward.*—"To proportion our DEFENSIVE *Passions,* to our *Dangers,* we call FORTITUDE;" which always implies "a just Mixture of calm Resentment and Animosity, and well-governed Caution." And this *Firmness of Mind* answers to the *Strength* and *Muscling* of the *Body.*—And "duly to adjust our PRIVATE *Passions* to our Wants, or to the respective Moment of the Good we affect or pursue, we call TEMPERANCE;" which does therefore always imply, in this large Sense of the Word, "a just Balance or Command of the Passions," and answers to the *Health* and *sound Temperament* of the Body.*

Duties to Society   The *second Class* of *Duties* arises from the PUBLIC or SOCIAL *Affections,* "the just Harmony or Proportion of which to the *Dangers* and *Wants* of others, and to the several *Relations* we bear, commonly goes by the Name of JUSTICE." This includes the Whole of our Duty to *Society,* to its *Parent,* and the *general Polity* of *Nature;* particularly *Gratitude, Friendship, Sincerity, natural Affection, Benevolence,* and the other *social Virtues:* This being the *noblest Temper* and *fairest Complexion* of the Soul, corresponds to the *Beauty* and *fine Proportion* of the Person. The Virtues comprehended under the former Class, especially *Prudence* and *Fortitude,* may likewise be transferred to this; and according to the various Circumstances in which they are placed, and the more confined or more extensive Sphere in which they operate, may be denominated PRIVATE, OECONOMICAL, or CIVIL *Prudence, Fortitude,* &c. These direct our Conduct with regard to the *Wants* and *Dangers* of those lesser or greater Circles with which we are connected.

---

* *Vid. Tim. Locr. de Anima Mundi.* [*On the Nature of the World and the Soul* was originally attributed to Timaeus of Locri, a fifth-century B.C. Greek writer from southern Italy upon whose thought Plato was said to have based his *Timaeus.* Contemporary scholars agree that it is a work of Middle Platonism, c. first century B.C. or first century A.D., and derived from Plato's work, rather than a source for it. In paragraphs 78–86 the author discusses the virtues and the health of body and soul. See Timaios of Locri, *On the Nature of the World and the Soul,* trans. and ed. Thomas H. Tobin, Texts and Translations Graeco-Roman Religion Series, no. 8 (Chico, Calif.: Scholars Press, 1985).]

The *third Class* of Duties respects the DEITY, and arises also from the   Duties to God
PUBLIC *Affections,* and the several glorious RELATIONS which he sustains to us, as our *Creator, Benefactor, Law-giver, Judge,* &c.

We chose to consider this *Set* of Duties in the last place, because,   Method
though prior in Dignity and Excellency, they seem to be *last* in Order
of Time, as thinking it the most simple and easy Method to follow the
gradual Progress of Nature, as it takes its Rise from Individuals, and
spreads through the *social* System, and still ascends upwards, till at
length it stretches to its all-mighty Parent and Head, and so terminates
in those Duties which are *highest* and *best.*

The Duties resulting from these *Relations,* are *Reverence, Gratitude,*   Piety
Love, Resignation, Dependence, Obedience, Worship, Praise; which, according to the Model of our finite Capacities, must maintain some sort
of Proportion to the Grandeur and Perfection of the Object whom we
venerate, love and obey. "This PROPORTION or HARMONY, is expressed by the general Name of PIETY or DEVOTION," which is always
stronger or weaker, according to the greater or less apprehended Excellency of its Object. This sublime Principle of Virtue, is the enlivening
Soul which animates the *moral System,* and that Cement which binds
and sustains the other Duties which *Man* owes to *himself* and to *Society.*
From hence, as will appear afterwards, *they* derive not only the firmest
Support, but their highest Relief and Lustre.

This then is the general Temper and Constitution of Virtue, and these   Divisions of
are the principal Lines or Divisions of Duty. To those good Disposi-   Conscience
tions, which respect the several Objects of our Duty, and to all Actions
which flow from such Disposition, the Mind gives its Sanction or Testimony. And this Sanction or Judgment concerning the moral Quality,
or the Goodness of Actions or Dispositions, Moralists call CON-
SCIENCE. When it judges of an Action that is to be performed, it is
called an *antecedent* Conscience; and when it passes Sentence on an Action which is performed, it is called a *subsequent* Conscience. The Ten-   Goodness of
dency of an Action to produce Happiness, or its external Conformity   an Action

Material   to a Law, is termed its *material* Goodness. But the good Dispositions
from which an Action proceeds, or its Conformity to Law in every re-
Formal   spect, constitutes its *formal* Goodness.

Natural and   Some Moralists of no mean Figure, reckon it necessary to constitute the
Moral   *formal* Goodness of an Action, that we reflect on the Action "with
Moral Complacency and Approbation. For mere *Affection,* or *a good
Temper,* whether it respects others, or ourselves, they call *natural* or *in-
stinctive* Goodness, of which the Brutes are equally capable with Man.
But when that Affection or Temper is viewed with Approbation, and
made the Object of a new Affection, this, they say, constitutes MORAL
GOODNESS or VIRTUE, in the strict Sense of the Word, and is the
Characteristic of MORAL or RATIONAL Agents."[5]

Whether   It must be acknowledged, that Men may be partially good, *i.e.* may in-
Approbation is   dulge some kind Affections, and some kind Actions, and yet may be
necessary to
complete the   vitious, or immoral on the Whole. Thus a Man may be affectionate to
Idea of Virtue   his Child, and injurious to his Neighbour; or compassionate to his
Neighbour, and cruel to his Country; or zealous for his Country, yet
inhuman to Mankind. It must also be acknowledged, that to make
every Degree and Act of good Affection the frequent Object of our Attention,—to reflect on these with Moral Approbation and Delight,—
to be convinced, on a full and impartial Review, that *Virtue* is most amiable in itself, and attended with the most happy Consequences, is
sometimes a great Support to Virtue, in many Instances necessary to
complete the virtuous Character, and always of use to give Uniformity
and Stability to virtuous Principles, especially amidst the numberless
Trials to which they are exposed in this mixed Scene of human Life. Yet

5. For example, Bishop Butler writes in the first paragraph of his *A Dissertation of
the Nature of Virtue,* appended to his *Analogy of Religion* (London, 1736), "Brute
creatures are impressed and actuated by various instincts and propensions: so also
we. But additional to this, we have a capacity of reflecting upon actions and characters, and making them an object of our thought: and on doing this, we naturally
and unavoidably approve some actions, under the peculiar view of their being virtuous and of good dessert; and disapprove others, as vicious and of ill dessert. . . ."

how many of our Fellow-Creatures do we esteem and love, who perhaps never coolly reflected on the Beauty or fair Proportions of Virtue, or turned it into a Subject of their Moral Approbation and Complacency! Philosophers, or contemplative Men, may very laudably amuse themselves with such charming Theories, and often do contemplate every the minutest Trace of Virtue about themselves, with a parental Fondness and Admiration, and by those amiable Images, reflected from themselves, they may perhaps be more confirmed in the Esteem of whatever is honest and praise-worthy. However, it is not generally among this recluse Set of Men, that we expect to find the highest Flights of Virtue; but rather among Men of Action and Business, who, through the Prevalence of a natural good Temper, or from generous Affections to their Friends, their Country, and Mankind, are truly and transcendently good. Whatever that Quality is which we approve in any Action, and count worthy our Esteem, and which excites an Esteem and Love of the Agent, we call the *Virtue, Merit,* or *formal Goodness* of that Action. And if Actions, invested with such a Quality, have the Ascendant in a Character, we call that Character *virtuous* or *good.* Now it is certain that those Qualities or Principles mentioned above, especially those of the public and benevolent kind, how simple, how instinctive soever, are viewed with Approbation and Love. The very Nature of that Principle we call *Conscience,* which approves these benevolent Affections, and whatever is done through their Influence, intimates that *Virtue* or *Merit* is present in the Mind before Conscience is exercised, and that its Office is only to observe it there, or to applaud it. For if Virtue is something that deserves our Esteem and Love, then it must exist before *Conscience* is exerted, or gives its Testimony. *Therefore* to say that the Testimony of Conscience is necessary to the *Being* or *Form* of a virtuous Action, is, in plain Terms, to affirm, that *Virtue* is not *Virtue,* till it is reflected on and approved as Virtue. The proper Business of *Reason,* in forming the *virtuous Character,* is to guide the several Affections of the Mind to their several Objects, and to direct us to that Conduct or to those Measures of Action, which are the most proper Means of acquiring them. Thus, with respect to *Benevolence,* which is the *Virtue* of a *Character,* or a principal Ingredient of *Merit,* its proper Object is the *public Good.* The Business of *Reason* then is to inform us wherein *consists the greatest public Good,* what Conduct and which Actions are the most effectual Means of promoting it. After all, the Motions of the Mind are so quick and imperceptible, and so complicated with each other, that perhaps seldom do any indulge the virtuous or good Affections without an approving Consciousness; and certainly the more that Virtue is contemplated with Admiration and Love, the more firm and inflexible will the Spectator be in his Attachment to it.

Divisions of Conscience
When the Mind is ignorant or uncertain about the Moment of an Action, or its Tendency to private or public Good, or when there are several Circumstances in the Case, some of which being doubtful, render the Mind dubious concerning the Morality of the Action, this is called a *doubtful* or *scrupulous* Conscience; if it mistakes concerning these, it is called an *erroneous* Conscience. If the *Error* or *Ignorance* is *involuntary* or *invincible,* the Action proceeding from that *Error,* or from that *Ignorance,* is reckoned *innocent,* or not *imputable.* If the Error or Ignorance is *supine* or *affected,* i.e. the Effect of Negligence, or of Affectation and wilful Inadvertence, the Conduct flowing from such Error, or such Ignorance, is *criminal* and *imputable.* Not to follow one's Conscience, though erroneous and ill-informed, is *criminal,* as it is the Guide of Life; and to counteract it, shews a depraved and incorrigible Spirit. Yet to follow an erroneous Conscience is likewise criminal, if that Error which misled the Conscience was the Effect of Inattention, or of any criminal Passion.*

How Conscience is to be rectified
If it be asked, "How an erroneous Conscience shall be rectified, since it is supposed to be the only Guide of Life, and Judge of Morals?" We answer, in the very same way that we would rectify *Reason,* if at any time it should judge wrong, as it often does, *viz.* By giving it proper and suf-

---

* *Vid.* Hutch. *Mor. Inst.* Lib. II. Cap. 3. [Francis Hutcheson, *Philosophiae moralis institutio compendiaria* (1742), 2nd ed., Glasgow, 1745. Following his death, Hutcheson's "Compends" were translated into English as *A Short Introduction to Moral Philosophy in Three Books, Containing the Elements of Ethics and the Law of Nature* (1747).]

ficient Materials for judging right, *i.e.* by enquiring into the whole State of the Case, the Relations, Connections, and several Obligations of the Actor, the Consequences, and other Circumstances of the Action, or the Surplusage of private or public Good which results, or is likely to result, from the Action or from the Omission of it. If those Circumstances are fairly and fully stated, the Conscience will be just and impartial in its Decision. For by a necessary Law of our Nature, it approves, and is well affected to the *Moral Form;* and if it seems to approve of *Vice* or *Immorality,* it is always under the Notion or Mask of some *Virtue.* So that strictly speaking, it is not Conscience which errs; for its Sentence is always conformable to the View of the Case which lies before it; and is *just,* upon the Supposition that the Case is truly such as it is represented to it. All the Fault is to be imputed to the Agent, who neglects to be better informed, or who, through Weakness or Wickedness, hastens to pass Sentence from an imperfect Evidence. Thus, he who persecutes another for the Sake of Conscience, or a Mistake in religious Opinion, does not approve of Injustice, or Cruelty, any more than his mistaken Neighbour who suffers by it; but thinking the Severity he uses conformable to the Divine Will or salutary to the Patient, or at least to the Society of the Faithful, whose Interest he reckons far preferable not only to the Interest of so small a Part, but to all the vast Remainder of Mankind; and thinking withal, that Severity is the only Means of securing that highest Interest, he passes a Sentence as just, and consequential from those Principles, as a Physician, who to save the whole Body, orders the Amputation of a gangrened Limb, thinking that the only Remedy. Perhaps, in the *latter* Case, an able Practitioner might have accomplished the Cure by a less dangerous Operation; and in the *former,* a better Casuist, or a greater Master in spiritual Medicine, might have contrived a Cure, full as sure, and much more innocent.

Having now given the general Divisions of *Duty* or *Virtue,* which exhibit its different Faces and Attitudes, as it stands directed to its respective Objects, let us next descend into Particulars, and mark its most minute Features and Proportions, as they appear in the Detail of human Life.

Of Man's Duty to Himself. Of the Nature of Good, and the Chief Good

Divisions of Good Every Creature, by the Constitution of his Nature, is determined to love himself, to pursue whatever tends to his Preservation and Happiness, and to avoid whatever tends to his Hurt and Misery. Being endued with Sense and Perception, he must necessarily receive *Pleasure* from some Objects, and *Pain* from others. Those Objects which give Pleasure are called *good,* and those which give Pain, *evil.* To the former he feels that Attraction or Motion we call *Desire,* or *Love:* to the latter that Impulse we call *Aversion,* or *Hatred.* To Objects which suggest neither Pleasure nor Pain, and are apprehended of no Use to procure one, or ward off the other, we feel neither *Desire* nor *Aversion,* and such Objects are called *indifferent.* Those Objects which do not of themselves procure Pleasure or Pain, but are the *Means* of procuring either, we call *useful* or *noxious.* Towards them we are affected in a subordinate manner, or with an *indirect* or *reflective,* rather than a *direct* and *immediate* Affection. All the original and particular Affections of our Nature, lead us out to, and ultimately rest in, the first kind of Objects, *viz.* those which give immediate Pleasure, and which we therefore call *good, directly so.* The calm Affection of *Self-love* alone is conversant about such Objects as are only *consequentially good,* or merely useful to ourselves.

Moral Good But besides those Sorts of Objects which we call good, merely and solely as they give Pleasure, or are Means of procuring it, there is an higher and nobler Species of Good, towards which we feel that peculiar

Movement we call *Approbation,* or *Moral Complacency,* and which *we therefore* denominate *Moral Good.* Such are our Affections, and the consequent Actions to them. The Perception of this is, as has been already observed, quite distinct in kind from the Perception of the other Species; and though it may be connected with *Pleasure* or *Advantage,* by the benevolent Constitution of Nature, yet it constitutes a Good independent of that Pleasure and that Advantage, and far superior not in Degree only, but in Dignity to both. The *other,* viz. the *Natural* Good, consists in obtaining those Pleasures which are adapted to the peculiar Senses and Passions susceptible of them, and is as various as are those Senses and Passions. *This,* viz. the *Moral Good,* lies in the right Conduct of the several Senses and Passions, or their just Proportion and Accommodation to their respective Objects and Relations; and this is of a more simple and invariable kind.

By our several Senses we are capable of a great Variety of pleasing Sensations. These constitute distinct Ends, or Objects ultimately pursuable for their own Sake. To these Ends, or ultimate Objects, correspond peculiar Appetites or Affections, which prompt the Mind to pursue them. When these are attained, there it rests and looks no farther. Whatever therefore is pursuable, not on its own Account, but as subservient or necessary to the Attainment of something else that is intrinsically valuable or for its own Sake, be that Value ever so great, or ever so small, we call a *Mean,* and not an *End.* So that *Ends,* and not *Means,* constitute the *Materials,* or the very *Essence* of our *Happiness.* Consequently Happiness, *i.e. human* Happiness, cannot be one simple uniform Thing, in Creatures constituted as we are, with such various Senses of Pleasure, or such different Capacities of Enjoyment. Now the same Principle, or Law of our Nature, which determines us to pursue any one End, or Species of Good, prompts us to pursue every other End, or Species of Good, of which we are susceptible, or to which our Maker has adapted an original Propension. But amidst the great Multiplicity of *Ends* or *Goods,* which form the various Ingredients of our Happiness, we perceive an evident *Gradation* or *Subordination,* suited to that Gradation of *Senses, Powers,* and *Passions,* which prevails in our mixed and various

Human
Happiness

Constitution, and to that ascending Series of Connections, which open upon us in the different Stages of our progressive State.

Gradation of
Goods

Thus the Goods of the *Body,* or of the *external Senses,* seem to hold the lowest Rank in this Gradation or Scale of Goods. These we have in common with the Brutes; and tho' many Men are brutish enough to pursue the Goods of the Body with a more than brutal Fury; yet when at any time they come in Competition with Goods of an higher Order, the unanimous Verdict of Mankind, by giving the last the Preference, condemns the first to the meanest Place. Goods consisting in exterior social Connections, as *Fame, Fortune, Power, Civil Authority,* seem to succeed next, and are chiefly valuable as the Means of procuring *natural* or *moral* Good, but principally the latter. Goods of the *Intellect* are still superior, as *Taste, Knowledge, Memory, Judgment,* &c. The highest are *moral* Goods of the Mind, directly and ultimately regarding ourselves, as *Command of the Appetites* and *Passions, Prudence, Fortitude, Benevolence,* &c. These are the great Objects of our Pursuit, and the principal Ingredients of our Happiness. Let us consider each of them, as they rise one above the other in this natural Series or Scale, and touch briefly on our Obligations to pursue them.

The Brevity of this Work will not permit us minutely to weigh the *real* or *comparative* Moment of the different kinds of Goods, which offer themselves to the Mind, or to scrutinize the particular Pleasures of which we are susceptible, either as to *Intenseness* or *Duration,* and the Enjoyment of which depends on Accidents rather than our Attention and Industry. We shall therefore confine ourselves to the Consideration of such Goods as lie properly within our own Sphere, and being the Objects of our Attention and Care, fall within the Verge of *Duty.*

Goods of
the Body

Those of the Body are *Health, Strength, Agility, Hardiness,* and *Patience of Change, Neatness,* and *Decency.*

Good Health

Good Health, and a regular easy Flow of Spirits, are in themselves sweet natural Enjoyments, a great Fund of Pleasure, and indeed the proper Seasoning which gives a Flavour and Poignancy to every other Pleasure.

The Want of Health unfits us for most Duties of Life, and is especially an Enemy to the social and human Affections, as it generally renders the unhappy Sufferer peevish and sullen, disgusted at the Allotments of Providence, and consequently apt to entertain suspicious and gloomy Sentiments of its Author. It obstructs the free Exercise and full Improvement of our Reason, makes us a Burthen to our Friends, and useless to Society. Whereas the uninterrupted Enjoyment of good Health, is a constant Source of good Humour, and good Humour is a great Friend to Openness and Benignity of Heart, enables us to encounter the various Ills and Disappointments of Life with more Courage, or to sustain them with more Patience; and, in short, conduces much, if we are otherwise duly qualified, to our acting our Part, in every Exigency of Life, with more Firmness, Consistency, and Dignity. Therefore, it imports us much to preserve and improve an Habit or Enjoyment, without which every other external Entertainment is tasteless, and most other Advantages of little Avail. And this is best done by a strict Temperance in Diet and Regimen, by regular Exercise, and by keeping the Mind serene and unruffled by violent Passions, and unsubdued by intense and constant Labours, which greatly impair and gradually destroy, the strongest Constitutions.

How preserved

Strength, Agility, Hardiness, and *Patience of Change,* suppose Health, and are unattainable without it; but they imply something more, and are necessary to guard it, to give us the perfect Use of Life and Limbs, and to secure us against many otherwise unavoidable Ills. The Exercise of the necessary manual, and of most of the elegant, Arts of Life, depends on Strength and Agility of Body; personal Dangers, private and public Dangers, the Demands of our Friends, our Families, and Country, require them; they are necessary in War, and ornamental in Peace; fit for the Employments of a Country and a Town Life, and they exalt the Entertainments and Diversions of both. They are chiefly obtained by moderate and regular Exercise.

Strength, Agility, &c.

How attained

Few are so much raised above Want and Dependence, or so exempted from Business and Care, as not to be often exposed to Inequalities and

Patience of Change

Changes of Diet, Exercise, Air, Climate, and other Irregularities. Now what can be so effectual to secure one against the Mischiefs arising from such unavoidable Alterations, as Hardiness and a certain Versatility of Constitution, which can bear extraordinary Labours, and submit to great Changes, without any sensible Uneasiness or bad Consequences. *How attained* This is best attained, not by an over-great Delicacy and minute Attention to Forms, or by an invariable Regularity in Diet, Hours, and Way of Living, but rather by a bold and discreet Latitude of Regimen. Besides, Deviations from established Rules and Forms of Living, if kept within the Bounds of Sobriety and Reason, are friendly to Thought and original Sentiment, animate the dull Scene of ordinary Life and Business, and agreeably stir the Passions, which stagnate or breed ill Humour in the Calms of Life.

Neatness, *Neatness, Cleanliness,* and *Decency,* to which we may add *Dignity* of
Decency, &c. *Countenance,* and *Demeanour,* seem to have something refined and moral in them. At least we generally esteem them Indications of an orderly, genteel, and well-governed Mind, conscious of inward Worth, or the Respect due to one's Nature. Whereas *Nastiness, Slovenliness, Aukwardness,* and *Indecency,* are shrewd Symptoms of something mean, careless, and deficient, and betray a Mind untaught, illiberal, unconscious of what is due to one's self or to others. How much Cleanliness conduces to Health needs hardly be mentioned; and how necessary it is to maintain one's Character and Rank in Life, and to render us agreeable to others as well as to ourselves, is as evident.—There are certain Motions, Airs and Gestures, which become the human Countenance and Form, in which we perceive a *Comeliness, Openness, Simplicity, Gracefulness;* and there are others, which, to our Sense of Decorum, appear *uncomely, affected, disingenuous,* and *aukward,* quite unsuitable to the native Dignity of our Face and Form. The *first* are in themselves the most easy, natural, and commodious, give one Boldness and Presence of Mind, a modest Assurance, an Address both awful and alluring, they bespeak Candour and Greatness of Mind, raise the most agreeable Prejudices in one's Favour, render Society engaging, command Respect, and often Love, and give Weight and Authority both in Conversation

and Business; in fine, they are the Colouring of Virtue, which shews it to the greatest Advantage in whomsoever it is; and not only imitate, but in some measure supply it where it is wanting. Whereas the last, *viz.* *Rudeness, Affectation, Indecorum,* and the like, have all the contrary Effects; they are burthensome to one's self, a Dishonour to our Nature, and a Nusance in Society. The former Qualities or Goods are best attained by a liberal Education, by preserving a just Sense of the Dignity of our Nature, by keeping the best and politest Company, but above all, by acquiring those virtuous and ennobling Habits of Mind, which are Decency in Perfection, which will give an Air of unaffected Grandeur, and spread a Lustre truly engaging over the whole Form and Deportment.

How attained

We are next to consider those Goods which consist in exterior social Connections, as *Fame, Fortune, Civil Authority, Power.*

Goods of exterior social Connections

The first has a twofold Aspect, as a Good, pleasant in itself, or gratifying to an original Passion, and then as expedient or useful towards a farther End. Honour from the Wise and Good, on Account of a virtuous Conduct, is regaling to a good Man; for then his Heart re-echoes to the grateful Sound. There are few quite indifferent, even to the Commendation of the Vulgar. Tho' we cannot approve that Conduct which proceeds entirely from this Principle, and not from good Affection or Love of the Conduct itself, yet as it is often a Guard and additional Motive to Virtue in Creatures, imperfect as we are, and often distracted by interfering Passions, it might be dangerous to suppress it altogether, however wise it may be to restrain it within due Bounds, and however laudable to use it only as a Scaffolding to our Virtue, which may be taken down when that glorious Structure is finished, but hardly till then. To pursue Fame for itself, is *innocent;* to regard it only as an Auxiliary to Virtue, is *noble;* to seek it chiefly as an Engine of public Usefulness, is still more noble, and highly praise-worthy. For tho' the Opinion and Breath of Men are transparent and fading Things, often obtained without Merit, and lost without Cause; yet, as our Business is with Men, and as our Capacity of serving them is generally increased in proportion

Fame

to their Esteem of us, therefore sound and well-established *moral* Applause may, and will be modestly, not ostentatiously sought after by the *Good;* not indeed as a solitary refined Sort of Luxury, but as a public and proper Instrument to serve and bless Mankind. At the same time they will learn to despise that Reputation which is founded on Rank, Fortune, and any other Circumstances or Accomplishments that are foreign to real Merit, or to useful Services done to others, and think that Praise of little avail which is purchased without Desert, and bestowed without Judgment.

Fortune, Power, &c. *Fortune, Power,* and *Civil Authority,* or whatever is called Influence and Weight among Mankind, are *Goods* of the *second* Division, that is, valuable or pursuable only as they are *useful,* or as Means to a farther End, *viz.* the procuring or preserving the immediate Objects of Enjoyment or Happiness to ourselves or others. Therefore to love such Goods on their own Account, and to pursue them as *Ends,* not the *Means* of Enjoyment, must be highly preposterous and absurd. There can be no Measure, no Limit to such Pursuit; all must be Whim, Caprice, Extravagance. Accordingly such Appetites, unlike all the *natural* ones, are increased by Possession, and whetted by Enjoyment. They are always precarious, and never without Fears, because the Object lies without one's self; they are seldom without Sorrow and Vexation, because no Accession of Wealth or Power can satisfy them. But if those Goods are considered only as the Materials or Means of private or public Happiness, then the same Obligations which bind us to pursue the latter, bind us How far pursuable likewise to pursue the former. We may, and no doubt we ought, to seek such a Measure of Wealth as is necessary to supply all our real Wants, to raise us above servile Dependence, and to provide us with such Conveniences as are suited to our Rank and Condition in Life. To be regardless of this Measure of Wealth, is to expose ourselves to all the Temptations of Poverty and Corruption, to forfeit our natural Independency and Freedom, to degrade, and consequently to render the Rank we hold, and the Character we sustain in Society, useless, if not contemptible. When these important Ends are secured, we ought not to murmur or repine that we possess no more; yet we are not secluded by any Obligation, moral or divine, from seeking more, in order to give us that happiest and most god-like of all Powers, the *Power* of *doing Good*. A supine Indolence in this respect is both absurd and criminal; *absurd*, as it robs us of an inexhausted Fund of the most refined and durable Enjoyments; and *criminal*, as it renders us so far useless to the Society to which we belong. "That Pursuit of Wealth which goes be- *Avarice* yond the former End, *viz.* the obtaining the Necessaries, or such Conveniencies of Life, as, in the Estimation of Reason, not of Vanity or Passion, are suited to our Rank and Condition, and yet is not directed to the latter, *viz.* the doing Good, is what we call AVARICE." And "that Pursuit of *Power*, which, after securing one's self, *i.e.* attained the proper *Ambition* Independence and Liberty of a rational social Creature, is not directed to the Good of others, is what we call *Ambition,* or the *Lust of Power.*" To what Extent the strict Measures of Virtue will allow us to pursue either Wealth, or Power, and Civil Authority, is not perhaps possible precisely to determine. That must be left to Prudence, and the peculiar Character, Condition, and other Circumstances of each Man. Only thus far a Limit may be set, that the Pursuit of either must encroach upon no other Duty or Obligation which we owe to ourselves, to Society, or to its Parent and Head. The same Reasoning is to be applied to *Power* as to *Wealth*. It is only valuable as an Instrument of our own Security, and of the free Enjoyment of those original Goods it may, and often does, administer to us, and as an Engine of more extensive Happiness to our Friends, our Country, and Mankind. In this Degree it may, and unless a greater Good forbids it, ought to be sought after; and when it is either offered to us, or may be obtained, consistently with a good Conscience, it would be criminal to decline it, and a selfish Indolence to neglect the necessary Means of acquiring it.

Now the best, and indeed the only Way to obtain a solid and lasting *How Fame* *Fame,* is an uniform inflexible Course of Virtue, the employing one's *and Power are* Ability and Wealth in supplying the Wants, and using one's Power in *attained* promoting or securing the Happiness, the Rights and Liberties of Mankind, joined to an universal Affability and Politeness of Manners. And surely one will not mistake the Matter much, who thinks the same

Course conducive to the acquiring greater Accessions both of Wealth
and Power; especially if he adds to those Qualifications a vigorous Industry, a constant Attention to the Characters and Wants of Men, to
the Conjunctures of Times, and continually varying Genius of Affairs,
and a steddy intrepid Honesty, that will neither yield to the Allurements, nor be over-awed with the Terrors of that corrupt and corrupting Scene in which we live. We have sometimes heard indeed of other
Ways and Means, as Fraud, Dissimulation, Servility, and Prostitution,
and the like ignoble Arts, by which the Men of the World (as they are
called, shrewd Politicians, and Men of Address!) amass Wealth, and
procure Power: but as we want rather to form a Man of Virtue, an honest, contented, happy Man, we leave to the Men of the World their own
Ways, and permit them, unenvied, and unimitated by us, to reap the
Fruit of their Doings.

Goods of the   The next Species of Objects in the Scale of Good, are the Goods of the
Intellect   *Intellect*, as *Knowledge, Memory, Judgment, Taste, Sagacity, Docility*, and
whatever else we call *intellectual* Virtues. Let us consider them a little,
and the *Means* as well as *Obligations* to improve them.

Their Moment   As *Man* is a *rational* Creature, capable of knowing the Differences of
Things and Actions;—as he not only sees and feels what is present, but
remembers what is past, and often foresees what is future;—as he advances, from small Beginnings, by slow Degrees, and with much Labour and Difficulty, to Knowledge and Experience:—as his Opinions
sway his Passions,—as Passions influence his Conduct,—and as his
Conduct draws Consequences after it, which extend, not only to the
present, but to the future Time, and therefore is the principal Source of
his Happiness or Misery, it is evident, that he is formed for intellectual
Improvements, and that it must be of the utmost Consequence for him
to improve and cultivate his intellectual Powers, on which those Opinions, those Passions, and that Conduct depend.*

* *Vid Philos. Sinic. Confuc. Lib.* I. §. 3, 4, &c. [*Confucius Sinarum Philosophus,
sive Scientia sinensis latine exposita.* Studio & opera Prosperi Intorcetta, Christiani

But besides the future Consequences and Moment of improving our *intellectual* Powers, their immediate Exercise on their proper Objects yields the most rational and refined Pleasures. Knowledge and a right Taste in the Arts of *Imitation* and *Design,* as *Poetry, Painting, Sculpture, Music, Architecture,* afford not only an innocent, but a most sensible and sublime Entertainment. By these the Understanding is instructed in ancient and modern Life, the History of Men and Things, the Energies and Effects of the Passions, the Consequences of Virtue and Vice; by these the Imagination is at once entertained and nourished with the Beauties of Nature and Art, lighted up and spread out with the Novelty, Grandeur, and Harmony of the Universe; and in fine, the Passions are agreeably rouzed, and suitably engaged with the greatest and most interesting Objects that can fill the human Mind. He who has a Taste formed to these ingenious Delights, and Plenty of Materials to gratify it, can never want the most agreeable Exercise and Entertainment, nor once have reason to make that fashionable Complaint of the Tediousness of Time. Nor can he want a proper Subject for the Discipline and Improvement of his Heart. For being daily conversant with *Beauty, Order,* and *Design,* in inferior Subjects, he bids fair for growing, in due Time, an Admirer of what is fair and well-proportioned in the Conduct of Life, and the Order of Society, which is only *Order* and *Design* exerted in their highest Subjects. He will learn to transfer the Numbers of Poetry to the Harmony of the Mind, and of well-governed Passions; and from admiring the Virtues of others in moral Paintings, come to approve and imitate them himself. Therefore to cultivate a *true* and *correct Taste,* must be both our *Interest* and our *Duty,* when the Circumstances of our Station give Leisure and Opportunity for it, and when the doing it is not inconsistent with our higher Obligations or Engagements to Society and Mankind.

The Pleasures they give

Knowledge and Taste

It is best attained by reading the best Books, where *good Sense* has more the Ascendant than *Learning,* and which retain more to *Practice* than to

How attained

Herdtrich, Francisci Rougemont, Philippi Couplet. . . . (Paris: Daniel Horthemels, 1687). This volume of Confucius's sayings, along with additional material, was edited and authored by four Jesuit priests and was the primary source of information about Confucian thought in eighteenth-century Europe.]

Speculation; by studying the best Models, *i.e.* those which profess to imitate Nature most, and approach the nearest to it, and by conversing
with Men of the most refined Taste, and the greatest Experience in Life.

Moment of
intellectual
Goods

As to the other *intellectual* Goods, what a Fund of Entertainment must
it be to investigate the Truth and various Relations of Things, to trace
the Operations of Nature to general Laws, to explain by these its manifold Phaenomena, to understand that Order by which the Universe is
upheld, and that Oeconomy by which it is governed; to be acquainted
with the human Mind, the Connections, Subordinations, and Uses of
its Powers, and to mark their Energy in Life! How agreeable to the ingenious Enquirer, to observe the manifold Relations and Combinations
of individual Minds in Society, to discern the Causes why they flourish
or decay, and from thence to ascend, through the vast Scale of Beings,
to that *general* Mind which presides over all, and operates unseen in
every System, and in every Age, through the whole Compass and Progression of Nature! Devoted to such Entertainments as these, the *Contemplative* have abandoned every other Pleasure, retired from the Body,
so to speak, and sequester'd themselves from social Intercourse; for
these the *Busy* have often preferred to the Hurry and Din of Life, the
calm Retreats of Contemplation; for these, when once they come to
taste them, even the *Gay* and *Voluptuous* have thrown up the lawless
Pursuits of Sense and Appetite, and acknowledged these mental Enjoyments to be the most *refined,* and indeed the *only* Luxury. Besides, by a
just and large Knowledge of Nature, we recognize the Perfections of its
Author; and thus Piety, and all those pious Affections which depend on
just Sentiments of his Character, are awakened and confirmed; and a
thousand superstitious Fears, that arise from partial Views of his Nature
and Works, will of course be excluded. An extensive Prospect of human
Life, and of the Periods and Revolutions of human Things, will conduce much to the giving a certain Greatness of Mind, and a noble Contempt of those little Competitions about Power, Honour, and Wealth,
which *disturb* and *divide* the Bulk of Mankind; and to promote a calm
Indurance of those Inconveniencies and Ills that are the common Ap-

pendages of Humanity. Add to all, that a just Knowledge of human Nature, and of those Hinges upon which the Business and Fortunes of Men turn, will prevent our thinking either too highly, or too meanly of our Fellow-Creatures, give no small Scope to the Exercise of Friendship, Confidence, and Good-will, and, at the same time, brace the Mind with a proper Caution and Distrust, those Nerves of Prudence, and give a greater Mastery in the Conduct of private as well as public Life. Therefore, by cultivating our Intellectual Abilities, we shall best promote and secure our Interest, and be qualified for acting our Part in Society with more Honour to ourselves, as well as Advantage to Mankind. Consequently to improve them to the utmost of our Power is our Duty; they are Talents committed to us by the Almighty Head of Society, and we are accountable to him for the use of them. But be it remembered withal, that how engaging soever the *Muses* and *Graces* are, they are chiefly valuable, as they are Handmaids to usher in and set off the *Moral Virtues,* from whose Service if they are ever divorced, they become Retainers to the meaner Passions, Panders to Vice, and convert Men (if we may use the Expression) into a refined Sort of Savages.

The Intellectual Virtues are best improved by accurate and impartial   How attained
Observation, extensive Reading, and unconfined Converse with Men of all Characters, especially with Those who, to private Study, have joined the widest Acquaintance with the World, and greatest Practice in Affairs; but above all, by being much in the World, and having large Dealings with Mankind. Such Opportunities contribute much to divest one of Prejudices and a servile Attachment to crude Systems, to open one's Views, and to give that Experience on which the most useful, because the most practical, Knowledge is built, and from which the surest Maxims for the Conduct of Life are deduced.

The highest Goods which enter into the Composition of Human Hap-   Moral Goods
piness are *Moral* Goods of the Mind, directly and ultimately regarding ourselves: as *Command of the Appetites* and *Passions, Prudence* and *Caution, Magnanimity, Fortitude, Humility, Love of Virtue, Love of God,*

Resignation, and the like. These sublime Goods are Goods by way of Eminence, Goods recommended and enforced by the most intimate and awful Sense and Consciousness of our Nature; Goods that constitute the Quintessence, the very Temper of Happiness, that Form and Complexion of Soul which renders us approveable and lovely in the Sight of God; Goods, in fine, which are the Elements of all our future Perfection and Felicity.

Their Moment   Most of the other Goods we have considered depend partly on ourselves, and partly on Accidents which we can neither foresee nor prevent, and result from Causes which we cannot influence or alter. They are such Goods as we may possess to-day and lose to-morrow, and which require a Felicity of Constitution, and Talents to attain them in full Vigour and Perfection, and a Felicity of Conjunctures to secure the Possession of them. Therefore did our Happiness depend altogether or chiefly on such transitory and precarious Possessions, it were itself most precarious, and the highest Folly to be anxious about it.—But though Creatures, constituted as we are, cannot be indifferent about such Goods, and must suffer in some degree, and consequently have our Happiness incomplete without them, yet they weigh but little in the Scale, when compared with Moral Goods. By the benevolent Constitution of our Nature these are placed within the Sphere of our Activity, so that no Man can be destitute of them unless he is first wanting to himself. Some of the wisest and best of Mankind have wanted most of the former Goods, and all the external kind, and felt most of the opposite Ills, such at least as arise from without; yet by possessing the latter, *viz.* the Moral Goods, have declared they were happy, and to the Conviction of the most impartial Observers have appeared happy. The worst of Men have been surrounded with every outward Good and Advantage of Fortune, and have possessed great Parts; yet, for want of Moral Rectitude, have been, and have confessed themselves, notoriously and exquisitely miserable. The Exercise of Virtue has supported its Votaries, and made them exult in the midst of Tortures almost intolerable; nay, how often has some false Form or Shadow of it sustained even the greatest Villains* and Bigots under the same Pressures! But no external Goods, no Goods of Fortune have been able to alleviate the Agonies, or expel the Fears of a guilty Mind, conscious of the deserved Hatred and Reproach of Mankind, and the just Displeasure of Almighty God. The other Senses and Capacities of Enjoyment are gratified when they obtain their respective Objects, and the Happiness of the corresponding Passions depends on their Success in their several Pursuits. Thus the Love of Honour, of Pleasure, of Power, and the like, are satisfied only when they obtain the desired Honour, Pleasure, or Power: when they fail of attaining these, they are disappointed, and Disappointment gives Disgust. But *Moral Good* is of so singular and sublime a Nature, that when the Mind is in pursuit of it, though it should prove unsuccessful in its Aims, it can rest in the Conduct without repining, without being dejected at the ill Success; nay, the Pleasure attending the Consciousness of upright Aims and generous Efforts absorbs the Disappointment, and makes inferior Ends disappear as of no amount in the great Aggregate or Surplusage of Good that remains. So that though Human Happiness, in the present State, consists of many separate and little Rivulets, which must often be left dry in the perpetual Flux and Reflux of Human Things, yet the main Stream, with which those lesser ones do generally communicate, flows from within, from the Heart of Man, and, if this be sound and clear, rolls on through Life with a strong and equal Current. Yet as many small Articles make up a pretty large Sum, and as those inferior Goods which enter into the Account, *Health, Fame, Fortune,* and the like, are often, even after our utmost Care, unattainable, or at least precarious, it is evidently of the utmost Consequence to be prepared against the Want or Loss of them, by having our Desires moderate, and our Passions under due Com-

---

*As Ravilliac, *who assassinated* Henry *the Fourth of* France; *and* Balthasar Geraerd, *who murdered* William *the First Prince of* Orange. [The assassinations committed by François Ravaillac (1578–1610) and Balthazar Gerard (1557–84) were religiously motivated, in each case a Catholic assassin killing a royal who was sympathetic to Protestant interests.]

mand. And let it be remembered, that it is not only of great Importance to our Ease and Security against Ill, but one of the highest Improvements of Virtue, to contemn those Things, the Contempt of which is truly great and heroic, and to place our Happiness chiefly in those virtuous Exercises and Affections which arise from a pure and well-disposed Mind; an Happiness which no Condition of Life can exclude, no Change of Fortune interrupt or destroy. This will arm and fortify the Mind against the Want of those inferior Goods, and against those Pains which result to the Generality of Mankind from the contrary Evils.

The mixed Condition of Human Life requires particular Virtues — As the present Condition of Human Life is wonderfully chequered with Good and Ill, and as no Height of Station, no Affluence of Fortune, can absolutely insure the Good, or secure against the Ill, it is evident that a great Part of the Comfort and Serenity of Life must lie in having our Minds duly affected with regard to both, *i.e.* rightly attempered to the Loss of one and the Sufferance of the other. For it is certain that outward Calamities derive their chief Malignity and Pressure from the inward Dispositions with which we receive them. By managing these right, we may greatly abate that Malignity and Pressure, and consequently diminish the Number, and weaken the Moment of the Ills of Life, if we should not have it in our Power to obtain a large Share of its Goods. There are particularly three Virtues which go to the forming this right Temper towards Ill, and which are of singular Efficacy, if not totally to remove, yet wonderfully to alleviate the Calamities of Life. These are *Fortitude,* or *Patience, Humility,* and *Resignation.* Let us consider them a little, and the Effects they produce.

Fortitude — *Fortitude* is that calm and steddy Habit of Mind, which either moderates our Fears, and enables us bravely to encounter the Prospect of Ill, or renders the Mind serene and invincible under its immediate Pressure. It lies equally distant from Rashness and Cowardice, and though it does not hinder us from feeling, yet prevents our complaining or shrinking under the Stroke. It always includes a generous Contempt of, or at least a noble Superiority to, those precarious Goods of which we can insure neither the Possession nor Continuance. The Man therefore who possesses this Virtue in this ample Sense of it, stands upon an Eminence, and sees human Things below him; the Tempest indeed may reach him, but he stands secure and collected against it upon the Basis of conscious Virtue, which the severest Storms can seldom shake, and never overthrow.

Humility is another Virtue of high Rank and Dignity, though often mistaken by proud Mortals for Meanness and Pusillanimity. It is opposed to *Pride,* which commonly includes in it a false or over-rated Estimation of our own Merit, an Ascription of it to ourselves as its only and original Cause, an undue Comparison of ourselves with others, and, in consequence of that supposed Superiority, an arrogant Preference of ourselves, and a supercilious Contempt of them. *Humility,* on the other hand, seems to denote that modest and ingenuous Temper of Mind, which arises from a just and equal Estimate of our own Advantages compared with those of others, and from a Sense of our deriving all originally from the Author of our Being. Its ordinary Attendants are Mildness, a gentle Forbearance, and an easy unassuming Humanity with regard to the Imperfections and Faults of others; Virtues rare indeed, but of the fairest Complexion, the proper Offspring of so lovely a Parent, the best Ornaments of such imperfect Creatures as we are, precious in the Sight of God, and which sweetly allure the Hearts of Men.—This Virtue was not altogether unknown to the more sober Moralists among the Ancients, who place *Submissio Animi* among the Train of Virtues; but it is taught in its highest Perfection, and enforced by the greatest Examples, and the strongest Motives, in the *Christian* Religion, which recommends and exalts this, as well as every other Moral and Divine Virtue, beyond every other System of Religion and Philosophy that ever appeared in the World; and teaches us throughout the whole of it, to refer every Virtue, and every Endowment, to their original Source, the Father of Lights, *from whom descends every good and perfect Gift.* Humility is a Virtue which highly adorns the Character in which it resides, and sets off every other Virtue; it is an admirable Ingredient of a contented Mind, and an excellent Security against many of those Ills in Life which are most sensibly felt by People of a delicate Nature. To be persuaded of this, we need only remember how many of our Uneasinesses arise from the Mortifications of our Pride—how almost every Ill we suffer, and all the Opposition we meet with, is aggravated and sharpened by the Reflection on our imaginary Merit, or how little we deserved those Ills, and how much we were entitled to the opposite Goods. Whereas, a sober Sense of what we are, and whose we are, and a Consciousness how far short our Virtue is of that Standard of Perfection to which we ought to aspire, will blunt the Edge of Injuries and Affronts, and make us sit down contented with our Share of the Goods, and easy under the Ills of Life, which this quick-sighted, unassuming Virtue will teach us often to trace to our own Misconduct, and consequently to interpret as the just and wholesome Correction of Heaven.

Resignation   *Resignation* is that mild and heroic Temper of Mind, which arises from a Sense of an infinitely wise and good Providence, and enables one to acquiesce, with a cordial Affection, in its just Appointments. This Virtue has something very peculiar in its Nature, and sublime in its Efficacy. For it teaches us to bear Ill not only with Patience and as being unavoidable, but it transforms, as it were, Ill into Good, by leading us to consider it, and every Event that has the least Appearance of Ill, as a Divine Dispensation, a wise and benevolent Temperament of Things, subservient to universal Good, and, of course, including that of every Individual, especially of such as calmly stoop to it. In this Light, the Administration itself, nay, every Act of it, becomes an Object of Affection, the Evil disappears, or is converted into a Balm which both heals and nourishes the Mind. For, though the first expected Access of Ill may surprize the Soul into Grief, yet that Grief, when the Mind calmly reviews its Object, changes into Contentment, and is by degrees exalted into Veneration and a divine Composure. Our private Will is lost in that of the Almighty, and our Security against any real Ill rests on the same Bottom as the Throne of him who lives and reigns for ever. He, therefore, who is provided with such Armour, taken, if we may say so, from the Armory of Heaven, may be proof against the sharpest Arrows of Fortune, and defy the Impotence of human Malice; and though he cannot be secure against those Ills which are the ordinary Appendages of Man's Lot, yet may possess that quiet contented Mind which takes off their Pungency, and is next to an Exemption from them. But we can only touch on these Things; a fuller Detail of our Obligations to cultivate and pursue these Moral Goods of the Mind, and the best Method of doing it, must be reserved to another and more proper Place.

Before we finish this Section, it may be fit to observe, that as the Deity is the supreme and inexhausted Source of Good, on whom the Happiness of the whole Creation depends; as he is the Object in Nature, and the only Object who is fully proportioned to the *Intellectual* and *Moral* Powers of the Mind, in whom they ultimately rest and find their most perfect Exercise and Completion, he is therefore termed the CHIEF GOOD of Man, OBJECTIVELY considered. And *Virtue,* or the proportioned and vigorous Exercise of the several Powers and Affections on their respective Objects, as above described, is, in the Schools, termed the CHIEF GOOD, FORMALLY considered, or its FORMAL Idea, being the inward Temper and native Constitution of Human Happiness.

Chief Good Objective and Formal

From the Detail we have gone thro', the following Corollaries may be deduced.

First, It is evident that the Happiness of such a *Progressive* Creature as Man can never be at a stand, or continue a fixed invariable Thing. His finite Nature, let it rise ever so high, admits still higher Degrees of Improvement and Perfection. And his Progression in Improvement, or Virtue, always makes way for a Progression in Happiness. So that no possible Point can be assigned in any Period of his Existence in which he is perfectly happy, that is, so happy as to exclude higher Degrees of Happiness. All his Perfection is only comparative. 2. It appears that many Things must conspire to complete the Happiness of so *various* a Creature as Man, subject to so many Wants, and susceptible of such different Pleasures. 3. As his Capacities of Pleasure cannot be all gratified at the same time, and must often interfere with each other in such a precarious and fleeting State as Human Life, or be frequently disappointed, perfect Happiness, *i.e.* the undisturbed Enjoyment of the sev-

Corollaries

eral Pleasures of which we are capable, is unattainable in our present State. 4. That State is most to be sought after, in which the fewest Competitions and Disappointments can happen, which least of all impairs any Sense of Pleasure, and opens an inexhausted Source of the most refined and lasting Enjoyments. 5. That State which is attended with all those Advantages, is a State or Course of Virtue. 6. THEREFORE, a State of *Virtue,* in which the Moral Goods of the Mind are attained, is the HAPPIEST STATE.

Duties to Society

CHAPTER I

Filial and Fraternal Duty

As we have followed the Order of Nature in tracing the History of Man, and those Duties which he owes to himself, it seems reasonable to take the same Method with those he owes to Society, which constitute the *second* Class of his *Obligations.*

His Parents are among the earliest Objects of his Attention, he becomes soonest acquainted with them, reposes a peculiar Confidence in them, and seems to regard them with a fond Affection, the early Prognostics of his future *Piety* and *Gratitude.* Thus does Nature dictate the first Lines of filial Duty, even before a just Sense of the Connection is formed. But when the Child is grown up, and has attained to such a Degree of Understanding, as to comprehend the *Moral Tye,* and be sensible of the Obligations he is under to his Parents; when he looks back on their tender and disinterested Affection, their incessant Cares and Labours in nursing, educating, and providing for him, during that State in which he had neither Prudence nor Strength to care and provide for himself, he must be conscious that he owes to them these peculiar Duties.

Connection of Parents

To reverence and honour them as the Instruments of Nature in introducing him to Life, and to that State of Comfort and Happiness which

Duties to Parents

he enjoys; and therefore to esteem and imitate their good Qualities, to alleviate and bear with, and spread, as much as possible, a decent Veil over their Faults and Weaknesses.

2. To be highly grateful to them for those Favours which it can hardly ever be in his Power fully to repay; to shew this Gratitude by a strict Attention to their Wants, and a solicitous Care to supply them; by a submissive Deference to their Authority and Advice, especially by paying great Regard to it in the Choice of a Wife, and of an Occupation; by yielding to, rather than peevishly contending with their Humours, as remembering how oft they have been persecuted by his; and in fine, by soothing their Cares, lightening their Sorrows, supporting the Infirmities of Age, and making the remainder of their Life as comfortable and joyful as possible.—To pay these Honours and make these Returns is, according to *Plato,* to pay the oldest, best, and greatest of Debts, next to those we owe to our supreme and common Parent. They are founded in our Nature, and agreeable to the most fundamental Laws of *Gratitude, Honour, Justice, Natural Affection,* and *Piety,* which are interwoven with our very Constitution; nor can we be deficient in them without casting off that Nature, and counteracting those Laws.

Duties to Brethren and Sisters
As his Brethren and Sisters are the next with whom the Creature forms a *Social* and *Moral* Connection, to them he owes a *Fraternal* Regard; and with them ought he to enter into a strict League of Friendship, mutual Sympathy, Advice, Assistance, and a generous Intercourse of kind Offices, remembering their Relation to common Parents, and that Brotherhood of Nature, which unites them into a closer Community of Interest and Affection.

CHAPTER II

Concerning Marriage

When Man arrives to a certain Age, he becomes sensible of a peculiar Sympathy and Tenderness towards the other Sex; the Charms of Beauty engage his Attention, and call forth new and softer Dispositions than he has yet felt. The many amiable Qualities exhibited by a fair Outside, or by the mild Allurement of Female Manners, or which the prejudiced Spectator without much Reasoning supposes those to include, with several other Circumstances, both natural and accidental, point his View and Affection to a particular Object, and of course contract that general rambling Regard, which was lost and useless among the undistinguished Croud, into a peculiar and permanent Attachment to one Woman, which ordinarily terminates in the most important, venerable, and delightful Connection in Life. *Connection with the other Sex*

The State of the Brute Creation is very different from that of Human Creatures. The former are cloathed, and generally armed by their Structure, easily find what is necessary to their Subsistence, and soon attain their Vigour and Maturity; so that they need the Care and Aid of their Parents but for a short while; and therefore we see that Nature has assigned to them vagrant and transient Amours. The Connection being purely *Natural,* and formed merely for propagating and rearing their Offspring, no sooner is that End answered than the Connection dissolves of course. But the Human Race are of a more tender and defenceless Constitution; their Infancy and Non-age continue longer; they advance slowly to Strength of Body, and Maturity of Reason; they need constant Attention, and a long Series of Cares and Labours to train them up to Decency, Virtue, and the various Arts of Life. Nature has, therefore, provided them with the most affectionate and anxious Tutors, to aid their Weakness, to supply their Wants, and to accomplish them in those necessary Arts, even their own Parents, on whom she has devolved this mighty Charge, rendered agreeable by the most alluring and powerful of all Ties, Parental Affection. But unless both concur in *The Grounds of this Connection* this grateful Task, and continue their joint Labours, till they have reared up and planted out their young Colony, it must become a Prey to every rude Invader, and the Purpose of Nature, in the original Union of the Human Pair, be defeated. Therefore our Structure as well as Condition is an evident Indication, that the Human Sexes are destined for a more intimate, for a moral and lasting Union. It appears likewise, that the principal End of Marriage is not to propagate and nurse up an Off-spring, but to educate and form Minds for the great Duties and exten-sive Destinations of Life. Society must be supplied from this original Nursery with useful Members, and its fairest Ornaments and Supports. But how shall the young Plants be guarded against the Inclemency of the Air and Seasons, cultivated and raised to Maturity, if Men, like Brutes, indulge to vagrant and promiscuous Amours?

Moral Ends of Marriage The Mind is apt to be dissipated in its Views, and Acts of Friendship and Humanity; unless the *former* be directed to a particular Object, and the *latter* employed in a particular Province. When Men once indulge to this Dissipation, there is no stopping their Career, they grow insen-sible to Moral Attractions, and by obstructing, or impairing, the decent and regular Exercise of the tender and generous Feelings of the human Heart, they in time become unqualified for, or averse to, the forming a Moral Union of Souls, which is the Cement of Society, and the Source of the purest domestic Joys. Whereas a rational, undepraved *Love,* and its fair Companion, *Marriage,* collect a Man's Views, guide his Heart to its proper Object, and by confining his Affection to that Object, do re-ally enlarge its Influence and Use. Besides, it is but too evident from the Conduct of Mankind, that the common Tyes of Humanity are too fee-ble to engage and interest the Passions of the Generality in the Affairs of Society. The Connections of Neighbourhood, Acquaintance, and general Intercourse, are too wide a Field of Action for many; and those of a *Public* or *Community* are so for more, and in which they *either care not, or know not how* to exert themselves. Therefore Nature, ever wise and benevolent, by implanting that strong Sympathy which reigns be-tween the Individuals of each Sex, and by urging them to form a par-ticular Moral Connection, the Spring of many domestic Endearments, has measured out to each Pair a particular *Sphere of Action,* proportioned to their Views, and adapted to their respective Capacities. Besides, by interesting them deeply in the Concerns of their own little Circle, she has connected them more closely with Society, which is composed of particular Families, and bound them down to their good Behaviour in that particular Community to which they belong. This *Moral Connection* is *Marriage,* and this *Sphere of Action* is a *Family.* It appears from what has been said that, to adult Persons, who have Fortune sufficient to provide for a Family, according to their Rank and Condition in Life, and who are endued with the ordinary Degrees of Prudence necessary to manage a Family, and educate Children, it is a Duty they owe to Society, to marry.

Some Pretenders to a peculiar Refinement in Morals think, however, that a *single State* is most conducive to the Perfection of our Nature, and to those sublime Improvements to which Religion calls us. Sometimes indeed the more important Duties we owe to the Public, which could scarce be performed, or not so well in the Married State, may require the single Life, or render the other not so honourable a Station in such Circumstances. But surely, it must be improving to the *Social* Affections to direct them to particular Objects whom we esteem, and to whom we stand in the nearest Relation, and to ascertain their Exercise in a Field of Action, which is both agreeable in itself, and highly advantageous to Society. The constant Exercise of Natural Affection, in which one is necessarily engaged in providing for, and training up one's Children, opens the Heart, and must inure the Mind to frequent Acts of Self-denial and Self-command, and consequently strengthen the Habits of Goodness. The Truth of this is but too evident in those married Persons who are so unfortunate as to have no Children, who for want of those necessary Exercises of Humanity are too generally overanxious about the World, and perhaps too attentive to the Affair of Oeconomy. Another Circumstance deserves to be remembered, that Men who are continually engaged in *Study* and *Business,* or anxiously intent on public Concerns, are apt to grow stern and severe, or peevish and morose, on account of the frequent Rubs they meet with, or the

An Objection answered

Fatigues they undergo in such a Course. The Female Softness is therefore useful to moderate their Severity, and change their Ill-humour into
domestic Tenderness, and a softer kind of Humanity. And thus their
Minds, which were over-strained by the Intenseness of their Application, are at once relaxed, and retuned for public Action. The Minds of
both Sexes are as much formed one for the other by a Temperament
peculiar to each, as their Persons. The *Strength, Firmness, Courage,
Gravity,* and *Dignity,* of the *Man,* tally to the *Softness, Delicacy, Tenderness of Passion, Elegance of Taste,* and *Decency of Conversation,* of the
Woman. The *Male* Mind is formed to *defend, deliberate, foresee, contrive,*
and *advise.* The *Female* One to *confide, imagine, apprehend, comply,* and
execute. Therefore the proper Temperament of these different Sexes of
Minds, makes a fine Moral Union; and the well-proportioned Opposition of different or contrary Qualities, like a due Mixture of Discords
in a Composition of Music, swells the Harmony of Society more than
if they were all Unisons to each other. And this Union of *Moral Sexes,*
if we may express it so, is evidently more conducive to the Improvement of each, than if they lived apart. For the *Man* not only protects
and advises, but communicates Vigour and Resolution to the *Woman.*
She, in her turn, softens, refines, and polishes him. In her Society he
finds Repose from Action and Care; in her Friendship, the Ferment
into which his Passions were wrought by the Hurry and Distraction of
public Life, subsides and settles into a Calm; and a thousand nameless
Graces and Decencies that flow from her Words and Actions, form him
for a more mild and elegant Deportment. His Conversation and Example, on the other hand, enlarge her Views, raise her Sentiments, sustain her Resolutions, and free her from a thousand Fears and Inquie-
tudes, to which her more feeble Constitution subjects her. Surely such
Dispositions, and the happy Consequences which result from them,
cannot be supposed to carry an unfriendly Aspect to any Duty he owes
either to *God,* or to *Man.*

Duties of   Of the *Conjugal* Alliance the following are the *natural Laws.* First, mu-
Marriage   tual Fidelity to the Marriage-bed. Disloyalty defeats the very End of
Marriage, dissolves the natural Cement of the Relation, weakens the

Moral Tye, the chief Strength of which lies in the Reciprocation of Affection; and by making the Offspring uncertain, diminishes the Care and Attachment necessary to their Education.

2. A Conspiration of Counsels and Endeavours to promote the common Interest of the Family, and to educate their common Offspring. In order to observe these Laws, it is necessary to cultivate, both before and during the married State, the strictest Decency and Chastity of Manners, and a just Sense of what becomes their respective Characters.

3. The Union must be inviolable, and for Life. The Nature of Friendship, and particularly of this Species of it, the Education of their Offspring, and the Order of Society, and of Successions which would otherwise be extremely perplexed, do all seem to require it. To preserve this Union, and render the matrimonial State more harmonious and comfortable, a mutual Esteem and Tenderness, a mutual Deference and Forbearance, a Communication of Advice, and Assistance, and Authority, are absolutely necessary. If either Party keep within their proper Departments, there need be no Disputes about Power or Superiority, and there will be none. They have no *opposite,* no *separate* Interests, and therefore there can be no just Ground for Opposition of Conduct.

From this Detail, and the present State of things, in which there is pretty near a Parity of Numbers of both Sexes, it is evident that *Polygamy* is an *unnatural* State; and tho it should be granted to be more fruitful of Children, which however it is not found to be, yet it is by no means so fit for rearing Minds, which seems to be as much, if not more, the Intention of Nature, than the Propagation of Bodies.

Polygamy

In what Cases Divorce may be proper, what are the just Obstacles to Marriage, and within what Degrees of Consanguinity it may be allowed, we have not room to discuss here, and therefore we refer the Reader to Mr. *Hutchinson's* ingenious *Moral Compend.* Book III. Chap. I.[6]

Divorce, &c.

6. Hutcheson, *Philosophiae moralis.*

CHAPTER III

Of Parental Duty

Connection of
Parents and
Children

The Connection of Parents with their Children is a natural Consequence of the matrimonial Connection, and the Duties which they owe
them, result as naturally from that Connection. The feeble State of
Children, subject to so many Wants and Dangers, requires their incessant Cares and Attention; their ignorant and uncultivated Minds demand their continual Instruction and Culture. Had human Creatures
come into the World with the full Strength of *Men,* and the Weakness
of Reason and Vehemence of Passions which prevail in *Children,* they
would have been too strong, or too stubborn, to have submitted to the
Government and Instruction of their Parents. But as they were designed for a Progression in Knowledge and Virtue, it was proper that
the Growth of their Bodies should keep pace with that of their Minds,
lest the Purposes of that Progression should have been defeated. Among
other admirable Purposes which this gradual Expansion of their outward as well as inward Structure serves, this is one, that it affords ample
Scope to the Exercise of many tender and generous Affections, which
fill up the domestic Life with a beautiful Variety of Duties and Enjoyments; and are of course a noble Discipline for the Heart, and an hardy
kind of Education for the more honourable and important Duties of
public Life.

The Authority
founded
on that
Connection

The above-mentioned weak and ignorant State of Children, seems
plainly to invest their Parents with such Authority and Power as is necessary to their Support, Protection, and Education; but that Authority
and Power can be construed to extend no farther than is necessary to
answer those Ends, and to last no longer than that Weakness and Ignorance continue; wherefore the Foundation or Reason of the Authority and Power ceasing, they cease of course. Whatever Power or Authority then it may be necessary or lawful for Parents to exercise during
the Non-age of their Children, to assume or usurp the same when they
have attained the Maturity or full Exercise of their Strength and Reason, would be tyrannical and unjust. From hence it is evident, that Par-

ents have no Right to punish the Persons of their Children more se-
verely than the Nature of their Wardship requires, much less to invade
their Lives, to encroach upon their Liberty, or transfer them as their
Property to any Master whatsoever. But if any Parent should be so unjust and inhuman as to consider and treat them like his other Goods
and Chattles, surely whenever they dare, they may resist, and whenever
they can, shake off that inhuman and unnatural Yoke, and be free with
that Liberty with which God and Nature has invested them.

The first Class of Duties which Parents owe their Children respect their
natural Life; and these comprehend Protection, Nurture, Provision, introducing them into the World in a manner suitable to their Rank and
Fortune, and the like. Duties of Parents

The second Order of Duties regards the *intellectual* and *moral* Life of
their Children, or their Education in such Arts and Accomplishments,
as are necessary to qualify them for performing the Duties they owe to
themselves and to others. As this was found to be the principal Design
of the matrimonial Alliance, so the fulfilling that Design is the most
important and dignified of all the parental Duties. In order therefore to
fit the Child for acting his Part wisely and worthily, as a *Man,* as a *Citizen,* and a *Creature of God,* both Parents ought to combine their joint
Wisdom, Authority, and Power, and each apart to employ those Talents
which are the peculiar Excellency and Ornament of their respective Sex.
The Father ought to *lay out* and *superintend* their Education, the
Mother to execute and manage the Detail of which she is capable. The
former should direct the manly Exertion of the intellectual and moral
Powers of the Child. His Imagination, and the manner of those Exertions, are the peculiar Province of the *latter.* The *former* should advise,
protect, command, and by his Experience, masculine Vigour, and that
superior Authority which is commonly ascribed to his Sex, brace and
strengthen his Pupil for *active* Life, for Gravity, Integrity, and Firmness
in Suffering. The Business of the *latter* is to bend and soften her *Male*
Pupil, by the Charms of her Conversation, and the Softness and Decency of her Manners, for *social* Life, for Politeness of Taste, and the Education

elegant Decorums of and Enjoyments of Humanity; and to improve and refine the Tenderness and Modesty of her *Female* Pupil, and form her to all those mild domestic Virtues, which are the peculiar Characteristics and Ornaments of her Sex.

> *Delightful Task! to rear the tender Thought,*
> *To teach the fair Idea how to shoot;*
> *To breathe th' enliv'ning Spirit, and to fix*
> *The generous Purpose in the glowing Breast.*[7]

To conduct the opening Minds of their sweet Charge through the several Periods of their Progress, to assist them in each Period in throwing out the latent Seeds of Reason and Ingenuity, and in gaining fresh Accessions of Light and Virtue; and at length, with all these Advantages, to produce the young Adventurers upon the great Theatre of human Life, to play their several Parts in the Sight of their Friends, of Society, and Mankind! How gloriously does Heaven reward the Task, when the Parents behold those dear Images and Representatives of themselves, inheriting their Virtues as well as Fortunes, sustaining their respective Characters gracefully and worthily, and giving them the agreeable Prospect of transmitting their Name with growing Honour and Advantage to a Race yet unborn!

CHAPTER IV

Herile and Servile Duty

The Ground of this Connection
In the natural Course of human Affairs it must necessarily happen, that some of Mankind will live in Plenty and Opulence, and others be reduced to a State of Indigence and Poverty. The former need the Labours of the latter, and the latter the Provision and Support of the former. This mutual Necessity is the Foundation of that Connection,

---

7. Lines 1149–53 from "Spring," the third part of the epic poem *The Seasons* (London, 1726–30, revised 1744) by the Scottish poet James Thomson (1700–48). Fordyce has elided the third line (1151), "To pour the fresh instruction o'er the mind."

whether we call it *Moral* or *Civil,* which subsists between Masters and
Servants. He who feeds another has a Right to some Equivalent, the The Conditions of Service
Labour of him whom he maintains, and the Fruits of it. And he who
labours for another, has a Right to expect that he should support him.
But as the Labours of a Man of ordinary Strength are certainly of
greater Value than mere Food and Cloathing; because they would actually produce more, even the Maintenance of a Family, were the La-
bourer to employ them in his own Behalf, therefore, he has an un-
doubted Right to rate and dispose of his Service for certain Wages above
mere Maintenance. And if he has incautiously disposed of it for the latter only, yet the Contract being of the *onerous* kind, he may equitably
claim a Supply of that Deficiency. If the Service be specified, the Servant is bound to that only; if not, then he is to be construed as bound
only to such Services as are consistent with the Laws of Justice and Humanity. By the voluntary Servitude to which he subjects himself, he for-
feits no Rights but such as are necessarily included in that Servitude,
and is obnoxious to no Punishment but such as a voluntary Failure in
the Service may be supposed reasonably to require. *The Offspring of such
Servants* have a Right to that Liberty which neither they, nor their Parents, have forfeited.

As to those, who because of some heinous Offence, or for some noto- The Case
of great
Offenders
rious Damage, for which they cannot otherwise compensate, are condemned to perpetual Service, they do not, on that account, forfeit all
the Rights of Men; but those, the Loss of which is necessary to secure
Society against the like Offences for the future, or to repair the Damage
they have done.

With regard to Captives taken in War, it is barbarous and inhuman to The Case of
Captives
make perpetual Slaves of them, unless some peculiar and aggravated
Circumstances of Guilt have attended their Hostility. The Bulk of the
Subjects of any Government engaged in War, may be fairly esteemed
innocent Enemies, and therefore they have a Right to that Clemency
which is consistent with the common Safety of Mankind, and the particular Security of that Society against which they are engaged. Though

ordinary Captives have a Grant of their Lives, yet to pay their Liberty as an Equivalent, is much too high a Price. There are other Ways of acknowledging or returning the Favour, than by surrendering what is far dearer than Life itself.* To those, who under Pretext of the Necessities of Commerce, drive the unnatural Trade of bargaining for human Flesh, and consigning their innocent, but unfortunate Fellow-creatures, to eternal Servitude and Misery, we may address the Words of a fine Writer; "Let Avarice defend it as it will, there is an honest Reluctance in Humanity against buying and selling, and regarding those of our own Species as our Wealth and Possessions."

As it is the Servant's Duty to serve his Master with Fidelity and Chearfulness, like one who knows he is accountable to the great Lord of the Universe, so the Master ought to exact nothing of his Servant beyond the natural Limits of Reason and Humanity, remembering that he is a Brother of the same Family, a Partner of the same Nature, and a Subject of the same great Lord.

CHAPTER V

Social Duties of the private Kind

Hitherto we have considered only the *Domestic, Oeconomical* Duties, because these are the first in the Progress of Nature. But as Man passes beyond the little Circle of a Family, he forms Connections with Relations, Friends, Neighbours, and others; from whence results a new Train of Duties of the more private social kind; as *Friendship, Chastity, Courtesy, Good-neighbourhood, Charity, Forgiveness, Hospitality.*

Man's Aptitude for Society Man is admirably formed for particular social Attachments and Duties. There is a peculiar and strong Propensity in his Nature to be affected with the Sentiments and Dispositions of others. Men, like certain musical Instruments, are set to each other, so that the Vibrations or Notes

* *Vid.* Hutches. *Moral Instit. Phil. Lib.* iii. *Cap.* 3. [Hutcheson, *Philosophiae moralis.*]

excited in one, raise correspondent Notes and Vibrations in the others. The Impulses of *Pleasure* or *Pain, Joy* or *Sorrow,* made on one Mind, are by an instantaneous Sympathy of Nature, communicated in some degree to all; especially when Hearts are (as an humane Writer expresses it) in *Unison* of Kindness; the Joy that vibrates in one, communicates to the other also. We may add, that tho' Joy thus imparted swells the Harmony, yet Grief vibrated to the Heart of a Friend, and rebounding from thence in sympathetic Notes, melts as it were, and almost dies away. All the Passions, but especially those of the social kind, are contagious; and when the Passions of one Man mingle with those of another, they increase and multiply prodigiously. There is a most moving Eloquence in the human Countenance, Air, Voice, and Gesture, wonderfully expressive of the most latent Feelings and Passions of the Soul, which darts them, like a subtle Flame, into the Hearts of others, and raises correspondent Feelings there: Friendship, Love, Good-humour, Joy, spread through every Feature, and particularly shoot from the Eyes their softer and fiercer Fires with an irresistible Energy. And in like manner, the opposite Passions of Hatred, Enmity, Ill-humour, Melancholy, diffuse a sullen and saddening Air over the Face, and flashing from Eye to Eye, kindle a Train of similar Passions. By these and other admirable Pieces of Machinery, Men are formed for Society and the delightful Interchange of friendly Sentiments and Duties, to increase the Happiness of others by Participation, and their own by Rebound, and to diminish, by dividing, the common Stock of their Misery.

The first Emanations of the *Social* Principle beyond the Bounds of a Family, lead us to form a nearer Conjunction of Friendship or Good-will with those, who are any wise connected with us by *Blood,* or *Domestic Alliance.* To them our Affection does, commonly, exert itself in a greater or less Degree, according to the Nearness or Distance of the Relation. And this Proportion is admirably suited to the Extent of our Powers and the Indigence of our State; for it is only within those lesser Circles of Consanguinity or Alliance, that the Generality of Mankind are able to display their Abilities or Benevolence, and consequently to uphold their Connection with Society and Subserviency to a public In-

Duties arising from private Relation

terest. Therefore it is our Duty to regard these closer Connections as the next Department to that of a Family, in which Nature has marked out for us a Sphere of Activity and Usefulness; and to cultivate the kind Affections which are the Cement of those endearing Alliances.

Ingredients of
Friendship Frequently, the view of distinguishing Moral Qualities in some of our Acquaintance may give birth to that more noble Connection we call FRIENDSHIP, which is far superior to the Alliances of Consanguinity. For these are of a superficial, and often of a transitory Nature, of which, as they hold more of *Instinct* than of *Reason,* we cannot give such a rational Account. But *Friendship* derives all its Strength and Beauty, and the only Existence which is durable, from the Qualities of the Heart, or from virtuous and lovely Dispositions. Or, should these be wanting, they or some Shadow of them must be supposed present. Therefore *Friendship* may be described to be, "The Union of two Souls, by means of *Virtue,* the common Object and Cement of their mutual Affection." Without Virtue, or the Supposition of it, Friendship is only a *Mercenary* League, an Alliance of Interest, which must dissolve of course when that Interest decays or subsists no longer. It is not so much any particular Passion, as a Composition of some of the noblest Feelings and Passions of the Mind. *Good Sense,* a *just Taste* and *Love of Virtue,* a *thorough Candor* and *Benignity of Heart,* or what we usually call a *Good Temper,* and a generous Sympathy of Sentiments and Affections, are the necessary Ingredients of this virtuous Connection. When it is grafted on Esteem, strengthened by Habit, and mellowed by Time, it yields infinite Pleasure, ever new and ever growing; is a noble Support amidst the various Trials and Vicissitudes of Life, and an high Seasoning to most of our other Enjoyments. To form and cultivate virtuous Friendship must be very improving to the Temper, as its principal *Object* is *Virtue,* set off with all the Allurement of Countenance, Air, and Manners, shining forth in the native Graces of manly honest Sentiments and Affections, and rendered *visible* as it were to the friendly Spectator in a Conduct unaffectedly great and good; and as its principal Exercises are the very Energies of Virtue, or its Effects or Emanations. So that wherever this amiable Attachment prevails, it will exalt our Admiration and

Attachment to Virtue, and, unless impeded in its Course by unnatural Prejudices, run out into a Friendship to the Human Race. For as no one can merit, and none ought to usurp, the sacred Name of a Friend, who hates Mankind, so, whoever truly loves *them,* possesses the most essential Quality of a true Friend.

The Duties of Friendship are a mutual Esteem of each other, unbribed by Interest, and independent of it, a generous Confidence, as far distant from Suspicion as from Reserve, an inviolable Harmony of Sentiments and Dispositions, of Designs and Interests, a Fidelity unshaken by the Changes of Fortune, a Constancy unalterable by distance of Time or Place, a Resignation of one's personal Interests to those of one's Friend, and a reciprocal, unenvious, unreserved Exchange of kind Offices.— But amidst all the Exertions of this Moral Connection, humane and generous as it is, we must remember that it operates within a narrow Sphere, and its immediate Operations respect only the Individual, and therefore, its particular Impulses must still be subordinate to a more public Interest, or be always directed and controuled by the more extensive Connections of our Nature.

Its Duties

When our Friendship terminates on any of the other Sex, in whom Beauty or Agreeableness of Person, and external Gracefulness of Manners, conspire to express and heighten the Moral Charm of a tender honest Heart; and sweet, ingenious, modest Temper, lighted up by good Sense, it generally grows into a more soft and endearing Attachment. When this Attachment is improved by a growing Acquaintance with the Worth of its Object, is conducted by Discretion, and issues at length, as it ought to do, in the Moral Connection formerly* mentioned, it becomes the Source of many amiable Duties, of a Communication of Passions and Interests, of the most refined Decencies, and of a thousand nameless deep-felt Joys of reciprocal Tenderness and Love, flowing from every Look, Word, and Action. Here Friendship acts with double Energy, and the *Natural* conspires with the *Moral*

Love and Chastity

* *See Chap. 3 of this Sect.*

Charm, to strengthen and secure the Love of Virtue. As the delicate Nature of Female Honour and Decorum, and the inexpressible Grace of a chaste and modest Behaviour, are the surest, and indeed the only means of kindling at first, and ever after of keeping alive this tender and elegant Flame, and of accomplishing the excellent Ends designed by it; to attempt by Fraud to violate one, or, under pretence of Passion, to sully and corrupt the other, and, by so doing, to expose the too often credulous and unguarded Object, with a wanton Cruelty, to the Hatred of her own Sex, and the Scorn of our's, and to the lowest Infamy of both, is a Conduct not only base and criminal, but inconsistent with that truly rational and refined Enjoyment, the Spirit and Quintessence of which is derived from the bashful and sacred Charms of Virtue kept untainted, and therefore ever alluring to the Lover's Heart.

Courtesy, Good-neighbour-hood, &c.   *Courtesy, Good-neighbourhood, Affability,* and the like Duties, which are founded on our private Social Connections, are no less necessary and obligatory to Creatures united in Society, and supporting and supported by each other in a Chain of mutual Want and Dependence. They do not consist in a smooth Address, an artificial or obsequious Air, fawning Adulations, or a polite Servility of Manners, but in a just and modest Sense of our own Dignity and that of others, and of the Reverence due to Mankind, especially to those who hold the highest Links of the Social Chain; in a discreet and manly Accommodation of ourselves to the Foibles and Humours of others; in a strict Observance of the Rules of Decorum and Civility; but above all in a frank obliging Carriage, and generous Interchange of good Deeds, rather than Words. Such a Conduct is of great Use and Advantage, as it is an excellent Security against Injury, and the best Claim and Recommendation to the Esteem, Civility, and universal Respect of Mankind. This inferior Order of Virtues unite the particular Members of Society more closely, and form the lesser Pillars of the civil Fabric; which, in many Instances, supply the unavoidable Defects of Laws, and maintain the Harmony and Decorum of Social Intercourse, where the more important and essential Lines of Virtue are wanting.

Charity and *Forgiveness* are truly amiable and useful Duties of the Social kind. There is a twofold Distinction of Rights commonly taken notice of by Moral Writers, *viz. Perfect* and *Imperfect.* To fulfil the former, is necessary to the Being and Support of Society; to fulfil the latter is a Duty equally sacred and obligatory, and tends to the Improvement and Prosperity of Society; but as the Violation of them is not equally prejudicial to the public Good, the fulfilling them is not subjected to the Cognizance of Law, but left to the Candor, Humanity, and Gratitude of Individuals. And by this means ample Scope is given to exercise all the Generosity, and display the genuine Merit and Lustre of Virtue. Thus the Wants and Misfortunes of others call for our charitable Assistance and seasonable Supplies. And the good Man, unconstrained by Law, and uncontrouled by human Authority, will chearfully acknowledge and generously satisfy this mournful and moving Claim; a Claim supported by the Sanction of Heaven, of whose Bounties he is honoured to be the grateful Trustee. If his own *perfect* Rights are invaded by the Injustice of others, he will not therefore reject their *imperfect* Right to Pity and Forgiveness, unless his Grant of these should be inconsistent with the more extensive Rights of Society, or the public Good. In that case he will have recourse to public Justice and the Laws, and even then he will prosecute the Injury with no unnecessary Severity, but rather with Mildness and Humanity. When the Injury is merely personal, and of such a Nature as to admit of Alleviations, and the Forgiveness of which would be attended with no worse Consequences, especially of a public kind, the good Man will generously forgive his offending Brother: and it is his Duty to do so, and not to take private Revenge, or retaliate Evil for Evil. For though Resentment of Injury is a natural Passion, and implanted, as was observed* above, for wise and good Ends; yet, considering the manifold Partialities which most Men have for themselves, was every one to act as Judge in his own Cause, and to execute the Sentence dictated by his own Resentment, it is but

Charity, Forgiveness

---

* *See Book* I. *Sect.* 2. & 4.

too evident that Mankind would pass all Bounds in their Fury, and the last Sufferer be provoked in his turn to make full Reprisals. So that Evil, thus encountering with Evil, would produce one continued Series of Violence and Misery, and render Society intolerable, if not impracticable. Therefore, when the Security of the Individual, or Good of the Public, does not require a proportionable Retaliation, it is agreeable to the general Law of Benevolence, and to the particular End of the Passion (which is to prevent Injury and the Misery occasioned by it) to forgive personal Injuries,* or not to return Evil for Evil. This Duty is one of the noble Refinements which *Christianity* has made upon the general Maxims and Practice of Mankind, and enforced with a peculiar Strength and Beauty, by Sanctions no less alluring than awful. And indeed the Practice of it is generally its own Reward; by expelling from the Mind the most dreadful Intruders upon its Repose, those rancorous Passions which are begot and nursed by Resentment, and by disarming and even subduing every Enemy one has, except such as have nothing left of Men, but the outward Form.

Hospitality The most enlarged and humane Connection of the private kind, seems to be the Hospitable Alliance, from which flow the amiable and disinterested Duties we owe to Strangers. If the Exercise of Passions of the most private and instinctive kind is beheld with Moral Approbation and Delight, how lovely and venerable must those appear, which result from a calm Philanthropy, are founded in the common Rights and Connections of Society, and embrace Men, not of a particular Sect, Party, or Nation, but all in general without Distinction, and without any of the little Partialities of Self-love.

---

* *See* Butler's *excellent Serm. (9th) on this Subject.* ["Upon Forgiveness of Injuries," Butler, *Fifteen Sermons.*]

CHAPTER VI

Social Duties of the Commercial Kind

The next Order of Connections are those which arise from the Wants and Weakness of Mankind, and from the various Circumstances in which their different Situations place them. These we may call *Commercial* Connections, and the Duties which result from them *Commercial* Duties, as *Justice, Fair-dealing, Sincerity, Fidelity to Compacts,* and the like.

Commercial Duties

It is observed somewhere by a Writer* of the first Rank, that though Nature is perfect in all her Works, yet she has observed a manifest and eminent Distinction among them. To all such as lie beyond the Reach of human Skill and Power, and are properly of her own Department, she has given the finishing Hand. These Man may design after and imitate, but he can never rival them, nor add to their Beauty or Perfection. Such are the Forms and Structure of Vegetables, Animals, and many of their Productions, as the Honeycomb, the Spider's Web, and the like. There are others of her Works which she has of design left unfinished, as it were, in order to exercise the Ingenuity and Power of Man. She has presented to him a rich Profusion of Materials of every kind for his Conveniency and Use; but they are rude and unpolished, or not to be come at without Art and Labour. These therefore he must apply, in order to adapt them to his Use, and to enjoy them in Perfection. Thus Nature has given him an infinite Variety of Herbs, Grain, Fossils, Minerals, Wood, Water, Earth, Air, and a thousand other crude Materials to supply his numerous Wants. But he must sow, plant, dig, refine, polish, build, and, in short, manufacture the various Produce of Nature, in order to obtain even the Necessaries, and much more the Conveniencies and Elegancies of Life. These then are the Price of his Labour and Industry, and, without that, Nature will sell him nothing. But as

Their Foundation

* *Lord* Bacon. [See, for example, Bacon's *De Augmentis,* book 2, chapter 2.]

the Wants of Mankind are many, and the single Strength of Individuals
small, they could hardly find the Necessaries, and much less the Conveniencies of Life, without uniting their Ingenuity and Strength in acquiring these, and without a mutual Intercourse of good Offices. Some
Men are better formed for some kinds of Ingenuity and Labour, and
others for other kinds; and different Soils and Climates are enriched
with different Productions; so that Men by exchanging the Produce of
their respective Labours, and supplying the Wants of one Country with
the Superfluities of another, do, in effect, diminish the Labours of each,
and increase the Abundance of all. This is the Foundation of all Commerce, or Exchange of Commodities and Goods one with another; in
order to facilitate which, Men have contrived different Species of *Coin*,
or *Money*, as a common Standard by which to estimate the comparative
Values of their respective Goods. But to render Commerce sure and effectual, *Justice, Fair-dealing, Sincerity*, and *Fidelity to Compacts* are absolutely necessary.

Justice, &c.   *Justice*, or *Fair-dealing*, or, in other Words, a Disposition to treat others
as we would be treated by them, is a Virtue of the first Importance, and
inseparable from the virtuous Character. It is the Cement of Society, or
that pervading Spirit which connects its Members, inspires its various
Relations, and maintains the Order and Subordination of each Part to
the Whole. Without it, Society would become a Den of Thieves and
Banditti, hating and hated, devouring and devoured, by one another.

Sincerity   *Sincerity* or *Veracity*, in our Words and Actions, is another Virtue or
Duty of great Importance to Society, being one of the great Bands of
mutual Intercourse, and the Foundation of mutual Trust. Without it,
Society would be the Dominion of Mistrust, Jealousy, and Fraud, and
Conversation a Traffic of Lies and Dissimulation. It includes in it a
Conformity of Words with our Sentiments, a Correspondence between
our Actions and Dispositions, a strict Regard to Truth, and an irreconcileable Abhorrence of Falsehood. It does not indeed require that we
expose our Sentiments indiscreetly, or tell all the Truth in every Case;
but certainly it does not and cannot admit the least Violation of Truth,

or Contradiction to our Sentiments. For if these Bounds are once passed, no possible Limit can be assigned where the Violation shall stop; and no Pretence of private or public Good, can possibly counterbalance the Ill Consequences of such a Violation. And we trust, the Order of Nature and Providence is such, that it seldom or never falls out, that so valuable a Sacrifice must be made in order to obtain the Ends of an extensive Benevolence. It belongs to *us* to do what appears right and conformable to the Laws of our Nature, and to leave Heaven to direct and over-rule Events or Consequences, which it will never fail to do, for the best.

Fidelity to Promises, Compacts, and *Engagements,* is likewise a Duty of such Importance to the Security of Commerce and Interchange of Benevolence among Mankind, that Society would soon grow intolerable without the strict Observance of it. *Hobbes,* and others who follow the same Track, have taken a wonderful deal of pains to puzzle this Subject, and to make all the Virtues of this Sort merely *artificial,* and not at all *obligatory,* antecedent to human Conventions. No doubt Compacts suppose People who make them, and Promises Persons to whom they are made, and therefore both suppose some Society more or less between those who enter into these mutual Engagements. But is not a Compact or Promise binding, till Men have agreed that they shall be binding? Or are they only binding because it is our Interest to be bound by them, or to fulfil them? Do not we highly approve the Man who fulfils them, even tho' they should prove to be against his Interest? And do not we condemn him as a Knave, who violates them on that account? A Promise is a voluntary Declaration, by Words, or by an Action equally significant, of our Resolution to do something in behalf of another, or for his Service. When it is made, the Person who makes it, is by all supposed under an Obligation to perform it. And he to whom it is made, may demand the Performance as his Right. That Perception of *Obligation* is a simple Idea, and is on the same Footing as our other Moral Perceptions, which may be described by Instances, but cannot be defined. Whether we have a Perception of such Obligation quite distinct from the Interest, either Public or Private, that may accompany

Fidelity to Promises, Compacts, &c.

the Fulfilment of it, must be referred to the Conscience of every Individual. And, whether the mere Sense of that Obligation, apart from its Concomitants, is not a sufficient Inducement or Motive to keep one's Promise, without having recourse to any selfish Principle of our Nature, must be likewise appealed to the Conscience of every honest Man. *Fairdealing* and *Fidelity to Compacts* require that we take no Advantage of the Ignorance, Passion, or Incapacity of others, from whatever Cause that Incapacity arises;—that we be explicit and candid in making Bargains, just and faithful in fulfilling our Part of them. And if the other Party violates his Engagements, Redress is to be sought for from the Laws, or from those who are intrusted with the Execution of them. In fine, the *Commercial* Virtues and Duties require that we not only do not invade, but maintain the Rights of others;—that we be fair and impartial in transferring, bartering, or exchanging Property, whether in Goods or Service; and be inviolably faithful to our Word and our Engagements, where the Matter of them is not criminal, and where they are not extorted by Force.—But on this the designed Brevity of the Work will not permit us farther to insist.

CHAPTER VII

Social Duties of the Political Kind

We are now arrived at the *last* and *highest* Order of Duties respecting Society, which result from the Exercise of the most generous and heroic Affections, and are founded on our most enlarged Connections.

Political Connections The *Social* Principle in Man is of such an expansive Nature, that it cannot be confined within the Circuit of a Family, of Friends, or a Neighbourhood: it spreads into wider Systems, and draws Men into larger Confederacies, Communities, and Commonwealths.—It is in these only that the higher Powers of our Nature attain the highest Improvement and Perfection of which they are capable. These Principles hardly find Objects in the solitary State of Nature. *There* the Principle of Action rises no higher at farthest than *Natural Affection* towards one's Offspring. There Personal or Family wants entirely engross the Creature's Attention and Labour, and allow no Leisure, or, if they did, no Exercise for Views and Affections of a more enlarged kind. In *Solitude* all are employed in the same way, in providing for the *Animal* Life. And even after their utmost Labour and Care, single and unaided by the Industry of others, they find but a sorry Supply of their Wants, and a feeble, precarious Security against Dangers from wild Beasts; from inclement Skies and Seasons; from the Mistakes or petulant Passions of their Fellow-creatures; from their Preference of themselves to their Neighbours; and from all the little Exorbitances of Self-love. But in *Society*, the mutual Aids which Men give and receive, shorten the Labours of each, and the combined Strength and Reason of Individuals give Security and Protection to the whole Body. There is both a Variety and Subordination of Genius among Mankind. Some are formed to lead and direct others, to contrive Plans of Happiness for Individuals, and of Government for Communities, to take in a public Interest, invent Laws and Arts, and superintend their Execution, and in short, to refine and civilize human Life. Others, who have not such good Heads, may have as honest Hearts, a truly public Spirit, Love of Liberty, Hatred of Corruption and Tyranny, a generous Submission to Laws, Order, and Public Institutions, and an extensive Philanthropy. And others, who have none of those Capacities either of Heart or Head, may be well-formed for Manual Exercises and Bodily Labour. The former of these Principles have no Scope in Solitude, where a Man's Thoughts and Concerns do all either center in himself, or extend no farther than a Family; into which little Circle all the Duty and Virtue of the Solitary Mortal is crouded. But Society finds proper Objects and Exercises for every Genius, and the noblest Objects and Exercises for the noblest Geniuses, and for the highest Principles in the human Constitution: particularly for that warmest and most divine Passion, which God hath kindled in our Bosoms, the Inclination of doing good and reverencing our Nature; which may find here both Employment, and the most exquisite Satisfaction. In Society a Man has not only more Leisure, but better Opportunities of applying his Talents with much greater Perfection and Success, especially as he is furnished with the joint Advice and

Assistance of his Fellow-creatures, who are now more closely united one
with the other, and sustain a common Relation to the same Moral System, or Community. This then is an Object proportioned to his most
enlarged Social Affections, and in serving it he finds Scope for the Exercise and Refinement of his highest Intellectual and Moral Powers.
THEREFORE *Society,* or a *State of Civil Government,* rests on these two
principal Pillars, "That in it we find Security against those Evils which
are unavoidable in Solitude—and obtain those Goods, some of which
cannot be obtained at all, and others not so well in that State, where
Men depend solely on their individual Sagacity and Industry."

From this short Detail it appears that *Man* is a SOCIAL Creature, and
formed for a SOCIAL State; and that *Society,* being adapted to the higher
Principles and Destinations of his Nature, must, of necessity, be his
NATURAL State.

Political
Duties

The Duties suited to that State, and resulting from those Principles and
Destinations, or in other Words, from our Social Passions and Social
Connections, or Relation to a Public System, are *Love of our Country,
Resignation and Obedience to the Laws, Public Spirit, Love of Liberty, Sac-
rifice of Life and all to the Public,* and the like.

Love of one's
Country

Love of our Country is one of the noblest Passions that can warm and
animate the human Breast. It includes all the limited and particular Affections to our Parents, Children, Friends, Neighbours, Fellow-
Citizens, Countrymen. It ought to direct and limit their more confined
and partial Action within their proper and natural Bounds, and never
let them encroach on those sacred and first Regards we owe to the great
Public to which we belong. Were we solitary Creatures, detached from
the rest of Mankind, and without any Capacity of comprehending a
public Interest, or without Affections, leading us to desire and pursue it,
it would not be our Duty to mind it, nor criminal to neglect it. But, as
we are PARTS of the *Public System,* and are not only capable of taking
in large Views of its Interests, but by the strongest Affections connected
with it, and prompted to take a Share of its Concerns, we are under the
most sacred Ties to prosecute its Security and Welfare with the utmost

Ardor, especially in times of public Trial. This *Love of our Country* does not import an Attachment to any particular Soil, Climate, or Spot of Earth, where perhaps we first drew our Breath, though those *Natural* Ideas are often associated with the *Moral* ones; and, like external Signs or Symbols, help to ascertain and bind them; but it imports an Affection to that *Moral System,* or *Community,* which is governed by the same Laws and Magistrates, and whose several Parts are variously connected one with the other, and all united upon the Bottom of a common Interest. Perhaps indeed every Member of the Community cannot comprehend so large an Object, especially if it extends through large Provinces, and over vast Tracts of Land; and still less can he form such an Idea, if there is no *Public, i.e.* if all are subjected to the Caprice and unlimited Will of one Man; but the Preference the Generality shew to their native Country; the Concern and Longing after it which they express, when they have been long absent from it; the Labours they undertake and Sufferings they endure to save or serve it; and the peculiar Attachment they have to their Country-men, evidently demonstrate that the Passion is *natural,* and never fails to exert itself, when it is fairly disengaged from foreign Clogs, and is directed to its proper Object. Wherever it prevails in its genuine Vigour and Extent, it swallows up all sordid and selfish Regards, it conquers the Love of *Ease, Power, Pleasure,* and *Wealth;* nay, when the amiable Partialities of *Friendship, Gratitude, private Affection,* or *Regards to a Family,* come in Competition with it, it will teach us bravely to sacrifice all, in order to maintain the Rights and *promote* or *defend* the Honour and Happiness of our Country.

Resignation and *Obedience to the Laws* and *Orders* of the Society to which we belong, are *Political* Duties necessary to its very Being and Security, without which it must soon degenerate into a State of Licence and Anarchy. The Welfare, nay, the Nature of Civil Society, requires that there should be a Subordination of Orders, or Diversity of Ranks and Conditions in it;—that certain Men, or Orders of Men, be appointed to super-intend and manage such Affairs as concern the Public Safety and Happiness;—that all have their particular Provinces assigned

Resignation and Obedience to the Laws, &c.

them;—that such a Subordination be settled among them, as none of
them may interfere with another;—and finally, that certain *Rules,* or
common *Measures of Action,* be agreed on, by which each is to discharge
his respective Duty to govern or be governed, and all may concur in
securing the Order and promoting the Felicity of the whole Political
Body. Those *Rules of Action* are the *Laws* of the Community, and those
different *Orders* are the several Officers, or Magistrates, appointed by
the Public to explain them, and super-intend or assist in their Execution. In consequence of this Settlement of Things, it is the Duty of each
Individual to obey the Laws enacted, to submit to the Executors of
them with all due Deference and Homage, according to their respective
Ranks and Dignity, as to the Keepers of the Public Peace, and the
Guardians of Public Liberty; to maintain his own Rank, and perform
the Functions of his own Station with Diligence, Fidelity, and Incor-
ruption. The Superiority of the *higher* Orders, or the Authority with
which the State has invested them, entitle them, especially if they employ their Authority well, to the Obedience and Submission of the
lower, and to a proportionable Honour and Respect from all. The Subordination of the lower Ranks claims Protection, Defence, and Security,
from the higher. And the Laws, being superior to all, require the Obedience and Submission of all, being the last Resort, beyond which there
is no Decision or Appeal.—Besides these natural and stated Subordinations in Society, there are others accidental and artificial, the *Opulent*
and *Indigent,* the *Great* and the *Vulgar,* the *Ingenious* and *Prudent,* and
those who are less so. The *Opulent* are to administer to the Necessities
of the *Indigent,* and the *Indigent* to return the Fruits of their Labours to
the *Opulent.* The *Great* ought to defend and patronize their *Dependents*
and *Inferiors,* and *They* in their turn, to return their combined Strength
and Assistance to the *Great.* The *Prudent* should improve the Ingenui-
ties of the Mind for the Benefit of the *Industrious,* and the *Industrious*
lend the Dexterities of their Strength for the Advantage of the *Prudent.*

Foundation of *Public Spirit, Heroic Zeal, Love of Liberty,* and the other *Political* Duties,
Public Spirit, do, above all others, recommend those who practise them to the Ad-
Love of
Liberty, &c. miration and Homage of Mankind; because as they are the Offspring

of the noblest Minds, so *are they* the Parents of the greatest Blessings to Society. Yet exalted as they are, it is only in equal and free Governments, where they can be exercised and have their due Effect. For there only does a true *Public* prevail, and there only is the *Public Good* made the Standard of the Civil Constitution. As the End of Society is the *Common Interest* and *Welfare* of the People associated, this End must, of necessity, be the *Supreme Law* or *Common Standard,* by which the particular Rules of Action of the several Members of the Society towards each other are to be regulated. But a *common Interest* can be no other than that which is the Result of the *common Reason,* or *common Feelings* of all. Private Men, or a particular Order of Men, have Interests and Feelings peculiar to themselves, and of which they may be good Judges; but these may be separate from, and often contrary to the Interests and Feelings of the rest of the Society; and therefore they can have no Right to make, and much less to impose, Laws on their Fellow-Citizens, inconsistent with, and opposite to those Interests and those Feelings. Therefore a *Society,* a *Government,* or *real Public,* truly worthy the Name, and not a Confederacy of Banditti, a Clan of lawless Savages, or a Band of Slaves under the Whip of a Master, must be such a one as consists of Freemen, chusing or consenting to Laws themselves; or, since it often happens that they cannot assemble and act in a *Collective* Body, delegating a sufficient Number of *Representatives, i.e.* such a Number as shall most fully comprehend, and most equally represent, their *common Feelings* and *common Interests,* to digest and vote Laws for the Conduct and Controul of the whole Body, the most agreeable to those common Feelings and common Interests.

A Society thus constituted by *common Reason,* and formed on the Plan of a *common Interest,* becomes immediately an Object of public Attention, public Veneration, public Obedience, a public and inviolable Attachment, which ought neither to be seduced by Bribes, nor awed by Terrors; an Object, in fine, of all those extensive and important Duties which arise from so glorious a Confederacy. To watch over such a System; to contribute all he can to promote its Good by his Reason, his Ingenuity, his Strength, and every other Ability, whether Natural or Ac-

Political Duties of every Citizen

quired; to resist, and, to the utmost of his Power, defeat every Incroach-
ment upon it, whether carried on by secret Corruption, or open Violence; and to sacrifice his Ease, his Wealth, his Power, nay Life itself,
and what is dearer still, his Family and Friends, to defend or save it, is
the Duty, the Honour, the Interest, and the Happiness of every Citizen;
it will make him venerable and beloved while he lives, be lamented and
honoured if he falls in so glorious a Cause, and transmit his Name with
immortal Renown to the latest Posterity.

Of the People As the PEOPLE are the Fountain of Power and Authority, the original
Seat of Majesty, the Authors of Laws, and the Creators of Officers to
execute them; if they shall find the Power they have conferred abused
by their Trustees, their Majesty violated by Tyranny, or by Usurpation,
their Authority prostituted to support Violence, or screen Corruption,
the Laws grown pernicious through Accidents unforeseen, or unavoidable, or rendered ineffectual thro' the Infidelity and Corruption of the
Executors of them; then it is their Right, and what is their Right is their
Duty, to resume that delegated Power, and call their Trustees to an Account; to resist the Usurpation, and extirpate the Tyranny; to restore
their sullied Majesty and prostituted Authority; to suspend, alter, or ab-
rogate those Laws, and punish their unfaithful and corrupt Officers.
Nor is it the Duty only of the united Body, but every Member of it
ought, according to his respective Rank, Power, and Weight in the
Community, to concur in advancing and supporting those glorious Designs.

Of Britons The Obligations of every *Briton* to fulfil the political Duties, receive a
vast Accession of Strength, when he calls to mind of what a noble and
well-balanced Constitution of Government he has the Honour to partake; a Constitution founded on *common Reason, common Consent,* and
common Good; a Constitution of free and equal Laws, secured against
arbitrary Will and *popular* Licence, by an admirable Temperament of
the governing Powers, controuling and controuled by one another.
How must every one who has tolerable Understanding to observe, or
tolerable Honesty to acknowledge its happy Effects, venerate and love

a Constitution, in which the Majesty of the People is, and has been frequently recognized; in which Kings are made and unmade by the
Choice of the People; Laws enacted or annulled only by their own Consent, and for their own Good, in which none can be deprived of their
Property, abridged of their Freedom, or forfeit their Lives, without an
Appeal to the Laws, and the Verdict of their Peers or Equals; a Constitution, in fine, the Nurse of Heroes, the Parent of Liberty, the Patron
of Learning and Arts, the Dominion of Laws, "the Pride of *Britain,* the
Envy of her Neighbours, and their Sanctuary too!"—How dissolute
and execrable must their Character and Conduct be, who, instead of
sacrificing their *Interest* and *Ambition,* will not part with the least Degree of either, to preserve inviolate, and entail in full Vigour to their
Posterity, such a glorious Constitution, the Labour of so many Ages,
and Price of so much Blood and Treasure; but would chuse rather to
sacrifice it, and all their own Independency, Freedom, and Dignity, to
personal Power and hollow Grandeur, to any little Pageant of a *King,*
who should prefer being the *Master of Slaves* to being the *Guardian of
Freemen,* and consider himself as the *Proprietor,* not the *Father* of his
People!—But Words cannot express the *Selfishness* and *Servility* of those
Men; and as little the public and heroic Spirit of such, if any such there
are, as have Virtue enough still left to stem the Torrent of Corruption,
and guard our sacred Constitution against the Profligacy and Prostitution of the Corruptors and the Corrupted.

Duty to God

Divine
Connections

Of all the *Relations* which the human Mind sustains, that which subsists between the *Creator* and his *Creatures,* the supreme *Lawgiver* and his *Subjects,* is the highest and the best. This Relation arises from the *Nature* of a *Creature* in general, and the *Constitution* of the *human Mind* in particular; the noblest Powers and Affections of which point to an *universal* Mind, and would be imperfect and abortive without such a Direction. How lame then must that System of Morals be, which leaves a *Deity* out of the Question! How disconsolate, and how destitute of its firmest Support!

Existence
of God

It does not appear, from any true History or Experience of the Mind's Progress, that any Man by any formal Deduction of his discursive Powers, ever reasoned himself into the Belief of a God. Whether such a Belief is only some *natural Anticipation* of Soul, or is derived from Father to Son, and from one Man to another, in the Way of *Tradition,* or is suggested to us in consequence of an *immutable Law of our Nature,* on beholding the august Aspect and beautiful Order of the Universe, we will not pretend to determine. What seems most agreeable to Experience is, that a *Sense* of its *Beauty* and *Grandeur,* and the *admirable Fitness* of one thing to another in its vast Apparatus, leads the Mind *necessarily* and *unavoidably* to a Perception of *Design,* or of a *designing Cause,* the Origin of all, by a Progress as simple and natural, as that by which a *beautiful Picture,* or a *fine Building,* suggests to us the Idea of an *excellent Artist.* For it seems to hold universally true, that wherever we discern a *Tendency,* or *Co-operation of Things, towards a certain End,* or producing a common Effect, there, by a *necessary Law of Association,* we apprehend *Design,* a *designing Energy,* or *Cause.* No matter whether the Objects are *natural* or *artificial,* still that Suggestion is unavoidable, and the *Connection* between the *Effect* and its *adequate Cause,* obtrudes itself on the Mind, and it requires no nice Search or elaborate Deduction of Reason, to trace or prove that Connection. We are particularly satisfied of its Truth in the Subject before us, by a kind of direct Intuition, and we do not seem to attend to the Maxim we learn in Schools, "That there cannot be an *infinite Series* of *Causes* and *Effects* producing and produced by one another." Nor do we feel a great Accession of Light and Conviction after we have learned it. We are conscious of our *Existence,* of *Thought, Sentiment,* and *Passion,* and sensible withal that these came not of ourselves, therefore we immediately recognize a *Parent-Mind,* an *Original Intelligence,* from whom we borrowed those little Portions of Thought and Activity. And while we not only feel *kind* Affections in ourselves, and discover them in others, but likewise behold all round us such a Number and Variety of Creatures, endued with Natures nicely adjusted to their several Stations and Oeconomies, supporting and supported by each other, and all sustained by a *common Order* of Things, and sharing different Degrees of Happiness, according to their respective Capacities, we are naturally and necessarily led up to the Father of such a numerous Offspring, the Fountain of such widespread Happiness. As we conceive this Being before all, above all, and greater than all, we naturally, and without Reasoning, ascribe to him every kind of Perfection, *Wisdom, Power,* and *Goodness without Bounds,* existing through all Time, and pervading all Space. We apply to him those glorious Epithets of our *Creator, Preserver, Benefactor,* the *supreme Lord* and *Law-giver* of the whole Society of rational intelligent Creatures.—Not only the Imperfections and Wants of our Being and Condition, but some of the *noblest Instincts* and *Affections* of our Minds, connect us with this great and universal Nature. The Mind, in its Progress from Object to Object, from one Character and Prospect of Beauty to another, finds some Blemish or Deficiency in each, and soon exhausts or grows weary and dissatisfied with its Subject; it sees no Char-

His Relation to the human Mind

acter of Excellency among Men, equal to that Pitch of Esteem which it
is capable of exerting; no Object within the Compass of human Things
adequate to the Strength of its Affection. Nor can it stop any where in
this self-expansive Progress, or find Repose after its highest Flights, till
it arrives at a Being of unbounded Greatness and Worth, on whom it
may employ its sublimest Powers without exhausting the Subject, and
give Scope to the utmost Force and Fulness of its Love, without Satiety
or Disgust. So that the Nature of this Being corresponds to the Nature
of Man; nor can his intelligent and moral Powers obtain their entire
End, but on the Supposition of such a Being, and without a real Sympathy and Communication with him. The native Propensity of the
Mind to reverence whatever is *great* and *wonderful* in Nature, finds a
proper Object of Homage in him who spread out the Heavens and the
Earth, and who sustains and governs the Whole of Things. The *Admi-
ration* of *Beauty,* the *Love* of *Order,* and the *Complacency* we feel in
Goodness, must rise to the highest Pitch, and attain the full Vigour and
Joy of their Operations, when they unite in him who is the Sum and
Source of all Perfection.

Immorality of   It is evident from the slightest Survey of Morals, that how punctual so-
Impiety   ever one may be in performing the Duties which result from our Relations to Mankind; yet to be quite deficient in performing those which
arise from our *Relation* to the *Almighty,* must argue a strange Perversion
of *Reason* or Depravity of *Heart.* If imperfect Degrees of Worth attract
our Veneration, and if the Want of it would imply an Insensibility, or,
which is worse, an Aversion to Merit, what Lameness of Affection and
Immorality of Character must it be to be unaffected with, and much
more to be ill-affected to a Being of superlative Worth! To love Society,
or particular Members of it, and yet to have no Sense of our Connection with its Head, no Affection to our common Parent and Benefactor; to be concerned about the Approbation or Censure of our Fellow-
Creatures, and yet to feel nothing of this kind towards Him who sees
and weighs our Actions with unerring Wisdom and Justice, and can
fully reward or punish them, betrays equal Madness and Partiality of
Mind. It is plain therefore beyond all doubt, that some Regards are due

to the great Father of all, in whom every lovely and adorable Quality combines to inspire Veneration and Homage.

As it has been observed already, that our *Affections* depend on our *Opinions* of their Objects, and generally keep pace with them, it must be of the highest Importance, and seems to be among the first Duties we owe to the Author of our Being, "to form the least imperfect, since we cannot form perfect, Conceptions of his *Character* and *Administration*." For such *Conceptions* thoroughly imbibed, will render our *Religion* rational, and our *Dispositions* refined. If our Opinions are diminutive and distorted, our Religion will be superstitious, and our Temper abject. Thus, if we ascribe to the Deity that false Majesty, which consists in the unbenevolent and sullen Exercise of mere *Will* or *Power,* or suppose him to delight in the Prostrations of servile Fear, or as servile Praise, he will be worshiped with mean Adulation, and a Profusion of Compliments. Farther, if he be looked upon as a stern and implacable Being, delighting in Vengeance, he will be adored with pompous Offerings, Sacrifices, or whatever else might be thought proper to sooth and mollify him. But if we believe *perfect Goodness* to be the Character of the Supreme Being, and that he loves those most who resemble him most, the Worship paid him will be rational and sublime, and his Worshipers will seek to please him, by imitating that Goodness which they adore.

Right Opinions of God

The Foundation then of all true Religion is *rational Faith.* And of a rational Faith these seem to be the chief Articles, to believe, "that an infinite all-perfect Mind exists, who has no opposite nor any separate Interest from that of his Creatures,—that he super-intends and governs all Creatures and Things,—that his Goodness extends to all his Creatures, in different Degrees indeed, according to their respective Natures, but without any Partiality or Envy,—that he does every thing for the best, or in a Subserviency to the Perfection and Happiness of the Whole,—particularly, that he directs and governs the Affairs of Men,—inspects their Actions,—distinguishes the *Good* from the *Bad,*—loves and befriends the former,—is displeased with and pities the latter in *this* World,—and will, according to their respective Deserts, reward one

Rational Faith

and punish the other in the *next;*—that, in fine, he is always carrying on a Scheme of Virtue and Happiness through an unlimited Duration,—and is ever guiding the Universe through its successive Stages and Periods, to higher Degrees of Perfection and Felicity." This is true *Theism,* the glorious Scheme of divine Faith; a Scheme exhibited in all the Works of God, and executed through his whole Administration.

Morality of Theism

This Faith well founded, and deeply felt, is nearly connected with a *true moral Taste,* and hath a powerful Efficacy on the Temper and Manners of the Theist. He who admires Goodness in others, and delights in the Practice of it, must be conscious of a reigning Order within, a Rectitude and Candor of Heart, which disposes him to entertain favourable Apprehensions of Men, and from an impartial Survey of things, to presume that *good Order* and *good Meaning* prevail in the Universe; and if good Meaning and good Order, then an *ordering,* an *intending Mind,* who is no Enemy, no Tyrant to his Creatures, but a *Friend,* a *Benefactor,* an *indulgent Sovereign.*

Immorality of Atheism

On the other hand, a bad Man, having nothing goodly or generous *to contemplate within,* no right Intentions, nor Honesty of Heart, suspects every Person and every Thing, and beholding Nature thro' the Gloom of a selfish and guilty Mind, is either averse to the Belief of a reigning Order, or, if he cannot suppress the unconquerable Anticipations of a governing Mind, he is prone to tarnish the Beauty of Nature, and to impute Malevolence, or Blindness and Impotence at least to the Sovereign Ruler. He turns the Universe into a forlorn and horrid Waste, and transfers his own Character to the Deity, by ascribing to him that uncommunicative Grandeur, that arbitrary or revengeful Spirit which he affects or admires in himself. As such a Temper of Mind naturally leads to *Atheism,* or to a *Superstition* full as bad; therefore as far as that Temper depends on the unhappy Creature in whom it prevails, the Propensity to Atheism or Superstition consequent thereto, must be *immoral.* Farther, if it be true that the Belief or Sense of a Deity is natural to the Mind, and the Evidence of his Existence reflected from his Works so full, as to strike even the most superficial Observer with Conviction, then the supplanting or corrupting that Sense, or the Want of due Attention to that Evidence, and in consequence of both, a *supine* Ignorance, or *affected* Unbelief of a Deity, must argue a bad Temper, or an immoral Turn of Mind. In the case of invincible Ignorance, or a very bad Education, though nothing can be concluded directly against the Character, yet whenever ill Passions and Habits pervert the Judgment, and by perverting the Judgment terminate in Atheism, then the Case becomes plainly criminal.

But let Casuists determine this as they will, a true Faith in the divine Character and Administration, is generally the Consequence of a virtuous State of Mind. The Man who is truly and habitually good, feels the *Love* of *Order*, of *Beauty*, and *Goodness*, in the strongest Degree, and therefore cannot be insensible to those Emanations of them which appear in all the Works of God, nor help loving their supreme Source and Model. He cannot but think, that he who has poured such Beauty and Goodness over all his Works, must himself delight in Beauty and Goodness, and what he delights in must be both amiable and happy. Some indeed there are, and it is Pity there should be any such, who, through the unhappy Influence of a wrong Education, have entertained dark and unfriendly Thoughts of a Deity, and his Administration, though otherwise of a virtuous Temper themselves. However it must be acknowledged, that such Sentiments have, for the most part, a bad Effect on the Temper; and when they have not, it is because the undepraved Affections of an honest *Heart* are more powerful in their Operation, than the speculative Opinions of an ill-formed *Head*. _{The Connection of Theism and Virtue}

But wherever right Conceptions of the Deity and his Providence prevail, when he is considered as the inexhausted Source of Light, and Love, and Joy, as acting in the joint Character of a *Father* and *Governor*, imparting an endless Variety of Capacities to his Creatures, and supplying them with every thing necessary to their full Completion and Happiness, what Veneration and Gratitude must such Conceptions thoroughly believed, excite in the Mind! How natural and delightful must it be to one whose Heart is open to the Perception of Truth, and of _{Duties of Gratitude, Love, &c.}

every thing *fair, great,* and *wonderful* in Nature, to contemplate and adore him, who is the first *fair,* the first *great,* and first *wonderful;* in whom *Wisdom, Power,* and *Goodness,* dwell vitally, essentially, originally, and act in perfect Concert! What *Grandeur* is here to fill the most enlarged Capacity, what *Beauty* to engage the most ardent Love, what a Mass of *Wonders* in such Exuberance of Perfection to astonish and delight the human Mind through an unfailing Duration!

Other Affections
If the *Deity* is considered as our supreme *Guardian* and *Benefactor,* as the *Father of Mercies,* who loves his Creatures with infinite Tenderness, and, in a particular manner, all good Men, nay, who delights in Goodness, even in its most imperfect Degrees; what Resignation, what Dependence, what generous Confidence, what Hope in God, and his allwise Providence, must arise in the Soul that is possessed of such amiable Views of him? All those Exercises of Piety, and above all a superlative Esteem and Love, are directed to God as to their *natural,* their *ultimate,* and indeed their only *adequate* Object; and though the immense Obligations we have received from him, may excite in us more lively Feelings of divine Goodness than a general and abstracted Contemplation of it, yet the Affections of *Gratitude* and *Love* are themselves of the generous disinterested kind, not the Result of Self-interest, or Views of Reward.* A perfect Character, in which we always suppose infinite Goodness, guided by unerring Wisdom, and supported by Almighty Power, is the proper Object of perfect Love; and tho' that Character sustains to us the Relation of a *Benefactor,* yet the Mind, deeply struck with that Perfection, is quite lost amidst such a Blaze of Beauty, and grows as it were insensible to those minuter Irradiations of it upon itself. To talk therefore of a *mercenary* Love of God, or which has *Fear* for its principal Ingredient, is equally impious and absurd. If we do not love the loveliest Object in the Universe for his own Sake, no Prospect of Good or Fear of Ill can ever bribe our Esteem, or captivate our Love. These Affections are too noble to be bought or sold, or bartered in the way of *Gain;*

---

* *See* Butler's *Sermon on the Love of God.* [Sermons 13 and 14 of Butler's *Fifteen Sermons* are titled "Upon the Love of God."]

Worth, or *Merit,* is their Object, and their Reward is something similar in kind. Whoever indulges such Sentiments and Affections towards the Deity, must be confirmed in the Love of Virtue, in a Desire to imitate its all-perfect Pattern, and in a chearful Security that all his great Concerns, those of his Friends, and of the Universe, shall be absolutely safe under the Conduct of unerring Wisdom, and unbounded Goodness. It is in his Care and Providence alone that the good Man, who is anxious for the Happiness of all, finds perfect Serenity, a Serenity neither ruffled by partial Ill, nor soured by private Disappointment.

When we consider the unstained Purity and absolute Perfection of the *Divine* Nature, and reflect withal on the Imperfection and various Blemishes of our own, we must sink, or be convinced we ought to sink, into the deepest Humility and Prostration of Soul before him, who is so wonderfully great and holy. When farther, we call to mind what low and languid Feelings we have of the Divine Presence and Majesty, what Insensibility of his fatherly and universal Goodness, nay what ungrateful Returns we have made to it, how far we come short of the Perfection of his Law, and the Dignity of our own Nature, how much we have indulged to the selfish Passions, and how little to the benevolent ones, we must be conscious that it is our Duty to repent of a Temper and Conduct so unworthy our Nature, and unbecoming our Obligations to its Author, and to resolve and endeavour to act a wiser and better Part for the future. The Connection of our Depravity and Folly with inward Remorse, and many outward Calamities, being established by the Deity himself, is a natural Intimation of his Present Displeasure with us; and a Propensity to continue in the same Course, contracted in consequence of the Laws of Habit, gives us just Ground of Fear, that we are obnoxious to his farther Displeasure, as that Propensity gives a Stability to our Vice and Folly, and forebodes our Perseverance in them.

Repentance, &c.

Nevertheless, from the Character which his Works exhibit of him, from those Delays or Alleviations of Punishment which Offenders often experience, and from the merciful Tenour of his Administration in many other Instances, the sincere Penitent may entertain good Hopes that his

Hopes of Pardon

Parent and Judge will not be strict to mark Iniquity, but will be propitious and favourable to him, if he honestly endeavours to avoid his former Practices, and subdue his former Habits, and to live in a greater Conformity to the Divine Will for the future. If any Doubts or Fears should still remain, how far it may be consistent with the Rectitude and Equity of the Divine Government to let his Iniquities pass unpunished, yet he cannot think it unsuitable to his paternal Clemency and Wisdom to contrive a Method of retrieving the penitent Offender, that shall unite and reconcile the Majesty and Mercy of his Government. If Reason cannot of itself suggest such a Scheme, it gives at least some Ground to expect it. But though *natural Religion* cannot let in more Light and Assurance on so interesting a Subject, yet it will teach the humble Theist to wait with great Submission for any farther Intimations it may please the supreme Governor to give of his Will; to examine with Candour and Impartiality, whatever Evidence shall be proposed to him of a *Divine Revelation,* whether that Evidence is *natural* or *supernatural;* to embrace it with Veneration and Chearfulness, if the Evidence is clear and convincing; and finally, if it bring to light any *new Relations* or *Connections, natural Religion* will persuade its sincere Votary faithfully to comply with the *Obligations,* and perform the *Duties* which result from those Relations and Connections.—This is *Theism, Piety,* the *Completion of Morality!*

Worship, Praise, Thanksgiving We must farther observe, that all those Affections which we supposed to regard the Deity as their *immediate* and *primary* Object, are vital Energies of the Soul, and consequently exert themselves into Act, and like all its other Energies, gain Strength or greater Activity by that Exertion. It is therefore our *Duty* as well as highest *Interest,* often at stated Times, and by decent and solemn Acts, to contemplate and adore the great Original of our Existence, the Parent of all Beauty, and of all Good; to express our Veneration and Love, by an awful and devout Recognition of his Perfections, and to evidence our Gratitude, by celebrating his Goodness, and thankfully acknowledging all his Benefits. It is likewise our Duty, by proper Exercises of Sorrow and Humiliation, to confess our Ingratitude and Folly, to signify our Dependence on God, and our

Confidence in his Goodness, by imploring his Blessing and gracious Concurrence in assisting the Weakness, and curing the Corruptions of our Nature; and finally, to testify our Sense of his Authority and our Faith in his Government, by devoting ourselves to do his Will, and resigning ourselves to his Disposal. These Duties are not therefore obligatory, because the Deity needs or can be profited by them; but as they are apparently *decent* and *moral,* suitable to the Relations he sustains of our *Creator, Benefactor, Law-giver,* and *Judge,* expressive of our State and Obligations, and improving to our Tempers, by making us more Rational, Social, God-like, and consequently more Happy.

We have now considered INTERNAL Piety, or the *Worship of the Mind,* that which is in Spirit and in Truth; we shall conclude this Section with a short Account of that which is EXTERNAL. *External* Worship is founded on the same Principles as *Internal,* and of as strict moral Obligation. It is either *private* or *public. Devotion,* that is *inward,* or *purely intellectual,* is too spiritual and abstracted an Operation for the Bulk of Mankind. The Operations of their Minds, such especially as are employed on the most sublime, immaterial Objects, must be assisted by their outward Organs, or by some Help from the Imagination, otherwise they will be soon dissipated by sensible Impressions, or grow tiresome if too long continued. Ideas are such fleeting things, that they must be fixed, and so subtle, that they must be expressed and delineated as it were, by sensible Marks and Images, otherwise we cannot attend to them, nor be much affected by them. THEREFORE *verbal Adoration, Prayer, Praise, Thanksgiving,* and *Confession,* are admirable Aids to *inward* Devotion, fix our Attention, compose and enliven our Thoughts, impress us more deeply with a Sense of the awful Presence in which we are, and, by a natural and mechanical sort of Influence, tend to heighten those devout Feelings and Affections which we ought to entertain, and after this manner reduce into formal and explicit Act.

External Worship

This holds true in an higher Degree in the case of PUBLIC Worship, where the Presence of our Fellow-creatures, and the powerful Contagion of the *social* Affections conspire to kindle and spread the devout

Public Worship

Flame with greater Warmth and Energy. To conclude: As *God* is the *Parent* and *Head* of the *social System,* as he has formed us for a *social State,* as by *one* we find the best Security against the Ills of Life, and in the *other* enjoy its greatest Comforts, and as by means of *both,* our Nature attains its highest Improvement and Perfection; and moreover, as there are *public Blessings* and *Crimes* in which we all share in some degree, and *public Wants* and *Dangers* to which all are exposed, it is therefore evident, that the various and solemn Offices of *public Religion,* are Duties of indispensible moral Obligation, among the best Cements of Society, the firmest Prop of Government, and the fairest Ornament of both.

Book III

Of Practical Ethics, or the Culture
of the Mind

We have now gone thro' a particular Detail of the several Duties we owe to OURSELVES, to SOCIETY, and to GOD. In considering the *first Order* of Duties, we just touched on the Methods of acquiring the different kinds of Goods, which we are led by Nature to pursue; only we left the Consideration of the Method of acquiring the *Moral* Goods of the Mind to a Section by itself, because of its singular Importance. This Section then will contain a brief Enumeration of the Arts of acquiring *Virtuous Habits,* and of eradicating *Vitious Ones,* as far as is consistent with the Brevity of such a Work; a Subject of the utmost Difficulty as well as importance in Morals; to which, nevertheless, the least Attention has been generally given by *Moral* Writers. This will properly follow a Detail of Duty, as it will direct us to such *Means* or *Helps* as are most necessary and conducive to the Practice of it.

Dignity and Importance of the Subject

In the first Part of this Inquiry we traced the Order in which the Passions shoot up in the different Periods of human Life. That Order is not accidental, or dependent on the Caprice of Men, or the Influence of Custom and Education; but arises from the Original Constitution and Laws of our Nature; of which this is one, *viz.* "That senseble Objects make the first and strongest Impressions on the Mind." These, by

Sensible Ideas and sensible Taste

119

means of our outward Organs being conveyed to the Mind, become Objects of its Attention, on which it reflects, when the outward Objects are no longer present, or, in other words, when the Impressions upon the outward Organs cease. These Objects of the Mind's Reflection are called *Ideas* or *Images.* Towards these, by another Law of our Nature, we are not altogether indifferent, but correspondent Movements of *Desire* or *Aversion, Love* or *Hatred,* arise, according as the Objects, of which they are Images or Copies, made an agreeable or disagreeable Impression on our Organs. Those *Ideas* and *Affections* which we experience in the *first* Period of Life, we refer to the BODY, or to SENSE; and the TASTE which is formed towards them, we call a SENSIBLE, or a merely NATURAL TASTE; and the Objects corresponding to them we in general call GOOD or PLEASANT.

Ideas of Beauty and a fine Taste
But, as the Mind moves forward in its Course, it extends its Views, and receives a *new* and more *complex* Set of Ideas, in which it observes *Uniformity, Variety, Similitude, Symmetry of Parts, Reference to an End, Novelty, Grandeur.* These compose a vast Train and Diversity of *Imagery,* which the Mind compounds, divides, and moulds into a thousand Forms, in the Absence of those Objects which first introduced it. And this more complicated Imagery suggests a new Train of *Desires* and *Affections,* full as sprightly and engaging as any which have yet appeared. This whole Class of *Perceptions* or *Impressions* is referred to the IMAGINATION, and forms an higher Taste than the *Sensible,* and which has an immediate and mighty Influence on the *finer* Passions of our Nature, and is commonly termed a FINE TASTE.

The Objects which correspond to this *Taste* we use to call *beautiful, harmonious, great,* or *wonderful,* or in general by the Name of BEAUTY.

Moral Ideas and a Moral Taste
The Mind still pushing onwards and increasing its Stock of Ideas, ascends from those to an higher Species of Objects, *viz.* the *Order* and *Mutual Relations* of *Minds* to each other, their reciprocal *Affections, Characters, Actions,* and various *Aspects.* In these it discovers a *Beauty,* a *Grandeur,* a *Decorum,* more interesting and alluring than in any of the former kinds. These Objects, or the Images of them, passing in review

before the Mind, do, by a necessary Law of our Nature, call forth another and nobler Set of Affections, as *Admiration, Esteem, Love, Honour, Gratitude, Benevolence,* and others of the like Tribe. This Class of *Perceptions* and their correspondent *Affections,* we refer because of their Objects (MANNERS) to a MORAL Sense, and call the *Taste* or *Temper* they excite MORAL. And the Objects which are agreeable to this *Taste* or *Temper* we denominate by the general Name of MORAL BEAUTY, in order to distinguish it from the other which is termed *Natural.*

These different Sets of *Ideas* or *Images* are the Materials about which the Mind employs itself, which it blends, ranges, and diversifies ten thousand different ways. It feels a strong Propension to connect and associate those Ideas among which it observes any *Similitude,* or any *Aptitude,* whether *original* and *natural,* or *customary* and *artificial,* to suggest each other. Thus it is ready to associate the Ideas of *Natural* and *Moral* Beauty, as both partake of the same Principle, *viz. Design, Harmony of Parts,* or *Reference to an End,* and are *Relative to Mind,* the common *Origin* of Both. A fine Face, or a graceful Deportment, *naturally* suggests Ideas of *Moral* Beauty. And many outward Badges, as Crowns, Crosiers, Purple Robes, and Statues, do often, by the Force of Custom, excite *Moral* Sentiments, as *Majesty, Piety, Justice, Virtue.* If any particular Sets of Ideas have been found, at any time, to co-exist in the same Objects, the Mind shall ever after have a Propensity to unite them, even when they no longer co-exist. Thus, because we have sometimes seen a *good Temper* accompany a *good Aspect, Virtue* annexed to *Politeness, Merit* to *Fame,* we are strongly inclined to fancy that they can never be disunited. When any Ideas or Sets of Ideas have been produced by certain Objects or Occasions immediately and presently, which Objects or Occasions have afterwards given rise to a different and perhaps quite opposite Set of Ideas or Impressions, the same Objects recurring, shall bring in view the *former* Set, while the *latter,* being posterior in time, shall be entirely forgot. Thus the *Drinker* or *Rake,* upon seeing his Bottle, and his Companion, or Mistress, shall amuse himself with all the gay Ideas of agreeable *Fellowship, Friendship, Gentleman-like Enjoyment, giving* and *receiving Pleasures,* which those Objects first excited,

Sources of Association

but, by an unhappy Self-delusion, shall over-look those *Head achs, Heart-achs,* that *Satiety,* and those other mortifying Impressions which accompanied though more laterly, his intemperate Indulgences.

Laws of But whatever the Reasons are, whether *Similitude, Co-existence, Causal-*
Association *ity,* or any other *Aptitude* or *Relation,* why any two or more Ideas are connected by the Mind at first, it is an established Law of our Nature, "That when two or more Ideas have often started in Company, they form so strong an Union, that it is very difficult ever after to separate them." Thus the *Lover* cannot separate the Idea of *Merit* from his *Mistress;* the *Courtier* that of *Dignity* from his *Title* or *Ribbon;* the *Miser* that of *Happiness* from his *Bags.* Here the Mind's Process is often the same as in its more abstracted Operations. When it has once been convinced of the Truth of any Geometrical Proposition, it may strongly retain the Connection of the Terms of the Proposition, suppose the Equality of the Angles of a Triangle to two Right ones, though it does not attend to, or has perhaps forgot, the intervening Ideas which shewed that Connection. In like manner, tho perhaps it was the Tendency of Wealth and Power, when well employed, to private Pleasure, or public Happiness, that gave the fond Admirers of either the first Notion of their Value, yet their Mind having once settled that *Connection,* frequently forgets the immediate Link, *viz.* the *wise* or *generous Use,* and by degrees come to admire Wealth and Power for themselves, fancying them *intrinsically* valuable, however they are used, and whether used or not. By these and many other ways the strongest Associations of Ideas are formed, the different Sets of Ideas before mentioned are shuffled together without Regularity or Distinction, often without any *Natural Alliance* or *Relation,* by mere Accident, Example, Company, Sympathy, Education, and sometimes by Caprice. So that any kind of *Natural Good* shall be combined with *Moral Beauty,* nay Ideas the most opposite in Nature shall be coupled together, so as hardly to be ever disunited in the Observer's Mind: as for instance, *Prudence* with *Craft, Honour* with *Injustice, Religion* with *Inhumanity, Corruption* or *Sedition* with *Patriotism.*—It is these Associations of *Worth* or *Happiness* with any of the different Sets of *Objects* or *Images* before specified, that form our *Taste,* or *Complex*

Idea of GOOD. By another Law of our Nature, "our *Affections* follow and are governed by this *Taste*. And to these *Affections* our *Character* and *Conduct* are similar and proportioned, on the general Tenour of which our *Happiness* principally depends."

As all our *Leading* Passions then depend on the Direction which our *Taste* takes, and as it is always of the same Strain with our *Leading* Associations, it is worth while to enquire a little more particularly how these are formed, in order to detect the secret Sources from whence our Passions derive their principal Strength, their various Rises and Falls. For this will give us the true Key to their Management, and let us into the right Method of correcting the *bad* and improving the *good.*

Leading Passions follow Taste

A very slight Inspection into human Nature suggests to us, that no kind of Objects make so powerful an Impression on us as those which are immediately impressed on our *Senses,* or strongly painted on our *Imaginations.* Whatever is purely *Intellectual,* as abstracted or scientific Truths, the subtile Relations and Differences of Things, has a fainter sort of Existence in the Mind; and though it may exercise and whet the *Memory,* the *Judgment,* or the *Reasoning Powers,* gives hardly any Impulse at all to the *Active* Powers, the *Passions,* which are the main Springs of Motion. On the other hand, were the Mind entirely under the Direction of *Sense,* and impressible only by such Objects as are present, and strike some of the outward Organs, we should then be precisely in the State of the Brute-Creation, and be governed solely by *Instinct* or *Appetite,* and have no Power to controul whatever Impressions are made upon us: Nature has therefore endued us with a MIDDLE FACULTY, wonderfully adapted to our MIXED State, which holds partly of *Sense* and partly of *Reason,* being strongly allied to the *former,* and the common Receptacle in which all the Notices that come from that quarter are treasured up, and yet greatly subservient and ministerial to the *latter,* by giving a Body, a Coherence, and Beauty to its Conceptions. This *middle* Faculty is called the IMAGINATION, one of the most busy and fruitful Powers of the Mind. Into this common Storehouse are likewise carried all those *Moral Images* or *Forms* which are derived from our

The Importance and Use of the Imagination

Moral Faculties of Perception, and there they often undergo new Changes and Appearances, by being mixed and wrought up with the Images and Forms of *Sensible* or *Natural* Things. By this Coalition of Imagery, *Natural Beauty* is dignified and heightened by *Moral Qualities* and *Perfections,* and *Moral Qualities* are at once exhibited, and set off by *Natural Beauty.* The *sensible* Beauty, or Good, is refined from its Dross by partaking of the *Moral,* and the *Moral* receives a Stamp, a visible Character and Currency from the *Sensible.*—But in order to judge of this mutual Influence, it will be proper to give a few Instances of the Process of the *Imagination,* or of the Energy of the *associating* Principle.

Its Energy in various Instances, in heightening sensible Pleasures

As we are first of all accustomed to *sensible* Impressions and *sensible* Enjoyments, we contract early a *Sensual Relish,* or *Love of Pleasure,* in the lower Sense of the Word. In order however to justify this Relish, the Mind, as it becomes open to *higher* Perceptions of *Beauty* and *Good,* borrows from thence a nobler Set of *Images,* as *fine Taste, Generosity, social Affection, Friendship, good Fellowship,* and the like; and, by dressing out the old Pursuits with these new Ornaments, gives them an additional Dignity and Lustre. By these ways the *Desire of a Table, Love of Finery, Intrigue,* and *Pleasure,* are vastly increased beyond their natural Pitch, having an Impulse combined of the Force of the *natural* Appetites and of the super-added Strength of those *Passions* which tend to the *Moral* Species.

In heightening the Pleasures of Beauty, Harmony, &c.

When the Mind becomes more sensible to those Objects or Appearances, in which it perceives *Beauty, Uniformity, Grandeur,* and *Harmony,* as fine Cloaths, elegant Furniture, Plate, Pictures, Gardens, Houses, Equipage, the Beauty of Animals, and particularly the Attractions of the Sex; to these Objects the Mind is led by *Nature,* or taught by *Custom,* the *Opinion* and *Example* of others, to annex certain Ideas of *Moral Character, Dignity, Decorum, Honour, Liberality, Tenderness,* and *Active* or *Social Enjoyment.* The Consequence of this Association is, that the Objects to which these are annexed, must rise in their Value, and be pursued with proportionable Ardor. The *Enjoyment* of them is often attended with *Pleasure,* and the mere *Possession* of them, where that is wanting, frequently draws *Respect* from one's Fellow-creatures: this *Respect* is, by many, equivalent to the Pleasure of *Enjoyment*. Hence it happens that the Idea of *Happiness* is connected with the mere *Possession*, which is therefore eagerly sought after, without any regard to the *generous Use*, or *honourable Enjoyment*. Thus the Passion resting on the *Means*, not the *End*, *i.e.* losing sight of its *natural* Object, becomes wild and extravagant.

In fine, any *Object*, or *External Denomination*, a *Staff*, a *Garter*, a *Cup*, a *Crown*, a *Title*, may become a *Moral* Badge, or Emblem of *Merit*, *Magnificence* or *Honour*, according as these have been found, or thought by the Possessors or Admirers of them, to accompany them; yet, by the Deception formerly mentioned, the *Merit* or the *Conduct* which entitled, or should entitle, to those Marks of Distinction, shall be forgot or neglected, and the *Badges* themselves be passionately affected, or pursued, as including every Excellency. If these are attained by any Means, all the Concomitants which *Nature*, *Custom*, or *Accidents* have joined to them, will be supposed to follow of course. Thus, *Moral Ends*, with which the unhappy Admirer is apt to colour over his Passion and Views, will, in his opinion, justify the most *Immoral Means*, as *Prostitution*, *Adulation*, *Fraud*, *Treachery*, and every Species of *Knavery*, whether more open, or more disguised. *In raising the Value of external Symbols, &c.*

When Men are once engaged in *Active* Life, and find that *Wealth* and *Power*, generally called INTEREST, are the great Avenues to every kind of Enjoyment, they are apt to throw in many engaging *Moral Forms* to the Object of their Pursuit, in order to justify their Passion, and varnish over the Measures they take to gratify it, as *Independency on the Vices* or *Passions* of others, *Provision* and *Security to themselves* and *Friends*, *Prudent Oeconomy* or *well-placed Charity*, *Social Communication*, *Superiority to their Enemies*, who are all Villains, *honourable Service*, and many other Ingredients of *Merit*. To attain such Capacities of *Usefulness* or *Enjoyment*, what Arts, nay what Meannesses can be thought blameable by those cool Pursuers of Interest?—Nor have they, whom the gay World is pleased to indulge with the Title of *Men of Pleasure*, their *In heightening the Value of Wealth, Power, &c.*

Imaginations less pregnant with *Moral Images,* with which they never fail to ennoble, or, if they cannot do that, to palliate their gross Pursuits. Thus *Admiration of Wit,* of *Sentiments* and *Merit, Friendship, Love, generous Sympathy, mutual Confidence, giving* and *receiving Pleasure,* are the ordinary Ingredients with which they season their Gallantry and pleasurable Entertainments; and by which they impose on themselves and endeavour to impose on others, that *their Amours* are the joint Issue of Good-sense and Virtue.

Its Influence on all the Passions
These *Associations,* variously combined and proportioned by the *Imagination,* from the chief *private* Passions, which govern the Lives of the Generality, as the *Love of Action,* of *Pleasure, Wealth,* and *Fame;* they influence the *Defensive,* and affect the *public Passions,* and raise *Joy* or *Sorrow,* as they are gratified or disappointed. So that in effect, these Associations of *Good* and *Evil, Beauty* and *Deformity,* and the Passions they raise, are the main *Hinges* of *Life* and *Manners,* and the great *Sources* of our *Happiness* or *Misery.* It is evident, therefore, that the whole of *Moral Culture* must depend on giving a right Direction to the *Leading Passions,* and duly proportioning them to the *Value* of the *Objects* or *Goods* pursued, under what Name soever they may appear.

Moral Culture, by Correcting our Taste or Imagination
Now, in order to give them this *right Direction* and *due Proportion,* it appears, from the foregoing Detail, that those *Associations* of Ideas, upon which the Passions depend, must be *duly* regulated; that is to say, as an exorbitant Passion for *Wealth, Pleasure,* or *Power,* flows from an *Association* or *Opinion* that more *Beauty* and *Good,* whether *Natural* or *Moral,* enters into the Enjoyment or Possession of them, than really belongs to either; *therefore,* in restoring those Passions to their just Proportion, we must begin with correcting the *Opinion,* or breaking the *false Association,* or, in other words, we must decompound the *Complex Phantom* of *Happiness* or *Good,* which we fondly admire; disunite those Ideas, that have no natural Alliance; and separate the *Original* Ideas of *Wealth, Power,* or *Pleasure,* from the foreign Mixtures incorporated with it, which enhance its Value, or give it its chief Power to enchant and seduce the Mind. For instance, let it be considered how poor and in-

considerable a Thing *Wealth* is, if it be disjoined from *real Use,* or from Ideas of *Capacity* in the Possessor *to do good* from *Independency, Generosity, Provision for a Family* or *Friends,* and *Social Communication* with others. By this *Standard* let its true Value be fixed; let its Misapplication, or unbenevolent Enjoyment be accounted sordid and infamous; and nothing worthy or estimable be ascribed to the *mere Possession* of it, which is not borrowed from its *generous Use.*

If that *complex* Form of *Good* which is called *Pleasure,* engages us, let it be analysed into its constituent Principles, or those Allurements it draws from the *Heart* and *Imagination,* in order to heighten the low part of the Indulgence; let the *separate* and *comparative* Moment of each be distinctly ascertained, and deduced from that gross part, and this Remainder of the accumulative Enjoyment will dwindle down into a poor, insipid, transitory thing. In proportion as the *Opinion* of the *Good* pursued abates, the *Admiration* must decay, and the *Passion* lose Strength of course. One effectual way to lower the *Opinion,* and consequently to weaken the *Habit* founded on it, is to practice lesser pieces of Self-denial, or to abstain, to a certain pitch, from the Pursuit or Enjoyment of the favourite Object; and, that this may be the more easily accomplished, one must avoid those Occasions, that Company, those Places and the other Circumstances that enflamed *one* and endeared the *other.* And, as a *Counter-process,* let *higher* or even different Enjoyments be brought in view, other Passions played upon the former, different Places frequented, other Exercises tried, Company kept with Persons of a different, or more correct way of thinking, both in *Natural* and *Moral* Subjects.

By Self-denial, and Counter-Process

As much depends on our setting out well in Life, let the *Youthful* Fancy, which is apt to be very florid and luxuriant, be early accustomed, by *Instruction, Example,* and significant *Moral Exercises,* nay by Looks, Gestures, and every other Testimony of just Approbation or Blame, to annex Ideas of *Merit, Honour* and *Happiness,* not to *Birth, Dress, Rank, Beauty, Fortune, Power, Popularity,* and the like *outward* Things, but to *Moral* and *truly virtuous Qualities,* and to those *Enjoyments* which

By a Sound and Natural Education

spring from a well-informed Judgment, and a regular Conduct of the Affections, especially those of the *social* and *disinterested* kind. Such dignified Forms of *Beauty* and *Good,* often suggested, and, by moving Pictures and Examples, warmly recommended to the *Imagination,* enforced by the Authority of *Conscience,* and demonstrated by *Reason* to be the surest Means of Enjoyment, and the only independent, undeprivable and durable Goods, will be the best Counter-balance to meaner Passions, and the firmest Foundation and Security to Virtue.

By rightly studying Human Nature

It is of great Importance to the forming a *just Taste,* or pure and large Conceptions of Happiness, to study and understand *Human Nature* well, to remember what a complicated System it is, particularly to have deeply imprinted on our Mind that GRADATION of *Senses, Faculties,* and *Powers of Enjoyment* formerly mentioned, and the *Subordination* of *Goods* resulting from thence, which Nature points out, and the Experience of Mankind confirms; who, when they think seriously, and are not under the immediate Influence of some violent Prejudice or Passion, prefer not the Pleasures of *Action, Contemplation, Society,* and most *Exercises* and *Joys* of the *Moral* kind, as *Friendship, Natural Affection,* and the like, to all *Sensual* Gratifications whatsoever. Where the different Species of Pleasure are blended into *one Complex Form,* let them be accurately distinguished, and be referred each to its proper *Faculty* and *Sense,* and examined apart what they have peculiar, what common with others, and what foreign and adventitious. Let *Wealth, Grandeur, Luxury, Love, Fame,* and the like, be tried by this Test, and their true Alloy will be found out.

By comparing the Moment and Abatements of different Goods

Let it be farther considered, whether the Mind may not be easy and enjoy itself greatly, though it want many of those Elegancies and Superfluities of Life which some possess, or that Load of Wealth and Power which others eagerly pursue, and under which they groan. Let the Difficulty of attaining, the Precariousness of possessing, and the many Abatements in enjoying over-grown Wealth and envied Greatness, of which the weary Possessors so frequently complain—as the Hurry of Business, the Burthen of Company, of paying Attendance to the *Few,* and giving it to the *Many,* the Cares of keeping, the Fears of losing, and the Desires of increasing what they have, and the other Troubles which accompany this pitiful Drudgery and pompous Servitude—let these and the like Circumstances be often considered that are conducive to the removing or lessening the *Opinion* of such Goods, and the attendant *Passions* or *Set* of *Passions* will decay of course.

Let the peculiar Bent of our Nature and Character be observed, whether we are most inclined to form Associations and relish Objects of the *Sensible, Intellectual,* or *Moral* kind. Let that which has the Ascendant be particularly watched, let it be directed to right Objects, be improved by proportioned Exercises, and guarded by proper Checks from an opposite Quarter. Thus, the *Sensible* turn may be exalted by the *Intellectual,* and a Taste for the Beauty of the *fine Arts,* and both may be made subservient to convey and rivet Sentiments highly *Moral* and *public spirited.* This inward Survey must extend to the *Strength* and *Weaknesses* of one's Nature, one's *Condition, Connections, Habitudes, Fortune, Studies, Acquaintance,* and the other Circumstances of one's Life, from which every Man will form the justest Estimate of his own Dispositions and Character, and the best Rules for correcting and improving them. And, in order to do this with more Advantage, let those *Times,* or *Critical Seasons* be watched, when the Mind is best disposed towards a Change, and let them be improved by vigorous *Resolutions, Promises,* or whatever else will engage the Mind to persevere in Virtue. Let the *Conduct,* in fine, be often reviewed, and the *Causes* of its *Corruption* or *Improvement* be carefully observed.

By observing our own Bent and Character, &c.

It will greatly conduce to refine the *Moral Taste* and strengthen the *virtuous Temper,* to accustom the Mind to the frequent Exercise of *Moral Sentiments* and *Determinations,* by reading *History, Poetry,* particularly of the *Picturesque* and *Dramatic* kind, the Study of the *fine Arts;* by conversing with the most eminent for Good-sense and Virtue; but above all by frequent and repeated Acts of *Humanity, Compassion, Friendship, Politeness* and *Hospitality.* It is Exercise gives Health and Strength. He that reasons most frequently becomes the wisest, and most enjoys the

By frequent Moral Exercises

Pleasures of Wisdom. He who is most often affected by Objects of Compassion in *Poetry, History,* or *real Life,* will have his Soul most open to Pity and its delightful Pains and Duties. So he also who practices most diligently the Offices of Kindness and Charity, will by it cultivate that Disposition, from whence all his Pretensions to personal Merit must arise, his present and his future Happiness.

By an honest Employment

An useful and honourable Employment in Life will administer a thousand Opportunities of this kind, and greatly strengthen a Sense of Virtue and good Affections, which must be nourished by right Training, as well as our Understandings. For such an Employment, by enlarging one's Experience, giving an Habit of Attention and Caution, or obliging one from Necessity or Interest, to keep a Guard over the Passions, and study the outward Decencies and Appearances of Virtue, will by degrees produce good Habits, and at length insinuate the Love of Virtue and Honesty for its own Sake.

By viewing Men and Manners in a fair Light

It is a great Inducement to the Exercise of Benevolence to view *Human Nature* in a favourable Light, to observe the Characters and Circumstances of Mankind on the *fairest* Sides, to put the best Constructions on their Actions they will bear, and to consider them as the Result of *partial* and *mistaken,* rather than *ill* Affections, or, at worst, as the Excesses of a pardonable Self-love, seldom or never the Effect of pure Malice.

By Consideration and pious Exercises

Above all, the *Nature* and *Consequences* of *Virtue* and *Vice,* their Consequences being the Law of our Nature and Will of Heaven; the Light in which they appear to our Supreme *Parent* and *Law-giver,* and the Reception they will meet with from him, must be often attended to. The Exercises of *Piety,* as *Adoration* and *Praise* of the *Divine* Excellency, *Invocation* of, and *Dependence* on his Aid, *Confession, Thanksgiving,* and *Resignation,* are habitually to be indulged, and frequently performed, not only as *medicinal,* but highly *improving* to the Temper.

To conclude: it will be of admirable Efficacy towards eradicating *bad* Habits, and implanting *good* ones, frequently to contemplate *Human Life,* as the great *Nursery* of our *future* and *immortal Existence,* as that *State* of *Probation,* in which we are to be *educated* for a *Divine Life.* To remember, that our *Virtues* or *Vices* will be *immortal* as ourselves, and influence our *future* as well as our *present* Happiness—and therefore, that every Disposition and Action is to be regarded as pointing beyond the *present* to an *immortal* Duration. An habitual Attention to this wide and important *Connection* will give a vast Compass and Dignity to our Sentiments and Actions, a noble Superiority to the Pleasures and Pains of Life, and a generous Ambition to make our *Virtue* as *immortal* as our *Being.*

By just Views of Human Life and its Connection with a future

Motives to Virtue
from Personal Happiness

Motives from personal Happiness We have already considered our *Obligations* to the Practice of *Virtue,* arising from the *Constitution* of our Nature, by which we are led to *approve* a certain *Order* and *Oeconomy* of *Affections,* and a certain *Course of Action* correspondent to it.*—But besides this, there are several Motives, which strengthen and secure Virtue, though not themselves of a *Moral* kind. These are, its *Tendency to personal Happiness,* and the *contrary Tendency of Vice.* "Personal Happiness arises, either from the State of a Man's own Mind, or from the State and Disposition of external Causes towards him."

Happiness of Virtue from within We shall first examine the "Tendency of Virtue to Happiness with respect to the State of a Man's own Mind."—This is a Point of the utmost Consequence in Morals, because, unless we can convince ourselves, or shew to others, that, by doing our *Duty,* or fulfilling our *Moral Obligations,* we consult the greatest Satisfaction of our own Mind, or our highest Interest on the whole, it will raise strong and often unsurmountable Prejudices against the Practice of Virtue, especially whenever there arises any Appearance of *Opposition* between our *Duty,* and our *Satisfaction* or *Interest.* To Creatures so desirous of Happiness, and averse to Misery as we are, and often so oddly situated amidst contend-

* *Vid. Book* I. *Sect.* 1, 2, &c.

ing Passions and Interests, it is necessary that Virtue appear not only an
honourable, but a *pleasing* and *beneficent* Form. And in order to justify
our Choice to ourselves, as well as before others, we must ourselves feel
and be able to avow in the Face of the whole World, that *her* Ways are
Ways of Pleasantness and her Paths the Paths of Peace. This will shew,
beyond all Contradiction, that we not only approve, but can give a sufficient Reason for what we do.

Let any Man, in a cool Hour, when he is disengaged from Business, and
undisturbed by Passion, as such cool Hours will sometimes happen, sit
down, and seriously reflect with himself what State or Temper of Mind
he would chuse to feel and indulge, in order to be easy and to enjoy
himself. Would he chuse, for that purpose, to be in a constant Dissipation and Hurry of Thought; to be disturbed in the Exercise of his
Reason; to have various, and often interfering Phantoms of Good play-
ing before his Imagination, soliciting and distracting him by turns, now
soothing him with amusing Hopes, then torturing him with anxious
Fears; and to approve this Minute what he shall condemn the next?
Would he chuse to have a strong and painful Sense of every petty Injury; quick Apprehensions of every impending Evil; incessant and insatiable Desires of Power, Wealth, Honour, Pleasure; an irreconcileable
Antipathy against all Competitors and Rivals; insolent and tyrannical
Dispositions to all below him; fawning, and at the same time envious,
Dispositions to all above him; with dark Suspicions and Jealousies of
every Mortal? Would he chuse neither to love nor be beloved of any, to
have no Friend in whom to confide, or with whom to interchange his
Sentiments or Designs; no Favourite, on whom to bestow his Kindness,
or vent his Passions; in fine, to be conscious of no Merit with Mankind,
no Esteem from any Creature, no good Affection to his Maker, no Concern for, or Hopes of his Approbation; but instead of all these, to hate,
and know that he is hated, to contemn, and know that he is contemned
by, all; by the Good, because he is so unlike; and by the Bad, because
he is so like themselves; to hate or to dread the very Being that made
him; and in short, to have his Breast the Seat of Pride and Passion, Pet-
ulance and Revenge, deep Melancholy, cool Malignity, and all the other

*Influence of
Vice on the
Temper of the
Mind*

Furies that ever possessed and tortured Mankind?—Would our calm
Enquirer after Happiness pitch on such a State, and such a Temper of
Mind, as the most likely means to put him in possession of his desired
Ease and Self-enjoyment?

Influence of
Virtue on the
Temper Or would he rather chuse a serene and easy Flow of Thoughts; a Reason
clear and composed; a Judgment unbiassed by Prejudice, and undis-
tracted by Passion; a sober and well-governed Fancy, which presents the
Images of Things true and unmixed with delusive and unnatural
Charms, and therefore administers no improper or dangerous Fuel to
the Passions, but leaves the Mind free to chuse or reject as becomes a
reasonable creature; a sweet and sedate Temper, not easily ruffled by
Hopes or Fears, prone neither to Suspicion nor Revenge, apt to view
Men and Things in the fairest Lights, and to bend gently to the Humours of others rather than obstinately to contend with them? Would
he chuse such Moderation and Continence of Mind, as neither to be
ambitious of *Power,* fond of *Honours,* covetous of *Wealth,* nor a Slave to
Pleasure; a Mind of course neither elated with Success, nor dejected
with Disappointment; such a modest and noble Spirit as supports
Power without Insolence, wears Honours without Pride, uses Wealth
without Profusion or Parsimony; and rejoices more in giving than in
receiving Pleasure; such Fortitude and Equanimity as rises above Misfortunes, or turns them into Blessings; such Integrity and Greatness of
Mind, as neither flatters the Vices, nor triumphs over the Follies of
Men; as equally spurns Servitude and Tyranny, and will neither engage
in low Designs, nor abet them in others? Would he chuse, in fine, such
Mildness and Benignity of Heart as takes part in all the Joys, and re-
fuses none of the Sorrows of others; stands well-affected to all Mankind; is conscious of meriting the Esteem of all, and of being beloved
by the best; a Mind which delights in doing good without any Shew,
and yet arrogates nothing on that account; rejoices in loving and being
beloved by its Maker, acts ever under his Eye, resigns itself to its Providence, and triumphs in his Approbation?—Which of these Dispositions would be his Choice, in order to be contented, serene and
happy?—The *former* Temper is VICE, the *latter* VIRTUE. Where *One*

prevails, there MISERY prevails, and by the Generality is acknowledged to prevail. Where the *other* reigns, there HAPPINESS reigns, and by the Confession of Mankind is acknowledged to reign. The *Perfection* of either Temper is *Misery,* or *Happiness in Perfection.* THEREFORE every *Approach* to *either Extreme,* is an *Approach* to *Misery,* or to *Happiness;* that is to say, every *Degree* of *Vice* or *Virtue* is accompanied with a *proportionable Degree* of *Misery* or *Happiness.*

But many are of opinion, and, by their Practice seem to avow the Opinion, that, by blending or softening the Extremes, and artfully reconciling *Virtue* with *Vice,* they bid fairer to strike a just *Medium* of Happiness, to pass more smoothly through Life, and to have more Resources in the present embarassed Scene. HONESTY (they acknowledge) "is, in the main, the best *Policy,* but it is often too blunt and surly, and always too scrupulous, and therefore to temper and season it with a little discreet Craft in critical and well-chosen Conjunctures, will, they think, make it more palatable to others and more profitable to one's self. *Kind* Affection is a good Thing in its own Place, and when it costs a Man nothing; but *Charity* begins at home; and one's Regard for others must still look that way, and be subservient to the main Chance. Besides, why suffer unnecessary Disquiet on the Account of others? Our own Happiness is Charge enough to us; and if we are not to be happy till others are so too, it is a mere *Utopian* Dream ever to expect it. One would not chuse to do Ill for the sake of Ill, but when *Necessity* requires it, the *lesser* Good must submit to the *greater,* that is, to our own *personal* Good; for in it, by the *first* and *fundamental* Law of our Nature, we are most interested. By such a Conduct we shall have least Reason to accuse ourselves, be most easy within, and best secured against the Misfortunes and Assaults of others."

An Objection from an imaginary Coalition of Virtue and Vice

This is the Language of great Partiality of Thought, as well as great Partiality of Heart.—But as it is one of the main Forts in which *Selfishness* and *Knavery* use to intrench themselves, it may be worth while to beat it down, to make way for the full Triumphs of their fair Adversary. That Man may neglect, or hurt their own Interest by an *indiscreet* Concern

The Temper and Condition of Half-honesty or Knavery

about that of others—that *Honesty* may sometimes degenerate into a *blunt Surliness,* or a *peevish Scrupulosity*—that important Occasions may demand the Sacrifice of a *less public,* to a *greater private* Good—that it were Folly to make one's self miserable, because others are not so happy as one would wish, we do not deny. But is there not the justest reason to suspect, that the *dishonest,* or the *half-honest* and *contracted* turn of Mind here pleaded for, is the very reverse of that *Temper* which begets true Satisfaction and Self-enjoyment, and of that *Character* which entitles to Credit, Security, and Success? The Man who doubts and hesitates, whether he may not, in some Instances, play the Knave, cannot, in any Sense, be termed honest. And surely, he cannot approve himself for that Conduct, which, by an inviolable Law of his Nature, he is compelled to condemn; and if he cannot approve himself for his Conduct, he is deprived of one of the sweetest Feelings of the human Heart. But, suppose he could disguise the immoral Deed or Disposition under the fair Name of some Virtue, or the Mask at least of a necessary Self-regard, as is often done, to elude the awful Decision of Conscience, which when uninfluenced is always unerring; yet he must be conscious he cannot stand the Test of *Judges less interested* than himself; and *must therefore* be under constant Dread of Discovery, and consequently of public Censure, with all its mortifying Attendants. This Dread must be so much the greater, if he has had Companions or Tools of his Knavery, which generally it must have in order to supply its native Impotence and Deficiency. This then is to be *insecure, obnoxious,* and *dependent,* and that too on the worst Set of Men, on whom one can have no hold but by their Vices, which, like undisciplined wild Beasts, often turn upon their Masters. Such an *insecure, obnoxious, dependent* State, must necessarily be a *State* of *Suspicion, Servitude* and *Fear,* which instead of begetting Serenity and Self-enjoyment, are the Parents of Disquiet and Misery. Besides, the fluctuating perpetually between opposite Principles, the Violence done to a native Sense of Honesty, the Reluctance against the first Advances of young and blushing Knavery, the hot and cold Fits of alternate Virtue and Vice, the Suspense and Irresolution of a Mind distracted between interfering Passions, are the first painful Symptoms of that dreadful Disease which afterwards lays waste every thing goodly and ingenuous, and raises Agonies intolerable to the Patient, and quite inconceivable by others. Whether such an inconsistent Conduct, divided between Vice and Virtue, will serve the Views of Interest proposed by it, will be afterwards examined.

As to the other Part of the Objection, let it be considered, that a Man of an enlarged benevolent Mind, who thinks, feels, and acts for others, is not subject to half the Disquietudes of the contracted selfish Soul;—finds a thousand Alleviations to soften his Disappointments, which the other wants;—and has a fair Chance for double his Enjoyments. His Desires are moderate, and his Wants few in comparison of the other's, because they are measured by Nature, which has Limits, not by Fancy or Passion, which has none. He is cautious, without being distrustful or jealous; careful, but not anxious; busy, but not distracted. He tastes Pleasure, without being dissipated; bears Pain, without Dejection or Discontent; is raised to Power, without turning giddy; feels few of the Pains of Competition, and none of the Pains of Envy.

Temper and Condition of the good benevolent Man

The principal Alleviations of his Calamities are these—that, though some of them may have been the Effect of his Imprudence, or Weakness, yet few of them are sharpened by a Sense of Guilt, and none of them by a Consciousness of Wickedness, which surely is their keenest Sting;—that they are common to him with the best of Men;—that they seldom or never attack him quite unprepared, but rather guarded with a Consciousness of his own Sincerity and Virtue, with a Faith and Trust in Providence, and a firm Resignation to its perfect Orders;—that they may be improved as Means of Correction, or Materials to give Scope and Stability to his Virtues;—and, to name no more, they are considerably lessened, and often sweetened to him by the general Sympathy of the Wise and Good.

The Alleviations of his Ills

His Enjoyments are more numerous, or, if less numerous, yet more intense than those of bad Men; for he shares in the Joys of others by Rebound; and every Increase of *general* or *particular* Happiness is a real Addition to his own. It is true, his friendly *Sympathy* with others

His Enjoyments

subjects him to some Pains which the hard-hearted Wretch does not feel; yet to give a loose to it is a kind of agreeable Discharge. It is such a Sorrow as he loves to indulge; a sort of pleasing Anguish, that sweetly melts the Mind, and terminates in a Self-approving Joy. Though the good Man may want Means to execute, or be disappointed in the Success of his benevolent Purposes, yet, as was formerly* observed, he is still conscious of good Affections, and that Consciousness is an Enjoyment of a more delightful Savour than the greatest Triumphs of successful Vice. If the *Ambitious, Covetous,* or *Voluptuous* are disappointed, their Passions recoil upon them with a Fury proportioned to their Opinion of the Value of what they pursue, and their Hope of Success; while they have nothing within to balance the Disappointment, unless it is an useful Fund of Pride, which *however frequently* turns mere Accidents into mortifying Affronts, and exalts Grief into Rage and Frenzy. Whereas the meek, humble, and benevolent Temper is its own immediate Reward, is satisfied from within, and as it magnifies greatly the Pleasure of Success, so it wonderfully alleviates, and in a manner annihilates, all Pain for the want of it.

From merited Esteem and Sympathy As the good Man is conscious of loving and wishing well to all Mankind, he must be sensible of his deserving the Esteem and Good-will of all; and this supposed Reciprocation of social Feelings, is, by the very Frame of our Nature, made a Source of very intense and enlivening Joys. By this Sympathy of Affections and Interests he feels himself intimately united with the Human Race; and being sensibly *alive* over the whole System, his Heart receives, and becomes responsive to every Touch given to any Part. So that, as an eminent *Philosopher*† finely ex-

---

* *See Book* 2. §. 2.
† *Vid.* Shaftsb. *Inq. into Virtue, Book* 2. [Anthony Ashley Cooper, third Earl of Shaftesbury (1671–1713), published a corrected version of his *An Inquiry Concerning Virtue, or Merit* (1699) in 1711 as part of his *Characteristics of Men, Manners, Opinions, Times.* A second revised edition appeared in 1714, after his death. In Book 2, section 2, part 1 (paragraph 176) of the *Inquiry* he observes, "So insinuating are these pleasures of sympathy, and so widely diffused through our whole lives, that

presses it, he gathers Contentment and Delight from the pleased and happy States of those around him, from Accounts and Relations of such Happinesses, from the very Countenances, Gestures, Voices and Sounds even of Creatures foreign to our kind, whose Signs of Joy and Contentment he can any way discern.

Nor do those generous Affections stop any other natural Source of Joy whatever, or deaden his Sense of any innocent Gratification. They rather keep the several *Senses* and *Powers of Enjoyment* open and disengaged, intense and uncorrupted by Riot or Abuse; as is evident to any one who considers the dissipated, unfeeling State of Men of *Pleasure, Ambition,* or *Interest,* and compares it with the serene and gentle State of a Mind at peace with itself, and friendly to all Mankind, unruffled by any violent Emotion, and sensible to every good-natured and alluring Joy. He who daily dwells with *Temperance* and *Virtue,* those everlasting Beauties and of the highest Order, cannot be insensible to the Charms of Society, or Friendship, the Attractions of virtuous Love, the Delights of Reading, or to any Beauty of a lower Species, the Unbendings of innocent Mirth, or whatever else sets the Soul at Ease, and gives him a Relish of his Being. By enjoying himself, he is in the best posture for enjoying every thing else. All is pure and well-ordered in such a Heart, and therefore whatever Pleasure is poured into it has an original Savour, not a single Drop is lost. For Virtue draws off all but the Dregs, and by mixing something of her own with the most ordinary Entertainments, refines them into exalted Enjoyments.

Do not interfere with other Joys

It were easy, by going through the different Sets of Affections mentioned formerly,* to shew, that it is only by maintaining the Proportion settled there that the Mind arrives at true Repose and Satisfaction. If *Fear* exceeds *that* Proportion, it sinks into Melancholy and Dejection. If *Anger* passes just Bounds, it ferments into Rage and Revenge, or sub-

The Misery of Excess in the Private Passions

---

there is hardly such a thing as satisfaction or contentment of which they make not an essential part."]

  * *See Book* I. §. I. 2.

sides into a sullen corroding Gloom, which embitters every Good, and
renders one exquisitely sensible to every Ill. The *Private* Passions, the
Love of Honour especially, whose Impulses are more generous as its
Effects are more diffusive, are Instruments of private Pleasure; but if
they are disproportioned to our *Wants,* or to the *Value* of their several
Objects, or to the *Balance* of other Passions, equally necessary, and
more amiable, they become Instruments of intense Pain and Misery.
For, being now destitute of that Counter-poise which held them at a
due pitch, they grow turbulent, peevish, and revengeful, the Cause of
constant Restlessness and Torment, sometimes flying out into a wild
delirious Joy, at other times settling into a deep splenetic Grief. The
Concert between Reason and Passion is then broke: all is Dissonance
and Distraction within. The Mind is out of Frame, and feels an Agony
proportioned to the Violence of the reigning Passion.

In the Public Affections · The Case is much the same, or rather worse, when any of the particular
kind Affections are out of their natural Order and Proportion; as hap-
pens in the case of *effeminate Pity, exorbitant Love, parental Dotage,* or
any *Party Passion,* where the just Regards to Society are supplanted.
The more *social* and *disinterested* the Passion is, it breaks out into the
wilder Excesses, and makes the more dreadful Havock, both within
and abroad, as is but too apparent in those Cases where a false Species
of *Religion, Honour, Zeal,* or *Party Rage* has seized on the natural Enthusiasm of the Mind, and worked it up to Madness. It breaks through
all Ties, *Natural* and *Civil,* counteracts the most sacred and solemn
Obligations, silences every other Affection, whether *Public* or *Private,*
and transforms the most gentle Natures into the most savage and inhuman. Such an exorbitant Passion is like the enormous Growth of a
natural Member, which not only draws from the Nourishment of the
rest, but threatens the Mortification of the whole Body, and in the
mean time occasions intolerable Pain and Anguish. In fine, all the
natural Affections, like the animal Spirits, or Humours of a strong
Body, if restrained from their proper Play, turn furious or melancholic,
and generally force their way by some violent Discharge, no less hurtful
to the Patient than offensive to those with whom he is connected.

Whereas the Man who keeps the *Balance* of *Affection* even, is easy and serene in his Motions; mild and yet affectionate; uniform and consistent with himself; is not liable to disagreeable Collisions of Interests and Passions; gives always place to the most friendly and humane Affections, and never to Dispositions or Acts of Resentment, but on high Occasions, when the *Security* of the *private,* or *Welfare* of the *public* System, or the *great Interests* of Mankind necessarily require a noble Indignation; and even then he observes a just Measure in Wrath; and last of all he proportions every Passion to the Value of the Object he affects, or to the Importance of the End he pursues.

Happiness of well-proportion'd Passions

To sum up this Part of the Argument, the *honest* and *good* Man has eminently the Advantage of the *knavish* and *selfish* Wretch in every respect. The Pleasures which the *last* enjoys flow chiefly from external Advantages and Gratifications; are superficial and transitory; dashed with long Intervals of Satiety, and frequent Returns of Remorse and Fear; dependent on favourable Accidents and Conjunctures; and subjected to the Humours of Men. But the *good* Man is satisfied from himself; his principal Possessions lie within, and therefore beyond the Reach of the Caprice of Men or Fortune; his Enjoyments are exquisite and permanent; accompanied with no inward Checks to damp them, and always with Ideas of Dignity and Self-Approbation; may be tasted at any time and in any Place.* The Gratifications of *Vice* are turbulent and unnatural, generally arising from the Relief of Passions in themselves intolerable, and issuing in tormenting Reflections; often irritated by Disappointment, always inflamed by Enjoyment; and yet ever cloyed with Repetition. The Pleasures of *Virtue* are calm and natural; flowing from the Exercise of kind Affections, or delightful Reflections

Sum of the Argument

---

* *Vid. the late ingenious Dial. on* Happiness *by* J. H. [James Harris (1709–80) of Salisbury was a nephew of Lord Shaftesbury, a member of Parliament, and an independent scholar best known for his *Hermes: or, a Philosophical Inquiry Concerning Language and Universal Grammar* (London, 1751). His essay on happiness was published as the third of *Three Treatises* (London, 1744). The first of the three treatises, "Concerning Art," was dedicated to his uncle, Lord Shaftesbury. The second treatise addressed music, painting, and poetry.]

in consequence of them; not only agreeable in the Prospect, but in the present Feeling; they never satiate, or lose their Relish; nay, rather the Admiration of Virtue grows stronger every Day; and not only is the Desire but the Enjoyment heightened by every new Gratification; and unlike to most others, it is increased, not diminished by Sympathy and Communication. In fine, the Satisfactions of Virtue may be purchased without a Bribe, and possessed in the humblest, as well as the most triumphant Fortune; they can bear the strictest Review, do not change with Circumstances, nor grow old with Time. Force cannot rob, nor Fraud cheat us of them; and, to crown all, instead of abating, they enhance every other Pleasure.

External Effects of Virtue — But the happy Consequences of *Virtue* are seen, not only in the Internal Enjoyments it affords a Man, but "in the favourable Disposition of External Causes towards him, to which it contributes."

On the Body — As VIRTUE gives the sober Possession of one's self and the Command of one's Passions, the Consequence must be Heart's Ease, and a fine natural Flow of Spirits, which conduce more than any thing else to Health and long Life. Violent Passions, and the Excesses they occasion, gradually impair and wear down the Machine. But the calm placid State of a temperate Mind, and the healthful Exercises in which *Virtue* engages her faithful Votaries, preserve the natural Functions in full Vigour and Harmony, and exhilarate the Spirits, which are the chief Instruments of Action. We might add, what will appear perhaps too refined, that as Virtue is the sound Temperament and beautiful Complexion of the Soul, so it even diffuses sometimes a congenial Air of Beauty over the Body, lights up, and spreads out the Countenance into a certain Openness, Chearfulness and Dignity, those natural Irradiations of inward Worth, which *Politeness,* that *Ape* of *Virtue,* may imitate, but can never fully attain.—In fine, *Temperance,* which has been called sometimes the *Mother,* and at other times the *Nurse* of the *Virtues,* is beautifully described by an ingenious Author,* to be that Virtue

---

* *See* Temple's *Miscell. Part* I. *Treat.* 6. [Sir William Temple (1608–99) was an En-

without Pride, and Fortune without Envy, that gives Indolence of Body and Tranquillity of Mind; the best Guardian of Youth and Support of old Age, the Tutelar Goddess of Health, and universal Medicine of Life, that clears the Head, strengthens the Nerves, enlightens the Eyes, and comforts the Heart.

It may by some be thought odd to assert, that *Virtue* is no Enemy to a Man's *Fortune* in the present State of Things.—But if, by *Fortune*, be meant a moderate or competent Share of *Wealth, Power,* or *Credit,* not overgrown Degrees of them, what should hinder the virtuous Man from obtaining that? He cannot cringe or fawn, it is true, but he can be civil and obliging as well as the Knave; and surely, his Civility is more alluring, because it has more Manliness and Grace in it than the mean Adulation of the other; he cannot cheat or undermine, but he may be cautious, provident, watchful of Occasions, and equally prompt with the Rogue in improving them; he scorns to prostitute himself as a Pandar to the Passions, or as a Tool to the Vices of Mankind, but he may have as sound an Understanding and as good Capacities for promoting their real Interests as the veriest Court-Slave; and then, he is more faithful and true to those who employ him. In the common Course of Business, he has the same Chances with the Knave of acquiring a Fortune, and rising in the World. He may have equal Abilities, equal Industry, equal Attention to Business; and in other respects he has greatly the Advantage of him. People love better to deal with him; they can trust him more; they know he will not impose on them, nor take Advantage of them, and can depend more on his Word than on the Oath or strongest Securities of others. Whereas what is commonly called CUNNING, which is the *Offspring* of *Ignorance,* and constant *Companion* of *Knavery,* is not only a mean-spirited, but a very short-sighted Talent, and a fundamental obstacle in the Road of Business. It may procure indeed immediate and petty Gains, but it is at-

On one's Fortune, Interest, &c.

glish diplomat and author. In the final essay of part one of his *Miscellanea,* 4th ed. (London, 1704–5), "An essay upon the cure of the gout by moxa," he discusses the contribution of temperance to good health.]

tended with dreadful Abatements, which do more than over-balance
them, both as it sinks a Man's Credit when discovered, and cramps
that Largeness of Mind, which extends to the remotest as well as the
nearest Interest, and takes in the most durable, equally with the most
transient Gains. It is therefore easy to see how much a Man's *Credit*
and *Reputation,* and consequently his Success, depend on his Honesty
and Virtue. The truly good Man has no Character to personate, no
Mask to wear; his Designs are transparent, and one Part of his Discourse and Conduct exactly tallies with another. Having no sordid
Views to promote, no mean Passions to serve, but wishing well to every
body, and doing all the Good he can, he is intrenched and guarded
round by *Innocence* and *Virtue;* and, though he is not secured against
Misfortunes, yet his Character and the Friends his Merit has procured
him will frequently retrieve him. Whereas *Tricking,* as one well expresses it, is a sort of Disguise, by which a Man hides himself in one
Place, and exposes himself in another. Besides, *Falshood* and *Roguery*
are variable unsettled Things, and the Source of a Conduct both ir-
resolute and inconsistent. They must often change hands, and be ever
contriving new Expedients as Accidents vary; and one lame Measure
must always limp on after another to support and back it. So that an
inexhausted Fund of Craft is necessary to play the Knave to any purpose, and to maintain for any time a counterfeit Character. When he
is once detected, his Credit is blown for ever; and, unless he is a great
Master in Dissimulation, his artificial Conduct will ever render him
obnoxious to Suspicion, which is ever sharp-sighted. Even the good
Man is not secure against the Attacks of Calumny, but he is armed
against its Sting. If he cannot silence, he will confute Detraction by
obstinately persisting in being virtuous and doing good; in time almighty Truth will prevail, and he might extort Veneration from the
Partial, as well as obtain a chearful Tribute from the *Candid* Judges of
Merit. But should the Cloud, in which Malice or Envy may have
involved his Virtue, never be entirely dissipated in his Life, yet Death,
that Soother of Envy and the Malevolent Passions, will totally dispel
any remaining Gloom, and display his Character in all its genuine and
unstained Glory. For the *Bed* of *Virtue* is a *Bed* of *Honour,* and he who

dies in it, cannot die *unlamented* by the *Good,* nor *unreverenced* by the *Bad.*

With regard to *Security* and *Peace* with his Neighbours, it may be thought perhaps, that the Man of a quiet forgiving Temper, and a flowing Benevolence and Courtesy, is much exposed to Injury and Affronts from every proud or peevish Mortal, who has the Power or Will to do Mischief. If we suppose indeed, this *Quietness* and *Gentleness* of Nature accompanied with *Cowardice* or *Pusillanimity,* this may often be the Case; but in reality, the good Man is bold as a Lion, and so much the bolder for being the calmer. Such a Person will hardly be a But to Mankind. The ill-natured will be afraid to provoke him, and the good-natured will not incline to do it. Besides, *true Virtue,* which is conducted by Reason, and exerted gracefully and without Parade, is a most insinuating and commanding Thing; if it cannot disarm Malice and Resentment at once, it will wear them out by Degrees, and subdue them at length. How many have, by Favours and prudently yielding, triumphed over an Enemy who would have been enflamed into tenfold Rage by the fiercest Opposition! In fine, *Goodness* is the most universally popular Thing that can be. Though the Prejudices or Passions of Men may sometimes dress it up in the Disguise of Weakness, or deface it with unlovely Features, yet let the Mask be dropt, and the lovely Form appear as it is, the most prejudiced will respect, the unprejudiced admire and love it, and all will be afraid, or at least ashamed, to traduce or offend a Thing so innocent and so God-like.

On one's Peace and Security

To conclude, the good Man may have some Enemies, but he will have more Friends, and having given so many Marks of private Friendship or public Virtue, he can hardly be destitute of a Patron to protect, or a Sanctuary to entertain him, or to entertain and protect his Children when he is gone. Tho' he should have little else to leave them, he bequeaths them the fairest, and generally the most unenvied Inheritance of a *good Name,* which, like good Seed sown in the Field of Futurity, will often raise up unsolicited Friends, and yield a benevolent Harvest of unexpected Charities. But should the Fragrance of the Par-

On one's Family

ent's Virtue prove offensive to a perverse or envious Age, or even draw
Persecution on the friendless Orphans, there is *one* in Heaven who will
be more than a Father to them, and recompense their Parent's Virtues
by showering down Blessings on them. The Thoughts of leaving them
in such good Hands sustain the honest Parent, and make him smile in
the Agonies of Death; being secure that that almighty Friend, who has
dispensed such a Profusion of Bounties to himself, cannot prove an
unkind Guardian, or an unfaithful Trustee to his fatherless Offspring.—This leads to consider a sublime Motive, and noble Mould
to Virtue, from whence it derives its firmest Support, and in which it
receives its highest Finishing and Lustre.

Motives to Virtue from
the Being and
Providence of God

Besides the interesting Motives mentioned in the last *Section,* there are
two great Motives to *Virtue,* strictly connected with *human Life,* and
resulting from the very *Constitution* of the *human Mind.* The First is
the BEING and PROVIDENCE of GOD; the Second is the IMMORTAL-
ITY of the Soul, with *future Rewards* and *Punishments.*

Two external Motives to Virtue

It appears from *Sect.* 4. of *Book* II that *Man,* by the *Constitution* of his
Nature, is designed to be a RELIGIOUS Creature. He is intimately connected with the *Deity,* and necessarily dependent on him. From that
Connection and necessary *Dependence* result various *Obligations* and
Duties, without fulfilling which, some of his sublimest Powers and Affections would be incomplete and abortive. If he be likewise an IM-
MORTAL Creature, and if his *present Conduct* shall affect his *future Happiness* in *another* State as well as in the *present,* it is evident that we take
only a *partial View* of the *Creature* if we leave out this important Property of his Nature, and make a *partial Estimate* of *human Life,* if we
strike out of the Account, or over-look that Part of his Duration which
runs out into Eternity.—We shall therefore consider the Motives which
arise from the former Connection in this *Section,* and those arising from
the latter in the *next.*

Their Importance

Piety   It is evident from the above-mentioned *Section,** that "to have a Respect to the *Deity* in our Temper and Conduct, to *venerate* and *love* his *Character*, to *adore* his *Goodness*, to *depend upon* and *resign* ourselves to his *Providence*, to *seek* his *Approbation*, and *act* under a *Sense* of his *Authority*, is a *fundamental Part* of *moral Virtue*, and the *Completion* of the *highest Destination* of *our Nature*."

A Support   But as *Piety* is an essential Part of Virtue, so likewise it is a *great Support*
to Virtue   and *Enforcement* to the Practice of it. To contemplate and admire a Being of such transcendent Dignity and Perfection as GOD, must naturally and necessarily open and enlarge the Mind, give a Freedom and Ampleness to its Powers, and a Grandeur and Elevation to its Aims. For, as an excellent *Divine*† observes, "the Greatness of an Object, and the Excellency of the Act of any AGENT about a transcendent Object, doth mightily tend to the Enlargement and Improvement of his Faculties." Little Objects, mean Company, mean Cares, and mean Business cramp the Mind, contract its Views, and give it a creeping Air and Deportment. But when it soars above mortal Cares and mortal Pursuits, into the Regions of Divinity, and converses with the greatest and best of Beings, it spreads itself into a wider Compass, takes higher Flights in Reason and Goodness, and becomes God-like in its Air and Manners. *Virtue* is, if one may say so, both the *Effect* and *Cause* of Largeness of Mind. It requires that one think freely, and act nobly. Now what can conduce more to Freedom of Thought and Dignity of Action, than to conceive worthily of God, to reverence and adore his unrivalled Excellency, to imitate and transcribe that Excellency into our own Na-

---

* *Sect.* 4. *Book* II.

† *Vid.* Whichcot'*s Serm. Part* II. *Serm.* VI. [The English divine Benjamin Whichcote (1609–83) spent most of his career in Cambridge, first as a Sunday lecturer at Trinity Church and later as Provost of King's College. Shaftesbury selected twelve of Whichcote's sermons and, writing an anonymous preface to the sermons, first published them in London in 1698 as *Select Sermons of Dr. Whichcote*. This book was later published in Edinburgh (1742) with a message to young ministers and divinity students from William Wishart, principal of Edinburgh University. See *Select Sermons of Dr. Whichcote, In Two Parts,* 281.]

ture, to remember our Relation to him, and that we are the Image and Representatives of his Glory to the rest of the Creation? Such Feelings and Exercises must and will make us scorn all Actions that are base, unhandsome, or unworthy our State; and the Relation we stand in to God, will irradiate the Mind with the Light of Wisdom, and ennoble it with the Liberty and Dominion of Virtue.

The Influence and Efficacy of *Religion* may be considered in another Light. We all know the Presence of a Friend, a Neighbour, or any Number of Spectators, but especially an august Assembly of them, to be a considerable Check upon the Conduct of one who is not lost to a Sense of Honour and Shame, and contributes to restrain many irregular Sallies of Passion. In the same manner we may imagine, that the Awe of some superior Mind, who is supposed privy to our secret Conduct, and armed with full Power to reward or punish it, will impose a Restraint on us in such Actions as fall not under the Controul or Animadversion of others. If we go still higher, and suppose our inmost Thoughts and darkest Designs, as well as our most secret Actions, to lie open to the Notice of the supreme and universal Mind, who is both the *Spectator* and *Judge* of human Actions, it is evident that the Belief of so august a Presence, and such awful Inspection, must carry a Restraint and Weight with it proportioned to the Strength of that Belief, and be an additional Motive to the Practice of many Duties which would not have been performed without it.—As our *Sense* of *Honour* or *Blame* is increased in proportion to the Esteem we have of those who bestow either, shall we suppose no Sensibility to the Applause, or Censure of him whom we believe to be the *Judge* as well as *Standard* of all Perfection? And if we suppose such a Sensibility, can we deny that it will operate on every Mind which feels it, both as an *Incentive* to deserve that Applause and as a *Guard* to avoid that Censure? We may suppose some Cases in which the virtuous Man, through the Force of Prejudices against him, and because of the false Lights in which his Actions are viewed, may be tempted to renounce the honest Cause by which he happens to incur Reproach or Ridicule. But if he can make his Appeal from the Opinions of Men to the Searcher of Hearts, it is evident that the Consciousness

A Guard and Enforcement to Virtue

of so high a Sanction may bear him out in his Course, and consequently be a Support to his Virtue, and in due time may teach him to despise the Strife of Tongues, nay the utmost Efforts of Malice and Envy.

But a good Man may likewise fall a Sacrifice to Power or to Injustice; his Life may be a Series of Misfortunes, and his Virtue may have exposed him to many of them; the Constitution and State of his Body, and peculiar Pressures on his Mind, may incapacitate him for enjoying the natural Fruits of Virtue, at least with an high Relish. How supporting in such a Case, nay how preservative must it be to his Integrity, and what an Antidote against that Gloom and Fretfulness which are apt to invade the Mind in such Circumstances of Trial, to believe that infinite Wisdom and Goodness preside in the Universe;—that every Event being under their Direction, is the Cause or Consequence of some greater Good to him, or to the whole;—that those Misfortunes which befall him are appointed by Heaven to correct his Follies, to improve or secure his Virtues, and consequently to increase his Happiness! These Sentiments thoroughly felt must and will serve as a Charm to sooth his Sorrows, and confirm his Loyalty and Resignation to the supreme Providence.

In Cases of the greatest Trial

In fine, let the Disposition of external Causes be ever so unfavourable to the good Man, yet, as he is conscious that the almighty Governor is his *Parent, Patron* and *Friend,* he may rest secure that he will either sustain and guard him in the midst of his Troubles, or direct and over-rule them to his greatest Good.

Exercises of Piety improving to Virtue

It may be observed farther, that "to live under an habitual Sense of the *Deity* and his great *Administration,* is to be conversant with *Wisdom, Order* and *Beauty* in the highest Subjects, and to receive the delightful Reflections and benign Feelings which these excite, while they irradiate upon him from every Scene of Nature and Providence." How improving must such Views be to the Mind, in dilating and exalting it above those puny Interests and Competitions which agitate and enflame the Bulk of Mankind against each other! What genial and propitious Influence on the Temper must the *Admiration* and *Love* of *Divine Goodness* have, when it is considered as diffused through infinite Space, to infinite Races of Creatures, and stretching from Eternity to Eternity! What Candor, Mildness, Benignity of Heart, and what Grandeur as well as Sweetness of Manners must it inspire? To conclude, with what alluring and commanding Energy must his *Benefits* call forth our *Gratitude,* his *Example* our *Imitation,* his *Wisdom, Power* and *Goodness,* our *Confidence* and *Hope,* his *Applause* our *Ambition* to deserve it? And how must his *Presence* strongly believed, or rather powerfully *felt,* enliven and fortify these and every other Principle of Virtue?

Motive to Virtue from the Immortality of the Soul, &c.

Metaphysical
Arguments for
its Immortality

The other Motive mentioned was the *Immortality* of the Soul, with *future Rewards* and *Punishments*. The *metaphysical* Proofs of the Soul's Immortality, are commonly drawn from its *simple, uncompounded,* and *indivisible* Nature, from whence it is concluded, that it cannot be corrupted or extinguished by a Dissolution or Destruction of Parts,—from its having a *Beginning* of *Motion* within itself, whence it is inferred, that it cannot discontinue and lose its Motion,—from the different Properties of *Matter* and *Mind,* the *Sluggishness* and *Inactivity* of *one,* and the immense *Activity* of the *other,* its prodigious Flight of *Thought* and *Imagination,* its *Penetration, Memory, Foresight,* and *Anticipations* of *Futurity,* from whence it is concluded, that a Being of so *divine* a Nature cannot be extinguished. But as these metaphysical Proofs depend on intricate Reasonings concerning the *Nature, Properties,* and *Distinctions* of *Body* and *Mind,* with which we are not very well acquainted, they are not obvious to ordinary Understandings, and are seldom so convincing even to those of higher Reach, as not to leave some Doubts behind them. Therefore perhaps it is not so safe to rest the Proof of such an important Article, on what many may call the Subleties of School-Learning. Those Proofs which are brought from *Analogy,* from the *moral Constitution* and *Phenomena* of the *human Mind,* the *moral Attributes* of God, and the *present Course of Things,* and which are therefore called the *moral* Arguments, are the plainest, and generally the most satisfying. We shall select only one or two from the rest.

In tracing the *Nature* and *Destination* of any Being, we form the surest   Moral Proof from Analogy
Judgment from his *Powers* of *Action,* and the *Scope* and *Limits* of these
compared with his *State,* or with that *Field* in which they are exercised.
If this Being passes through different States, or Fields of Action, and we
find a *Succession* of Powers adapted to the different Periods of his Progress, we conclude that he was destined for those successive States, and
reckon his Nature *Progressive.* If, besides the immediate Set of Powers
which fit him for Action in his present State, we observe another Set
which appears superfluous, if he was to be confined to it, and which
point to another or higher one, we naturally conclude, that he is not
designed to remain in his present State, but to advance to that for which
those supernumerary Powers are adapted. Thus we argue that the *Insect,*
which has Wings forming or formed, and all the Apparatus proper for
Flight, is not destined always to creep on the Ground, or to continue
in the torpid State of adhering to a Wall, but is designed in its Season
to take its Flight in Air. Without this farther Destination, the admirable
Mechanism of Wings and the other Apparatus, would be useless and
absurd. The same kind of Reasoning may be applied to Man, while he
lives only a sort of *vegetative* Life in the Womb. He is furnished even
there with a beautiful Apparatus of Organs, Eyes, Ears, and other delicate Senses, which receive Nourishment indeed, but are in a manner
folded up, and have no proper Exercise or Use in their present Con-
finement.* Let us suppose some intelligent Spectator, who had never
any Connection with Man, nor the least Acquaintance with human Affairs, to see this odd Phenomenon, a Creature formed after such a manner, and placed in a Situation apparently unsuitable to such various
Machinery, must he not be strangely puzzled about the Use of his com-

---

* *Vid.* Ludov. Viv. *de Rel. Christ. Lib.* II. *de Vita Uteri,* &c. [The reference is to
the Spanish humanist Juan Luis Vives (1492–1540), friend and correspondent of
Erasmus and Thomas More, whose unfinished apologia for Christianity *De veritate
fidei Christianae* was published in 1543. In book 1, chapter 7, "De vita uteri, et de hac
nostra, et altera," Vives compares the passage from the womb to life outside the
womb to the passage from death into life after death. See *Ioannis Ludovici Valentini
Opera Omnia* (Valencia: Montfort, 1782–90; reprint London: Gregg Press, 1964),
vol. 8, 51–53.]

plicated Structure, and reckon such a Profusion of Art and admirable Workmanship lost on the Subject; or reason by Way of Anticipation, that a Creature, endued with such various, yet unexerted Capacities, was destined for a more enlarged Sphere of Action, in which those latent Capacities shall have full Play? The vast Variety, and yet beautiful Symmetry and Proportions of the several Parts and Organs with which the Creature is endued, and their apt Cohesion with, and Dependence on, the curious Receptacle of their Life and Nourishment, would forbid his concluding the Whole to be the Birth of Chance, or the bungling Effort of an unskilful Artist, at least would make him demur a-while at so harsh a Sentence. But if, while he is in this State of Uncertainty, we suppose him to see the Babe, after a few successful Struggles, throwing off his Fetters, breaking loose from his little dark Prison, and emerging into open Day, then unfolding his recluse and dormant Powers, breathing in Air, gazing at Light, admitting Colours, Sounds, and all the *fair Variety* of Nature, immediately his Doubts clear up, the Propriety and Excellency of the Workmanship dawn upon him with full Lustre, and the whole Mystery of the *first* Period is unravelled by the opening of this new Scene. Though in this *second* Period the Creature lives chiefly a kind of *animal* Life, *i.e.* of *Sense* and *Appetite,* yet by various Trials and Observations, he gains Experience, and by the gradual Evolution of the Powers of *Imagination,* he ripens apace for an *higher* Life, for exercising the Arts of *Design* and *Imitation,* and of those in which Strength or Dexterity are more requisite than Acuteness or Reach of Judgment. In the succeeding *rational* or *intellectual* Period, his *Understanding,* which formerly crept in a lower, mounts into an higher Sphere, canvasses the Natures, judges of the Relations of Things, forms Schemes, deduces Consequences from what is past, and from present as well as past, collects future Events. By this Succession of States, and of correspondent Culture, he grows up at length into a *moral,* a *social,* and a *political* Creature. This is the last Period, at which we perceive him to arrive in this his mortal Career. Each *Period* is introductory to the next succeeding one; each *Life* is a Field of Exercise and Improvement for the next higher one, the Life of the *Foetus* for that of the *Infant,* the Life of the *Infant* for that of the *Child,* and all the lower for the highest and best.*—But is this the last Period of Nature's Progression? Is this the utmost Extent of her Plot, where she winds up the Drama, and dismisses the Actor into eternal Oblivion? Or does he appear to be invested with supernumerary Powers, which have not full Exercise and Scope, even in the last Scene, and reach not that Maturity or Perfection of which they are capable; and therefore point to some higher Scene, where he is to sustain another and more important Character than he has yet sustained? If any such there are, may we not conclude by Analogy, or in the same Way of Anticipation as before, that he is destined for that After-part, and is to be produced upon a more august and solemn Stage, where his sublimer Powers shall have proportioned Action, and its Nature attain its Completion?

If we attend to that *Curiosity,* or prodigious *Thirst of Knowledge,* which is natural to the Mind in every Period of its Progress, and consider withal the endless Round of Business and Care, and the various Hardships to which the Bulk of Mankind are chained down, it is evident, that in this present State, it is imposible to expect the Gratification of an Appetite at once so insatiable and so noble. Our *Senses,* the ordinary Organs by which Knowledge is let into the Mind, are always imperfect, and often fallacious; the Advantages of assisting, or correcting them, are possessed by few; the Difficulties of finding out Truth amidst the various and contradictory Opinions, Interests, and Passions of Mankind, are many; and the Wants of the Creature, and of those with whom he is connected, numerous and urgent; so that it may be said of most Men, that their *intellectual* Organs are as much shut up and secluded from proper Nourishment and Exercise in that little Circle to which they are confined, as the *bodily* Organs are in the Womb. Nay, those who to an aspiring Genius have added all the Assistances of Art, Leisure, and the

Powers in Man which point to an After-Life

Intellectual

---

* *See* Butler'*s Analogy, Part* I. [Bishop Joseph Butler's *The Analogy of Religion, Natural and Revealed, to the Constitution and Course of Nature* was published in London in 1736. Part 1 is an examination of natural religion. In chapter 5 of part 1, "Of a State of Probation, as Intended for Moral Discipline and Improvement," Butler discusses natural moral development.]

most liberal Education, what narrow Prospects can even they take of this unbounded Scene of Things from that little Eminence on which they stand? And how eagerly do they still grasp at new Discoveries, without any Satisfaction or Limit to their Ambition?

Moral Powers But should it be said, that Man is made for *Action,* and not for *Speculation,* or fruitless Searches after Knowledge, we ask, for what kind of Action? Is it only for *bodily* Exercises, or for *moral, political,* and *religious* ones? Of all these he is capable, yet by the unavoidable Circumstances of his Lot, he is tied down to the *former,* and has hardly any Leisure to think of the *latter,* or, if he has, wants the proper Instruments of exerting them. The *Love of Virtue, of one's Friends* and *Country,* the *generous Sympathy with Mankind,* and *heroic Zeal of doing Good,* which are all so *natural* to great and good Minds, and some Traces of which are found in the lowest, are seldom united with proportioned Means or Opportunities of exercising them; so that the *moral* Spring, the noble Energies and Impulses of the Mind, can hardly find proper Scope, even in the most fortunate Condition; but are much depressed in some, and almost entirely restrained in the Generality, by the numerous Clogs of an indigent, sickly, or embarrassed Life. Were such mighty Powers, such God-like Affections planted in the human Breast to be folded up in the narrow Womb of our present Existence, never to be produced into a more *perfect* Life, nor to expatiate in the ample Career of Immortality?

Unsatisfied Let it be considered, at the same time, that no Possession, no Enjoy-
Desires of ment within the Round of Mortal Things is commensurate to the De-
Existence and sires, or adequate to the Capacities of the Mind. The most envied Con-
Happiness, dition has its Abatements, the happiest Conjuncture of Fortune leaves
&c. many Wishes behind, and after the highest Gratifications the Mind is carried forward in Pursuit of new ones without End. Add to all, the fond *Desire* of *Immortality,* the secret *Dread* of *Non-existence,* and the high unremitting *Pulse* of the Soul beating for *Perfection,* joined to the Improbability or the Impossibility of attaining it *here;* and then judge whether this elaborate Structure, this magnificent Apparatus of

inward Powers and Organs, does not plainly point out an *Here-after,* *and intimate Eternity to Man?* Does Nature give the finishing Touches to the lesser and ignobler Instances of her Skill, and raise every other Creature to the Maturity and Perfection of his Being, and shall she leave her principal Workmanship unfinished? Does she carry the *Vegetative* and *Animal* Life in *Man* to their full Vigour, and highest Destination, and shall she suffer his *Intellectual,* his *Moral,* his *Divine* Life to fade away, and be for ever extinguished? Would such Abortions in the moral World be congruous to that *Perfection of Wisdom and Goodness,* which upholds and adorns the *Natural?*

We must therefore conclude, from this Detail, that the *Present State,* even at its best, is only the WOMB of Man's Being, in which the noblest Principles of his Nature are in a manner fettered, or secluded from a correspondent Sphere of Action, and therefore destined for a future and unbounded State, where they shall emancipate themselves, and exert the Fulness of their Strength. The most accomplished Mortal, in this low and dark Apartment of Nature, is only the *Rudiments* of what he shall be, when he takes his Etherial Flight, and puts on Immortality. Without a Reference to that State, *Man* were a mere Abortion, a rude unfinished Embryo, a Monster in Nature. But this being once supposed, he still maintains his Rank, of the Master-piece of the Creation; his latent Powers are all suitable to the *Harmony* and *Progression* of Nature, his noble Aspirations, and the Pains of his Dissolution, are his Efforts toward a *second* Birth, the Pangs of his Delivery into Light, Liberty, and Perfection; and *Death,* his Discharge from Gaol, his Separation from his Fellow-Prisoners, and Introduction into the Assembly of those heroic Spirits who are gone before him, and of their great eternal Parent. The Fetters of his Mortal Coil being loosened, and his Prison-Walls broke down, he will be bare and open on every Side to the Admission of *Truth* and *Virtue,* and their fair Attendant, *Happiness;* every *Vital* and *Intellectual* Spring will evolve itself, with a divine Elasticity, in the free Air of Heaven. He will not then peep at the Universe and its glorious Author through a dark Grate, or a gross Medium, nor receive the Reflections of his Glory through the strait Openings of sen-

Therefore Man immortal

sible Organs, but will be *all Eye, all Air, all Etherial and Divine Feeling**.—Let one part however of the Analogy be attended to, that, as in the Womb we receive our Original Constitution, Form, and the essential *Stamina* of our Being, which we carry along with us into the Light, and which greatly affect the succeeding Periods of our Life; so our Temper and Condition in the *future* Life will depend on the Conduct we have observed, and the Character we have formed in the *present* Life. We are *here* in *Miniature* what we shall be at *full Length here-after.* The first *rude Sketch,* or *Out-lines* of *Reason* and *Virtue,* must be drawn at present, to be afterwards enlarged to the *Stature* and *Beauty* of Angels.

Immortality a Guard and Incentive to Virtue This, if duly attended to, must prove not only a *Guard,* but an admirable *Incentive* to Virtue. For he who faithfully and ardently follows the Lights of Knowledge, and pants after higher Improvements in Virtue, will be wonderfully animated and inflamed in that Pursuit, by a full Conviction that the Scene does not close with Life—that his Struggles arising from the Weakness of Nature, and the Strength of Habit, will be turned into Triumphs—that his Career in the Tracks of Wisdom and Goodness will be both swifter and smoother—and those generous Ardors with which he glows towards *Heaven, i.e.* the *Perfection* and *Immortality of Virtue,* will find their adequate Object and Exercise in a Sphere proportionably enlarged, incorruptible, immortal. On the other hand, what an inexpressible Damp must it be to the good Man, to dread the total Extinction of that *Light* and *Virtue,* without which *Life,* nay *Immortality* itself, were not worth a single Wish?

Proof from the Inequality of present Distributions Many Writers draw their Proofs of the Immortality of the Soul, and of a future State of Rewards and Punishments, from the unequal Distribution of these here. It cannot be dissembled that wicked Men often escape the *outward* Punishment due to their Crimes, and do not feel the *inward* in that measure their Demerit seems to require, partly from the Callousness induced upon their Nature by the Habits of Vice, and

---

* *Vid. Relig. of Nat.* §. 9. [Wollaston, *The Religion of Nature Delineated,* section 9, "Truths belonging to a Private Man, and respecting (directly) only himself."]

partly from the Dissipation of their Minds abroad by Pleasure or Business—and sometimes good Men do not reap all the natural and genuine Fruits of their Virtue, through the many unforeseen or unavoidable Calamities in which they are involved. This no doubt, upon the Supposition of an all-wise and good Providence, where an Argument, and a strong one too, for a future State, in which those Inequalities shall be corrected. But unless we suppose a *prepollent good Order* in the present Scene of Things, we weaken the Proof of the *Divine* Administration, and the Presumption of any better Order in any future Period of it.

From *Section the second* of this *Book* it appears, that *Virtue* has present Rewards, and *Vice* present Punishments annexed to it, such Rewards and Punishments as make *Virtue,* in most Cases that happen, far more eligible than *Vice;* but, in the infinite Variety of Human Contingencies, it may sometimes fall out, that the inflexible Practice of Virtue shall deprive a Man of considerable Advantages to himself, his Family or Friends, which he might gain by a well-timed piece of Roguery, suppose by betraying his Trust, voting against his Conscience, selling his Country, or any other Crime, where the Security against Discovery shall heighten the Temptation. Or, it may happen, that a strict Adherence to his Honour, to his Religion, to the Cause of Liberty and Virtue, shall expose him, or his Family, to the Loss of every thing, nay to Poverty, Slavery, Death itself, or to Torments far more intolerable. Now, what shall secure a Man's Virtue in Circumstances of such Trial? What shall enforce the Obligations of Conscience against the Allurements of so many Interests, the Dread of so many and so terrible Evils, and the almost unsurmountable Aversion of human Nature to excessive Pain? The Conflict is the greater, when the Circumstances of the Crime are such as easily admit a Variety of Alleviations from *Necessity, Natural Affection, Love to one's Family,* or *Friends,* perhaps in Indigence? These will give it even the Air of Virtue. Add to all, that the Crime may be thought to have few bad Consequences,—may be easily concealed—or imagined possible to be retrieved in a good measure, by future good Conduct. It is obvious to which Side most Men will lean in such a Case, and how much need there is of a Balance in the opposite Scale, from

Belief of Immortality, &c. a great Support amidst Trials

the Consideration of a *God,* of a *Providence,* and of an *immortal State* of *Retribution,* to keep the Mind firm and uncorrupt in those or like Instances of singular Trial, or Distress.

In the general Course of Life

But without supposing such peculiar Instances, a Sense of a Governing Mind, and a Persuasion that Virtue is not only befriended by him here, but will be crowned by him hereafter with Rewards suitable to its Nature, vast in themselves, and immortal in their Duration, must be not only a mighty Support and Incentive to the Practice of Virtue, but a strong Barrier against Vice. The Thoughts of an almighty Judge and of an impartial future Reckoning, are often alarming, inexpressibly so, even to the stoutest Offenders. On the other hand, how supporting must it be to the good Man, to think that he acts under the Eye of his Friend, as well as Judge! How improving, to consider the *present State* as connected with a *future* one, and every Relation in which he stands as a *School* of *Discipline* for his *Affections,* every *Trial* as the *Exercise* of some *Virtue,* and the virtuous Deeds which result from both, as introductory to higher Scenes of *Action* and *Enjoyment!* Finally, how transporting is it to view *Death* as his *Discharge* from the *Warfare* of *Mortality,* and a triumphant *Entry* into a State of Freedom, Security and Perfection in which Knowledge and Wisdom shall break upon him from every Quarter; where each Faculty shall have its proper Object, and his Virtue, which was often damped or defeated here, shall be enthroned in undisturbed and eternal Empire!

Advantages of the Christian Scheme, and its Connection with Natural Religion or Morality

On reviewing this short *System* of *Morals,* and the *Motives* which support and enforce it, and comparing both with the CHRISTIAN *Scheme,* what *Light* and *Vigour* do they borrow from thence! How clearly and fully does CHRISTIANITY lay open the *Connections* of our Nature, both *material* and *immaterial,* and *future* as well as *present!* What an ample and beautiful Detail does it present of the *Duties* we owe to *God,* to *Society* and *Ourselves,* promulgated in the most simple, intelligible, and popular manner; divested of every Partiality of Sect or Nation; and adapted to the general State of Mankind! With what bright and alluring *Examples* does it illustrate and recommend the Practice of those Duties;

and with what mighty *Sanctions* does it enforce that Practice! How strongly does it describe the *Corruptions* of our Nature; the *Deviations* of our Life from the *Rule* of *Duty;* and the *Causes* of both! How marvellous and benevolent a Plan of *Redemption* does it unfold, by which those *Corruptions* may be remedied, and our *Nature* restored from its *Deviations,* to transcendent Heights of *Virtue* and *Piety!* Finally, what a fair and comprehensive Prospect does it give us of the *Administration* of *God,* of which it represents the *present State* only as a *small Period;* and a *Period* of *Warfare* and *Trial!* How solemn and unbounded are the Scenes which it opens beyond it; the *Resurrection* of the *Dead;* the *General Judgment;* the *Equal Distribution* of *Rewards* and *Punishments* to the *Good* and the *Bad;* and the full *Completion* of *Divine Wisdom* and *Goodness* in the *final Establishment* of *Order, Perfection* and *Happiness!*—How glorious then is that SCHEME of RELIGION, and how worthy of *Affection* as well as of *Admiration,* which, by making such *Discoveries,* and affording such *Assistances,* has disclosed the unfading Fruits and Triumphs of VIRTUE, and secured its Interests beyond the Power of TIME and CHANCE!

Conclusion

We have now considered the CONSTITUTION and CONNECTIONS of MAN, and deduced the several DUTIES resulting from *both.* We have investigated some of the METHODS by which his *Constitution* may be preserved in a *sound* and *healthful* State, or *restored* to it. We have enquired into the FINAL CAUSES of his *Constitution,* and found its admirable *Harmony* with his *Situation.* And, lastly, we have enumerated the principal MOTIVES which inforce the *Practice* of the *Duties,* incumbent on a Creature *so constituted,* and *so situated.* *Recapitulation*

From this Deduction it appears, that "MAN is a *Creature* endued with a Variety of *Senses, Powers* and *Passions,* subject to a Variety of *Wants* and *Dangers,* environed with many NATURAL, and capable of forming many CIVIL *Connections;* bound to many *Duties* in consequence of *Result* such a *Nature,* such a *Situation,* and such *Connections,* and susceptible of many *Enjoyments* in the Discharge of them."—It farther appears, that "the Sum of those *Duties* may be reduced to such a Conduct of his *Senses, Powers* and *Passions,* as is duly *proportioned* to his *Wants,* to his *Dangers,* and to his *Connections;*—that this *Conduct* is most approved in the mean time, and yields the most refined and lasting *Pleasures* afterwards;—that particularly, the Exercise of the *public Affections* is attended with *Enjoyments,* the greatest in DIGNITY and *Duration;*—and in the *largest Sum* of such *Pleasures* and *Enjoyments* his highest HAPPINESS consists. THEREFORE, to keep those refined Sources of Enjoyment always open, and, in cases of Competition, to sacrifice the *Lower* kinds, *i.e.* those of *Sense* and *Appetite,* to the *Higher, i.e.* to those of *Reason,* of *Virtue* and *Piety,* is not real *Self-Denial,* but the truest *Wisdom* and the justest *Estimate* of *Happiness.*—And to shut up the nobler Springs, or to sacrifice the *higher* to the *lower* kinds, is not *Self-Indulgence,* but the *Height* of *Folly,* and a wrong *Calculation* of *Happiness.*"

The happiest Youth *Therefore* HE who, in his YOUTH, improves his *Intellectual* Powers in the Search of Truth and useful Knowledge; and refines and strengthens his *Moral* and *Active* Powers, by the Love of Virtue, for the Service of his Friends, his Country and Mankind; who is animated by true Glory, exalted by sacred Friendship for *Social,* and softened by virtuous Love for *Domestic* Life; who lays his Heart open to every other mild and generous Affection, and who, to all these adds a sober masculine *Piety,* equally remote from *Superstition* and *Enthusiasm,* that MAN enjoys the most agreeable *Youth;* and lays in the richest Fund for the honourable *Action,* and *happy* Enjoyment of the *succeeding Periods* of Life.

The happiest Manhood *He* who, in MANHOOD, keeps the *Defensive* and *Private Passions* under the wisest Restraint; who forms the most select and virtuous Friendships; who seeks after *Fame, Wealth* and *Power* in the Road of *Truth* and *Virtue,* and, if he cannot find them in that Road, generously despises them; who, in his *private* Character and Connections gives fullest Scope to the tender and manly Passions, and in his *public* Character and Connections serves his Country and Mankind, in the most upright and disinterested manner: who, in fine, enjoys the *Goods* of Life with the greatest *Moderation,* bears its *Ills* with the greatest *Fortitude;* and in those various Circumstances of *Duty* and *Trial* maintains and expresses an habitual and supreme *Reverence* and *Love of God;* THAT MAN is the *worthiest* Character in *this Stage* of Life; passes through it with the highest Satisfaction and Dignity; and paves the Way to the most easy and honourable *Old-age.*

Finally, HE who, in the DECLINE OF LIFE preserves himself most exempt from the Chagrins incident to that Period; cherishes the most *equal* and *kind Affections;* uses his *Experience, Wisdom* and *Authority* in the most *fatherly* and *venerable* manner; acts under a *Sense* of the *Inspection,* and with a View to the *Approbation* of his *Maker;* is daily aspiring after Immortality, and ripening apace for it; and having sustained his Part with Integrity and Consistency to the last, quits the Stage with a modest and graceful Triumph; THIS is the *best,* this is the *happiest* OLD-MAN. *The happiest Old-age*

Therefore that *whole Life* of *Youth, Manhood* and *Old-age* which is spent after this manner, is the BEST and the HAPPIEST LIFE. *The happiest Life*

"*He,* who has the strongest *Original Propension* to such Sentiments and Dispositions, has the best NATURAL Temper." "*He,* who *cultivates* them with the greatest Care, is the most VIRTUOUS Character." "HE, who *knows* to *indulge* them in the most *discreet* and *consistent* manner, is the WISEST." "And HE, who, with the *largest Capacities,* has the best Opportunities of indulging them, is the most FORTUNATE." *The good Man* *The Virtuous, The Wise, the Fortunate Man*

"To form our Life upon this Plan is to FOLLOW NATURE," that is to say, "to act in a *Conformity* to our *Original Constitution,* and in a *Subordination* to the *Eternal Order* of *Things.* And, by acting in this manner, (so benevolently are we formed by our common Parent!) we effectually promote and secure our highest Interest." THUS, at last it appears, (and who would not rejoice in so *Divine* a *Constitution?*) that "DUTY, WISDOM and HAPPINESS *coincide,* and are *one.*" *A Life according to Nature* *Duty, Wisdom and Happiness are one*

The Sum and
Perfection of
Virtue

To conclude: "VIRTUE is the highest *Exercise* and *Improvement* of REA-SON; the *Integrity,* the *Harmony,* and *just Balance* of AFFECTION; the *Health, Strength* and *Beauty* of the MIND." "The PERFECTION of *Virtue* is to give REASON *free* Scope; to obey the Authority of CONSCIENCE with *Alacrity;* to exercise the *Defensive Passions* with FORTITUDE; the *Private* with TEMPERANCE; the *Public* with JUSTICE; and all of them with PRUDENCE; that is, in a due *Proportion* to each other, and an entire *Subserviency* to a *calm diffusive* BENEVOLENCE;—to *adore* and *love* GOD with a *disinterested* and *unrivalled* AFFECTION; and to *acquiesce* in his *Providence* with a *joyful Resignation.*" "Every *Approach* to this *Standard* is an *Approach* to *Perfection* and HAPPINESS. And every *Deviation* from it, a *Deviation* to VICE and MISERY."

A noble
and joyful
Corollary

From this whole REVIEW of HUMAN NATURE, the most *divine* and *joyful* of all *Truths* breaks upon us with full Evidence and Lustre; "That MAN is liberally provided with *Senses* and *Capacities* for *enjoying Happiness;* furnished with *Means* for *attaining* it; *taught* by his NATURE where it *lies; prompted* by his PASSIONS *within,* and his CONDITION *without,* powerfully to seek it; and, by the *wise* and *benevolent* ORDER of *Heaven,* often *conducted* to the WELFARE of the PARTICULAR, and always made *subservient* to the GOOD of the UNIVERSAL SYSTEM."

FINIS.

A brief Account of the Nature, Progress, and Origin of Philosophy
delivered by
the late Mr. David Fordyce, P. P. Marish. Col: Ab^dn
to his Scholars, before they begun their Philosophical course.
Anno 1743/4.

1. Philosophy, a thing much talked of but little understood by the generality, is defined by Cicero the great interpreter of the Greecian Philosophy: The knowledge of things divine & humane.[1] But the definition of it given by Pythagoras seems to express the nature with much more clearness & precisness. He calls Philosophy the knowledge of things which are of being, which have a real existence. Or still more distinctly, Philosophy may be described to be The Study & knowledge of the nature & laws of things, & their established connections with proper reasonings upon them.

2. The (το παν) Universe, or which system of things is independant on man, who is only a part; & perhaps a very inconsiderable one of the great whole. For the Supreme Being by whom the World was made has formed the natures & connections of things, & by laws adapted to the peculiar constitutions of his Creatures, & productive of the greatest good upon the whole, does wisely produce every change & event that happens in the Universe. The operation of the Deity by those laws or according to those settled rules, & the regular & uniform alterations of things produced by them, are named the Course or Phenomena of Nature or the providence of God.

3. The almighty God has placed upon this Earth a great variety of sensible & intellectual beings rising the one above the other in a beau-

---

1. See note 3 to *The Elements*.

tiful state of perfection; yet on man alone has he bestowed senses &
powers which fit him for examining the Nature & laws of the universe,
with abilities to deduce from thence in some measure the knowledge of
the Deity of nature, & his own obligations in duty.

4. But tho men have those superior powers they cannot attain to
knowledge without labour & attention. We come into the world destitute of the knowledge of things, ignorant of ourselves & of our connections with those beings that surround us, & of the relation of things
to each other. By slow degrees we receive our different perceptions or
Ideas of things above us & learn by Experience what feelings we shall
have in certain given circumstances, & what connections our Ideas have
among themselves, & by what means alterations may be made in things
without us or in the perceptions of ourselves & others; hence it is evident that setting aside sovereign instruction, true knowledge must be acquired by slow degrees from experience & observation, & that it will
always be proportionate to the largeness & extent of our Experience.

5. The powers of our minds, tho noble of themselves & admirably
fitted for our present state of probation, & this infancy of our existence
are limited & narrow, & unable at one view to take in the whole August
Drama of Nature or Providence which is presented to us & acted before
us. For while we are intent upon one scene, an infinity of others skip &
pass by us without being Observed, & of that to which we do attend
many parts escape the notice of the most accurate Spectator. Was man
therefore to owe his whole stock of knowledge to the gleanings of his
own observation during this short period of his present life, his Acqui-
sitions would be very inconsiderable; But to remedy this inconveniency
the bountiful Author of our Nature has made us social creatures & by
giving us power to communicate our Observations to one another, has
enabled us to reap the benefit of the experience of others who have examined different parts of nature or perhaps the same part more accurately than ourselves.

6. The knowledge then of the nature, laws & connections of things
is, as has been observed, Philosophy; and they who apply to the study
of these, & from thence deduce rules for the conduct & improvement
of human life, are Philosophers. They who consider things as they are

or as they exist, & draw right conclusions from thence, are true Philosophers. But they who without regard to fact or nature indulge themselves in framing systems to which they afterwards reduce all appearances, are, notwithstanding their ingenuity & subtilty, to be reckoned only the corrupters & enemies of true learning.

7. From this short deduction concerning the nature of Philosophy, & the Origin of our knowledge, it will appear that in the early ages of the world, the beginnings of Philosophy have been very inconsiderable & its progress slow. For before Societies were constituted & arts & sciences invented & separated, the attention of the generality of mankind was turned upon procuring the necessaries of life. And their wandring & unsettled way of life before the establishment of States & politics was doubtless a very great Obstacle to the progress of knowledge which takes deepest root & spreads widest amidst Ease & Security. We may therefore expect to find the beginnings of Arts & Sciences in those places where the first Governments & societies were formed.

8. As the East Countries were first peopled & formed into Empires & Governments, Science took its rise in them, & spread from thence thro' the rest of the world. Now the first & most Ancient kingdom seems to have been that of Egypt; for the joint testimony of all antiquity concurs in asserting that the neighbouring Nations borrowed from this Mother Land both their religion & philosophy; indeed we only grope in the dark about the high Egyptian antiquities as there are few or no monuments of Egyptian wisdom transmitted to us. The books ascribed to Hermes Trismegistis[2] tho' very antient are spurious. The way their Priests had of concealing their science & philosophy, not only in Characters unknown to the vulgar but likewise in Hieroglyphics or Sacred sculpture & other mysterious symbols which none understood but the priests, or those initiated by them, & their great shyness in admitting initiates to the mysteries, are among the principal reasons of our igno-

2. Hermes Trismegistus, "the thrice great Hermes," is the name given to the Egyptian god Thoth, alleged author of works on alchemy, astrology, and magic.

rance of the Egyptian learning. Diodorus[3] informs us that their chief
study lay in Geometry, Arithmetick & Astronomy; & indeed the situation, & circumstances of their Country which was Annually overflown
by the Nile put them upon studying them, that they might the better
ascertain & secure their property; And Arithmetic was not only necessary to assist them in their measurings & geometrical Problems, but was
peculiarly necessary in the common practice & commerce of life, in so
great & civilized a nation. Their Astronomy was chiefly adapted to the
uses of Agriculture, & the settling their Calendar & Festivals. Politics
& its inseparable attendant morals were likewise much studied here:
their Architecture & the other elegant Arts of life, they seem to have
carried to the utmost length, having exhibited the noblest specimens of
Symmetry & grandeur in their publick works. They were likewise the
first who collected Libraries, those treasures of Science, which they
called The store house of the remedies of the soul.

9. Next to the Egyptians, the Assyrians, Persians & Indians are re-
corded for the wisdom of their Magi & Brachmans of whose principles
we have but a very lame account left us. The Assyrians are reckoned
among the first who applied to Letters; & the first imperial School was
at Babylon, which continued till Nebuchadnezar the great & Daniel's
time. The Chaldaeans were reckoned their wise men, who were also
called their Magi. Daniel was set over their Colleges & Accademies by
the King; whence 'tis probable that they applied to studies of a legiti-
mate kind, & to natural knowledge as well as to Astrology & other insignificant Arts. They were celebrated chiefly for their Skill in Geneaol-
ogy & Astronomy. Pythagoras went among them to learn the motion
of the Stars & the origin of the World on the two principal heads of
natural Philosophy, viz. (Κοσμοσυσασις & Κοσμογονια or) the Constitution & generation of things. They thought that the matter of the
world was eternal, but that it had the form & order from the divine

---

3. Diodorus Siculus was a first century B.C. Greek historian whose history of the
world is a major source for these lectures.

providence. They ascribed the invention of their Philosophy to Zoroaster who reduced it to a System.

The Persians did the same, whose Magi or wise men presided over the education of the royal Children. They studied philosophy, divinity & politics, & taught the period & renovation of the world. They believed that the elements & Stars of heaven were Gods, of whom they chiefly adored the Fire & Sun; & by the name of Jupiter understood the whole circumference of the heavens.

The Indian Brachmans or Gymnosophists affected a solitary way of life, & underwent great Austerity. They taught a future state, & inculcated the offices of Justice & Virtue. Besides their morals, they applied to Physiology & Astronomy, & believed the formation of our World from water, but of the Universe from other principles; The Soul's incorruptibility and the (παλινγενεσια or) regeneration of all things. In a word all the ancient kingdoms boasted of their learned men.

The Phenicians had their Sanhuniathon⁴ & were celebrated as the first who invented or at least introduced letters & Characters under Cadmus into Greece. They were likewise famous for their skill in Astronomy, Navigation, Arithmetic, Mechanics, & the other Arts of a civilized life; to which indeed their extensive commerce with the rest of the World did in a manner entitle them.

The Chinese were celebrated for their skill in Religion, Politics & Morals, which they principally owed to their great Confucius. Even the barbarous northern nations, the Germans, Britons & the ancient Celts had their learned Druids & Bards whose knowledge was chiefly traditionary, (or πατροπαροδοτος) for we do not hear that they committed any thing to writing, which is the reason why we know so little about their Philosophy or Maxims.

10. But leaving those things which are buried in obscurity we proceed to Greece, that favourite Country, where Arts & Sciences made quickest progress & arrived at their greatest perfection. And here we

---

4. Scholars dispute the existence of Sanchuniathon, whose writing on ancient Phoenicia Philo of Byblos claims to have drawn upon in his *Phoenician History*.

may trace the greek learning from its Original having proper records to depend on. These inform us that Greece was form'd with Colonies from Egypt and the other Eastern Nations, who we may believe carried the Religion & Arts of their Parent Country along with them; And indeed the learning of Ancient Greece wore the strongest Features of Resemblance to the Egyptian, consisting chiefly in Fables & Allegories, short but pithy sentences & dark Enigma's.

11. The Poets Orpheus, Linus, & Hesiod are amongst the earliest Philosophers of Greece, for the Philosophic, Poetic, & often legislative characters were joined in the same persons; there being as yet no separation of the Sciences. The subjects which those old Poets sung required a considerable acquaintance with nature being the (θεαγονια or) Birth of the Gods or the generation of things. Hesiod[5] whose (θεαγονια) Birth of the Gods has been preserved to our day, has interwoven with his poems many moral reflections & precepts which show him well acquainted with morals & life. Orpheus employed musick or numbers & verse, to humanize & soften the minds of his rude & savage Cotemporaries, & to insinuate his moral precepts with a more persuasive & irresistable charm. In a word all the greek Poets of note seem to have made no inconsiderable progress in Philosophy. And indeed if we consider: as an Imitator of Nature every Poet must be a Philosopher, for how can one copy what he knows not or imitate it?

12. The first who made it their business to instruct their Country men, & upon that account were dignifyed with the name of (Σοφοι or) Wise men, were the Seven famous Contemporaries, commonly called the seven wise men of Greece, viz. Thales of Miletus, Pittacus of Mytellene, Bias of Pryene, Solon of Athens, Cleobulus of Lindus, Miso of Lycaonia, & Chylo of Lacedemon. They flourished betwixt the 40th and 50th Olympiad ⟨620–580 B.C.⟩, & excepting Thales were all legislators in their respective States. The credit of Solon was much increas'd by a remarkable instance of his modesty, which happened on the fol-

---

5. Hesiod, c. eighth century B.C., provides an account of the origin of the world and the genealogy of the gods in his *Theogony*.

lowing occasion. Some young men of Ionia bought a draught of the Milesian fishermen; when the net was drawn, there was found in it a golden Tripod of great value; hereupon there arose a dispute & the Oracle of Delphi was consulted, which returned this answer, That it should be given to the wisest. The Milesians presented it to Thales, he sent it to Bias, he again to Pittacus, & so going thro' all the seven, it came at last to Solon, who affirming the Deity to be the wisest, consecrated the Tripod to Apollo. The knowledge of the (σοφοι) wise men was communicated in short sentences or Apothegms, several of which are transmitted to us by ancient writers, such as (γνωθι σεαυτον) know thyself. They who have a mind to know more particulars about the early Sages may consult Diogenes Laertius & Plutarch.[6]

13. Thales was the founder of the Ionic Sect or School, as it was called, & flourished 500 years after the taking of Troy. He was one of the first Philosophers who travelled for the improvement of knowledge of Men & things, & who treated of nature simply without the disguise of Fable or shadowings of Allegory. He taught the immortality of the Soul, marked the solstices & Equinoxes, inscribed Triangles in Circles, & foretold the Eclipses of the Sun. He thought water the first principle of all things. And Anaxagoras his follower set a Mind over this fluid mass, & explained the digestion of this mass into order by the sole power of Gravity. The Ionic Philosophers thought that the Celestial Regions consisted of a thing subtile, or fluid; that the Planets were opaque bodies & the fixed stars firey. Nor were they ignorant of the earth's motion.

After Thales philosophy became a profession, & was taught by Anaximander & Pythagoras & his disciples. The latter was the founder of the Italic School, heard Thales, & Phericydes & flourished about the 60th Olympiad ⟨540–536 B.C.⟩, that is, the 6th or 7th Century before Christ. He, to wit Pythagoras, travelled likewise in search of knowledge

6. Diogenes Laertius, a Greek historian of philosophy of the early third century A.D., is the author of *Lives and Opinions of Eminent Philosophers*. Plutarch (A.D. c. 50–c. 125) writes of the lives and characters of the Greek philosophers in *Parallel Lives*.

thro' Egypt, Chaldea & Phenicia; he spent 22 years among the Egyptian Priests, visited the Oracles of Delphi, Delos & Crete, was initiated into all the mysteries of the Barbarians, as well as Greecians, & instructed in the whole learning of the East. He left Samos, & went to the south of Italy, called at that time Magna Greecia, now the kingdom of Naples, & set up a School at Crotona about the 62^d Olympiad ⟨532 B.C.⟩. Pythagoras formed his Philosophy on the Egyptian plan, which he delivered chiefly in numbers & numerical Symbols; for he reckoned numbers the Causes & principles of things, & accordingly held the number four (τετραχις) in great veneration, which some explain of the Jewish (τετραγραμματον or) the name Jehovah.

It was not till after five years silence in a great variety of preparation in previous trials that his Scholars were admitted to the full knowledge of his Doctrine. He made great improvements in Geometry, Arithmetic & Music, & applied proportion of numbers & harmony to every thing, or at least made them his ordinary Symbols. He invented the 47th Proposition of Euclid's first Book, & is said to have offered an Hecatomb on that account. He was so modest ⟨he refused⟩ the Appellation of (σοφος) Wise, & assumed that humble one of (φιλοσοφος) a lover of Wisdom.

He divided Philosophy into theoretical & practical: the end of the first is truth and to wonder at nothing, & that of the other Virtue & the liberty of the Soul, which he reckoned confined in the body as in a prison. His doctrine of the Transmigration of Souls is well known. To promote the enlargement or disengagement of the mind, he prescribed a very spare diet; forbade the eating of flesh, or killing of animals either for food or sacrifice; he himself lived on honey, bread, herbs & water. His direction to enquire into the actions of the day every evening is justly celebrated. He observed so much Order design & proportion in the structure of the Universe, that he gave it the name (Κοσμος) Order. He wrote several books which are all lost. The golden verses of Pythagoras, tho they contain the sum of the Pythagorean Doctrine, were not wrote by him but by Epicharmus or Empedocles. Pythagoras thought the Earth moveable & placed the Sun in the Center, which from him is called the Pythagorean System; he placed the Comets without Air & set them among the planets, & reckoned that the heavens were fluid & oetherial, & that the stars were so many worlds. You will find more particulars concerning Pythagoras & his Doctrine related by Diogenes Laertius, Iamblicus & Porphery, who have wrote his Life, & intermixed with it many ridiculous Stories. Of the Italic School were Architus Tarentinus, Ocellus, Lucanus, Epicharmus, Empedocles, Timaeus Locrus, and a great many Others.

14. To Thales in the Ionic School succeeded Anaximander a Milesian, who invented Gnomic's or Dialing,[7] & observed the obliquity of the Zodiac & likewise observed Equinoxes. To him again succeeded Anaximenes who held that Air was the first principle of all things. After him came Anaxagoras, who tho' born to a great Fortune, left all to apply to Philosophy. In the 20th year of his Age, the first of the 75th Olympiad ⟨480 B.C.⟩, he went to Athens, where he continued 30 years, & for his great wisdom got the name of (Νους) or Mind. He was banished from Athens in the 3^{d} year of the 82^{d} Olympiad ⟨450 B.C.⟩, & retiring to Lampsachon spent the rest of his days there. Archilaus was the Scholar of Anaxagoras, master of Socrates the celebrated Athenian Philosopher. About the time of Anaximander & Archilaus flourished Xenophanes the Colophonian the founder of the Eleatic Sect, which was a miscellaneous School consisting of philosophers differing in Nation, Opinions & Manners. Xenophanes thought there were innumerable worlds, infinite Suns, & Moons eternal & unchangeable. Parmenides, one of this Sect admitted an Origin of things, & that from Fire & Earth as Elements. Herein he agreed with Archilaus; for the Eliatics differ little from the Ionics about the origin of things, if they admitted any. For some of them took away all motion, without which there can be neither generation nor corruption. Some include Leusippus & Democrates in this Sect who brought in the hypothesis of Atoms, & with that a sounder way of Philosophizing by considering the State, motion, figure, situation & bulk of bodies, estimating their powers & explaining their

---

7. Anaximander of Miletus (c. 610–c. 547 B.C.) is credited with inventing the "gnomon," or upright pointer of the sundial to track hours and seasons.

effects from thence, not seeking as the Italic & other Philosophers, the principles of bodies & their power among numbers, proportions, ideas & the like. Leusippus owned the earths motion about its Axis & was followed by Democrates in physics, who conversed with the Magi, the Chaldean Priests & Arabians. The Attention of the Ionics from Thales's time, had been almost wholly employed in natural Philosophy or Physics, in which very small progress was made, for a reason to be mentioned afterwards. It was SOCRATES that gave the proper turn to learning, & therefore is justly reckoned the Father of true Philosophy.

15. SOCRATES was born at Athens in the 77th Olympiad ⟨472–469 B.C.⟩, his father was Sophroniscus a statuary, & his mother Phaenoreta, a midwife. He followed for some time his father's profession, but soon discovered such a genius and love for learning that CRITO, a rich Athenian, took him from the shop & gave him a liberal Education. Having observed of how little advantage the Philosophy then in repute was in life, Socrates, as Cicero expresses it, recalled Philosophy from the hidden & Obscure subjects about which his Predecessors had busied themselves & brought it down to common Life, to enquire into Good & Evil, Virtue & Vice & their Consequences. Hence, he is said to have fetcht Philosophy from the heavens, & to have introduced it into Cities houses & families. Man was the subject of his Philosophy, & its scope was to make men wiser, better & fitter for social & private life by inculcating the duties of Religion & Virtue. His method of teaching was remarkable, being admirably adapted to human nature. It was by asking Questions, beginning at the most plain & simple & proceeding from the answers given to others of a higher, more general & abstracted nature; he himself all the while affirming nothing. His method was founded upon the belief he had of the pre-existence of Souls, whose former knowledge was lost by being immersed in the body, & brought to remembrance again by instruction, or the method of interrogation. On this account he humourously used to say that his Art had some Affinity to his Mothers; for tho barren himself he assisted in bringing forth the Births of Others, or educing those latent principles of knowledge with which the mind of man was originally stored. His modesty was so great that he constantly said that he knew nothing save only that he knew

nothing; & was for this saying honoured with the title of the wisest man by the Oracle of Apollo. We are not however to conclude from this that Socrates was a Sceptic; he seems only to have had a just Sense of the weakness of human Understanding, to have shunned determining in speculative points, & thought the great end of Philosophy was to enforce with proper inducements the practice of Virtue. He saw through the absurdity of the popular religion & thought that God made the world, knew all things & governed the Universe by his providence. He taught the immortality of the Soul & supported that doctrine by a variety of arguments, & besides inculcated a future state of rewards for the good & punishments for the wicked, & in a word he made such improvements in moral Philosophy that he seemed to have been the first that had just notions of the nature of man & his duty. In order to lay the deeper foundations for a genuine Philosophy, he endeavoured to remove the rubbish that lay in his way, those false opinions, inveterate prejudices, & high pretensions to wisdom which overrun Greece at that time. For this purpose, by his interrogatory method of reasoning, from him called the Socratic way, & likewise by a delicate & refined Irony, he exposed the Sophists, those high pretenders to wisdom who, without any real knowledge, pretended to know every thing & who professed to teach the Art of Speaking for & against every thing, a Race of men who then pestered the several Cities of Greece, & took upon them the care & education of the youth. In so ridiculous a light did he place them by his well timed & artful railery, & so thoroughly did he confute the sham pretensions of those Quacks & smatterers in learning that they concerted a design to bring about his ruin. Aristophanes the Comedian at their instigation introduced him upon the Stage, & by dressing him up in a false & unnatural Character made this great man, who with a patience truly philosophical was a Spectator of the play, ridiculous to the people.[8] At last one Miletus accused him before the Senate of despising the Gods whom the city believd, & introducing new deities, and of corrupting the youth by his Philosophy; to the lasting reproach of his Judges this extra-

8. Aristophanes (c. 448–380 B.C.) ridicules Socrates in *The Clouds*.

ordinary & virtuous person was condemned to Death. The day before the execution of this sentence he reasoned with his friends concerning the immortality of the Soul, & expressed a particular pleasure in the hopes of meeting with Homer, Hesiod & other great men, who had died before him. In the evening the executioner brought him a Cup of poison, which with a chearful & undaunted mind he drunk of, & soon after expired in the 1ˢᵗ year of the 95ᵗʰ Olympiad ⟨400 B.C.⟩. The Athenians were soon so much ashamed of this infamous deed that they put his Accusers to death.

Tis generally thought that Socrates wrote nothing. We have a full account of his life & Philosophy in the writings of his Scholars, Xenophon, Aeschines & Plato. In the memorable things of Socrates wrote by Xenophon we have the best account of his reasoning, & likewise in the dialogues of Aeschines; for Plato in his dialogues has intermixt a great many of his own ⟨ideas⟩ which Socrates never taught, & has likewise adorned them with a profounder erudition, & more laboured & florid eloquence than Socrates used in his common conversation. Among his Schollars were Xenophon, Aeschines, Plato, Aristippus, Phaedo, Euclid of Megara, Cebes & many others.

16. Xenophon & Aeschines both Athenians were particular favourites of Socrates & committed his conversations in that simple & familiar way & manner in which Socrates talked & debated, some of which have happily reached our times. Xenophon was the son of Gyrgilles & was born about the 82ᵈ Olympiad ⟨452 B.C.⟩.⁹ He was in the Peloponnesian war along with Socrates & ever after followed a military life. He attended Cyrus the younger in his expedition into Asia against Artaxerxes the King of Persia; & is justly celebrated for that amazing instance of his wisdom & Valour, the conducting the extraordinary retreat of the Greeks after the defeat of Cyrus. He died at Corinth about the 105ᵗʰ Olympiad ⟨360 B.C.⟩. His books are reckoned among the purest of the Greek Classics, & discover him to have been a fine Gentleman, an able Captain & a great Scholar. Cebes of Thebes, an-

9. Laertius identifies Gryllus as the father of Xenophon.

other of Socrates's Scholars, wrote several Dialogues one of which viz. *The Tablature* or *Picture,* that admirable draught of human life, has escaped the injury of time.[10]

17. Aristippus of Cyrene, a Scholar of Socrates but differing widely from the practice of his Master, founded the Cyrenaic Sect; they entirely rejected Virtue as a principle of Action, amiable in itself, & said that Justice & Honesty were only the institution of men. They made pleasure the ultimate end of all their actions, & Virtue had no farther place in their System than it was thought expedient or necessary to produce pleasure. This Sect was also called Hedonic, from the name ($\H\delta ov\eta$) or Pleasure, & was divided into a great many Branches, one of which, called Theodorians from Theodorus their head, made profession of downright Atheism. Phaedo the Elian & Euclid of Megara were two other Scholars of Socrates. The first was the Author of the Eliac, & the last of the Megaric Sect. Tho' we have no remains of the Eliac philosophy, yet we have reason to believe it differed very little from the Socratic. The Megaric Sect applied themselves mostly to the study of Logic & from thence were named ($\Delta\iota\alpha\lambda\epsilon\kappa\tau\iota\kappa ov$ or) Reasoners or Logicians.

18. Antisthenes another Scholar of Socrates founded the Sect of the Cynics & had the famous Diogenes for his Scholar. They had learned from Socrates that morality was the usefullest of all Sciences, & from this they concluded absurdly enough that all other arts & sciences were to be despised. Their foundamental Maxim was to live in conformity to virtue, which they said was sufficient to make men happy. They sought Liberty & Independency as the greatest Good. The Gods, said they, stand in need of nothing & those that stand in need of few things do most resemble them. To procure this happy independency they pretended to look upon honour & Riches with perfect indifferency, & to renounce all the inconveniencies of Life. Diogenes would have no other habitation than a Tub, & when he found that he could drink

---

10. Cebes' *The Picture of Human Life* was highly esteemed in the eighteenth century for its moral teaching. Robert Dodsley included a translation of *The Picture* at the conclusion of *The Preceptor.*

out of the hollow of his hand, he threw away his wooden cup as a superfluity. Alexander the Great, coming to visit Diogenes in his Tub, asked him what he desired of him. "Nothing," said the Philosopher, "but that you would not stand between me & the Sun." The Cynics under pretence of following nature & living independently observed no decency in their conduct, & treated all the world with the utmost Contempt. The Stoicks shot out as a Branch from this Sect, who, from an Enthusiasm of temper pushed their Philosophy beyond the bounds of Nature, & placed Virtue in a total exemption from passion, or at least from the smallest degree of perturbation of Mind. So that they alledged their virtuous man was happy in evry state & circumstance of Life. (Liber, honouratus, pulcher, Rex denique Regum.)[11] We have several noble relicks of the Stoical philosophy transmitted down to us from ancient times, in which we find the noblest precepts for the conduct of life & particularly for attaining that tranquility of mind & indifference about external things, without some degrees of which no man can be tollerably happy in this mixed uncertain & complicated scene of things. The Stoics however were more celebrated for their morals than for their Physics. They believed the conflagration of the world, called God the artificer of all things (the $\lambda o\gamma o\nu$ $\delta\eta\mu\iota o\upsilon\rho\chi o\nu$ $\kappa\alpha\iota$ $\tau\epsilon\chi\nu\iota\kappa o\nu$) under whom they placed passive Matter. They distinguished between ($\sigma o\iota\chi\epsilon\iota\alpha$)[12] Elements & ($\alpha\rho\chi\alpha\iota$) Principles, reckoning the latter ungenerated, uncorporeal & uncompounded. By the former perhaps they understood the simple unformed ($\chi\upsilon\lambda\eta$) Mass, & distinguished it from Body. They believed that a Fire was the first of Bodies which were made, & the rest of the Elements of it & of both all kind of mixed bodies, which, they said, were again resolved into fire. They called the Sun ($\pi\upsilon\rho$ $\epsilon\iota\lambda\iota\kappa\rho\iota\nu\eta s$) Pure Fire, the Moon, ($\gamma\epsilon\omega\delta\epsilon\sigma\epsilon\rho\alpha$) of an earthly matter, & the Stars ($\pi\upsilon\rho\iota\nu\alpha$) of a firey nature, & likewise that some of them were higher than others in which they are supported by the modern Philosophy. Their Fate signified the unchangeable &

11. Horace, *Epistulae,* bk. 1, ep. 1, line 107: "Free, honored, morally excellent, King, at last, of kings."

12. $\sigma\tau o\iota\chi\epsilon\iota\alpha$, although $\sigma o\iota\chi\epsilon\iota\alpha$ appears in the text.

immoveable order & series of things by which the Gods themselves were governed in their productions of things.

19. Of all the Scholars of Socrates, Plato made the greatest figure. He was born at Athens in the 88th Olympiad ⟨428 B.C.⟩. After he had heard & studied under Socrates he travelled into Egypt & Italy, & returning to Athens he taught Philosophy in the Accademy, the Gymnasium or place of exercise in the suburbs of the City, environed with woods & adorned with beautiful walks named from Accademus a private Gentleman to whom it first belonged.

Inter Sylvas Accademi quarere Verum.[13]

Hence his followers got the name of Accademics. The Philosophy which he taught was a compound of the Socratic & Pythagoric Doctrines, & was chiefly divided into these three parts: Ethics, Physics & Dialectics. The knowledge of the platonic Philosophy is to be got from the works of its Author, which are justly held in the greatest esteem. He wrote in the way of Dialogues, in which Socrates makes one of the principal speakers, & generally confutes the bombast or subtle sophists by the depths of his Socratic reasoning, joined with an exquisite strain of raillery. His Books (*De republica & Legibus*) of the Commonwealth & the Laws, show him to have been an able Politician & deep Scholar. The Platonics did (as the Pythagoreans) apply more to the contemplation of Ratios & abstract proportions than of matter & its properties. We have a sketch of Plato's Philosophy in his *Timaeus.* He assigned geometrical figures to the Elements, & compounds & places them geometrically. He makes three principles of all things, the (Νους) Deity, (Χυλη) Matter, & his (Ιδεα) Idea or exemplary cause, or rather his proportion & ideas. Many traces of the old learning & the Ancient world are to be found in his *Timaeus,* his *Politicus* & *Phaedo,* which he brought from Egypt & the pillar of Hermes. His genius in Theology & morality was by the ancients esteemed divine.

20. Arcesilaus one of the successors of Plato about the time of the

---

13. Horace *Epistulae,* bk. 2, ep. 2, line 45: "In the woods of Accademus we seek truth."

107th Olympiad ⟨352 B.C.⟩ founded the Middle Accademy. His way was to doubt of every thing in arguing for and against all manner of questions. He went a great deal farther than Socrates in Sceptical Philosophy, & said that he could not be certain even of this, that he knew nothing. Carneades did afterwards soften this Scepticism a little by allowing that there was no truth which did not admit of some belief, yet there were such degrees of probability as were sufficient to determine men. This was the new or third Accademy. Carneades was sent from Athens in company with Diogenes the Cynic & Critolaus the peripatetic on an Embassy to Rome about the 599th year after the building of the City. He & the other two taught in different places of the City, & were resorted to by the Roman Youth, who drank in their Philosophy with the utmost avidity, which made Old Cato the Censor move in the Senate to dispatch them as soon as possible, lest the Roman Youth who he said were grown enthusiastically mad after Greecian Arts & learning should be diverted from a military Life to the study of Philosophy.

21. Aristotle the most famous of Plato's Scholars was born at Stagiola,[14] a City of Thrace in the first year of the 99th Olympiad ⟨384 B.C.⟩. When he was 17 years of Age he came to Athens, where he soon distinguished himself & became a favourite disciple of Plato. In the 4th year of the 109th Olympiad ⟨341 B.C.⟩ at the request of King Philip he went into Macedonia and became Tutor to Alexander the great, not only in Ethics & Politics but in all the other Sciences. In the first year of the 111th Olympiad ⟨336 B.C.⟩ Philip dyd & Aristotle returned to Athens where he taught in the Lycaeum, (a place in the suburbs built by Pericles for exercising the Citizens in) walking up & down therein. Hence he & his schollars got the name of Peripatetics (or Walkers). He was the first who reduced the scattered precepts of Philosophy into a System & left Treatises wrote professedly on Logic, Metaphysics, Ethics & Physics. All which shew a Judgment & accuteness of penetration superior to most men. He wrote on Rhetoric, Poetry & natural History & other Subjects. In the two former treatises he discovers a great insight

14. Stagira, although Stagiola appears in the text.

in the human nature & large acquaintance with fine writing. And indeed he is universally acknowledged to have been a very comprehensive & extraordinary Genius. The grand principle of his Ethics is, that every Virtue consists in the Mean or Middle between two extremes both of which are Vicious.

The Peripatetic principles may be gathered from Aristotle's writings & are well explained by Cicero in so far as they differ from the Stoical principles. To Aristotle in the peripatetic School succeeded Theophrastus, Strato, Lycon, Aristo, Critolaus, Diodorus &c. The Aristotelians believed the world to be eternal as well as to its form as to its matter; & all the creatures in it begitting & begotten in an infinite series with all its plants & various furniture. Aristotle thought the heavens were of Adamant & the Stars fixed like golden Nails in the roofs of their orbits & these Orbs chained together, & All the whole world rolled about in 24 hours time; that the planets were carried about by contrary motions, that the matter of the heavens is quite different from all other & immutable into any other. He introduced his Substantial forms & specific Qualities to explain the Actions & forces of Bodies. He said that sensation was performed by an intentional species, that Providence descended not below the Moon, that the Soul was the $Ev\tau\epsilon\lambda\epsilon\chi\epsilon\iota\alpha$, a Cant word that signified nothing; he was uncertain of the immortality of the Soul.

22. Epicurus the author of another Sect named Epicureans was born in the 3ᵈ year of the 109ᵗʰ Olympiad ⟨341 B.C.⟩. He began very early to read Philosophy particularly the writings of Democritus, from whence he chiefly borrowed his Physics. Having purchased a pleasant Garden at Athens, he lived there with his friends & disciples, & taught Philosophy. He ascertained that the world was formed by a fortuitous concourse of Atoms falling & clashing one with another in infinite directions thro' an immense void, without the interposition of an intelligent principle. Tho' he allowed the existence of the Gods, yet he said they took no care or concern about the world or its affairs, but lived at a great distance in immortal Peace & in inglorious indolence, & by this means subverted the foundations of all religion which is built upon a sense of our Connection with God & dependance upon him, as the Almighty

Maker & Governor of the World. He affirmed that Pleasure was the chief end of all our Actions & the Chief Good, & that Virtue was no farther to be followed than as it produces & tends to pleasure. But they are much mistaken, who think that Epicurus gave himself up to all manner of Debauchery; On the contrary he recommended Temperance & the other Virtues as conducive to true happiness. Yet some of his followers made a very bad use of his Doctrine, indulging themselves in the greatest sensuality, & having no notion of moral happiness. The School in the Garden was continued till the days of Augustus under the successive management of Hermochus, Polystratus, Dyonisius, Basilides &c. Epicurus made Sense the supreme Standard by which we judge of truth, said the Sun was no bigger than a foot & a half, & that the Earth was rooted to an infinite extent downward. We have a large Account of the Epicurean Doctrine in Diogenes Laertius & Cicero & Lucretius Carus an elegant Latin Poet has given us a compleat System of his Philosophy (of which he was a professed Admirer) in his poem (*De rerum natura*) of the nature of things. Epicurus died in the second year of the 127th Olympiad ⟨270 B.C.⟩.

23. Zeno, contemporary with Epicurus, founded the Stoical Sect directly opposite to the principles of Epicurus. He was at first Scholar to Crates the Cynic, then to Stilpo the Megaric & afterwards heard Diodorus, Cronus and Polemon. He set up a School in the (ποικιλη σοα)[15] Painted Walk at Athens, & thence, his Disciples got the name of Stoics. The most Considerable part of the Stoical Philosophy was their Morality whose fundamental Principles were, That Virtue was the alone good & Vice the only Ill; that pleasure was not good nor pain evil; that the passions were preternatural perturbations entirely to be rooted out; that men were not born for themselves but for their Country & Society, & that the whole of mans duty was to live according to Nature. The (Απαθια or) entire freedom from the passions of human nature was certainly impossible to be attained & perhaps was more than the Stoics meant when they recommended the mastery over our appetites & pas-

---

15. ποικιλη στοα, although ποικαλησοα appears in the text.

sions. For they seem to have taken our passions in too limited a sense for mental disorders or such violent impulses & propensities of Soul as are inconsistent with the exercise of reason & destructive of it; & in this sense, no doubt they are carefully to be subdued. But both Zeno & Epicurus seem to have erred in not considering the whole of Mans Nature; For Epicurus viewed him only as a sensible Being capable of pleasure & pain; whereas Zeno regarded only the moral part of his Constitution. The peripatetic Philosophers seem to have had juster notions of the matter when they considered Man as a Creature formed for the enjoyment both of Natural & moral good, that is, As a Sensible & Moral Being; & said that the passions were implanted in his nature for valuable purposes, & therefore were not to be extirpated but governed by his Reason. The Stoicks imagined the World (or το παν) to be an Animal whereof God was the soul. They maintained a Fate or Destiny to which Gods & men were equally subjected. They cultivated Dialecticks, but made little progress in Physics. In short they were a natural Shoute ⟨shoot⟩ from the Cynics, only they refined upon & carried their Philosophy to a higher pitch. To Zeno in the Stoical School succeeded Cleanthus, Chrysippus, Diogenes, Antipater, Panatius & Posidonius.

24. Among the Old Greek Philosophers of note were Parmenides, Leusippus, Democritus & Heraclitus, who all, especially the two last, improved the corpuscular Physics which Epicurus perfected. Pyrrho, contemporary with Aristotle, having read the books of Democritus & having heard various Philosophers, gave rise to another Sect called Sceptics, Pyrronistics and sometimes Zetetics. They held nothing certain, doubting every thing, & said nothing was to be understood or comprehended. As Absurd as these principles were Pyrrho had his admirers & followers, such were Simon,[16] Hecataeus, Eurylochus & Sextus Empyricus; nay we find still that he has likewise his Admirers in Modern times who carry his Philosophy to as extravagant a Pitch as the evil of man can devise or his Fancy wish.

25. Among this variety of different Sects of Philosophers it is reason-

16. Timon, although Simon appears in the text.

able to believe their several Systems were neither wholly true nor wholly false. Polemo of Alexandria did therefore in the reign of Augustus introduce the Eclektic Philosophy. They who embraced this method espoused none of the Systems in the Gross but took such doctrines from each as seemed most reasonable, every man judging for himself, & allowing the same liberty to others.

Having now pointed out the principal Stages & periods of Philosophy among the Greecians, it remains just to touch at the Barbarian Philosophy & its Origen. The opinions of those whom the Greeks entitled Barbarians were delivered mostly without proof or reasoning & received because of the Authority of the Teacher, or the reasons are too weak & insufficient to convince. We have an instance of this in the Conflagration of the world, whose Causes & process they neither explain, nor attempted to prove its truth. The same thing may be said with regard to the periods of the World, the pre-existence & revolution of Souls. The Ancient Philosophy never laboured about Theories or the demonstration of things from their Causes or Effects, which the modern has attempted not without Success; But theirs was short & easy by way of Questions & Answers, so that it plainly appears to have been propagated by Tradition. Some derive it from the Hebrews, from Moses & Abraham; But the former himself was a Disciple of the Egyptians so that the Egyptian learning was before him. And as to the Arabian, Job who was a renowned & learned Arabian, is reckoned elder than Moses for several reasons, 1st Because that pious Man counteracted the law of Moses in offering Sacrifices for himself, after the examples of Noah & others before the Law. 2^d Because there is no mention made of Moses or his exploits in his Book. 3^d From the measure of his life which ought to be placed about the third age after the Deluge, for he lived about 200 years. Besides his history seems to savour of great Antiquity. He Mentions the first kind of Idolatry, that of the Sun & Moon. He speaks of Sculpture the most ancient kind of writing, when he talks of recording his Calamities; His wealth is counted by his Flocks; he mentions no Sabbath or instituted Law, & followed the precepts of Noah. Josephus derives learning from Abraham, but without proof from Sacred or prophane History. Besides 'tis improbable that he shoude instruct the Egyptians in the space of the two years he lived among them. Therefore it is more probable that the Sciences derived their Origin from a higher Source, even Noah, the common parent of the Jews & Nations. He is said to have delivered moral precepts to his descendants, called the precepts of the Noachides, & therefore why not Opinions & Doctrines also? In short it is highly probable that he knew the greatest part of the wisdom of the long lived Antidiluvian Patriarchs since he had 600 years commerce with them, & Consequently that from him as from the fountain head were derived those streams of ancient learning which flowed through the Old world, of which only some small drops have descended to us.

26. There is a Contest betwixt the Egyptians & Hebrews about their precedency & antiquity in learning. That none of the Philosophers travelled among the latter to gather knowledge is a plain evidence that they were not renowned for Letters. We do not read that they excelled in natural or mathematical knowledge, tho Solomon certainly was an eminent Naturalist. Their Schools were formed for Religion & Prophecy rather than for the Sciences. No nation did ever abound so much in prophets & inspired men. So that a divine virtue seems to have been peculiar to their Soil & Climate. They pretended to have preserved among them from the beginning a Cabala or secret Science containing the mysteries of the natural & invisible world; But two things are wanting in this Science, first the establishing & aggreeing upon certain common principles, Secondly, their ascertaining the Use & Signification of words. And indeed this boasted Science of theirs seems to have been a mysterious Gibberish or an obscure Phraseology rather than the knowledge of things. As to their four worlds of Emanation, Creation, Formation & Fabrication, we know little of them, & their explications of them are themselves inexplicable. Their ancient Cabbala might have some foundation, however deformed & vitiated by the moderns, & perhaps treated of the Origin & Gradations of things, or the scale of beings; But being traditionary it came soon to be lost & so the modern Doctors or Rabbies in order to fill up this Void, & to maintain an imaginary Character of ancient Learning threw in their multiplied fictions till at length it grew up or swelled into the enormous size of the

present Cabbala. The Cabbalists thought that Gods or their Ensoph contained all things within himself at first, & only evolved or unfolded himself when the World was made, & that it perishes again by its reflux or resolution into the Divinity. (The opinion of the Stoicks was too gross, for they restricted every thing to matter, & understood by Jupiter the Simple Ether, into which they thought the whole world would be finally resolved, & then after a state of time would reassume its primitive form & appearance.) The Essenes an ancient Sect among the Jews resembled the Brachmans in their manners & studies; their Life was most simple & primitive & they applied themselves to the study of the divine nature & the Origin of things.

27. 'Tis thought by Sir Isaac Newton[17] that learning flourished early in Arabia or at least in Idumaea a Country of it. Learning flourished there from the time of Job to the Age of Solomon if the Queen of Sheba was of Arabia, as is highly probable. Job was a renowned Sage among the Arabs, & had a great knowledge of nature as is evident from his book which is the first & Oldest monument of Arabic wisdom. In it are many Arabisms to be found. 'Tis probable the Magi or Wise men of the East who came to adore our Saviour at his birth were of Arabia, because the presents they brought were only of an Arabian growth, & because the East is commonly used in Scripture to signify Arabia. The Zabii or Zabaisti[18] (the same with the Sabaeans & their Priests) were famous among the Arabians, & were a very ancient nation: The Jews say that Abraham was educated in their Religion at first, but that after he worshipped the true God he left them & inveighed against their Doctrines. Maimonides will have Moses to have chiefly regarded their Rites &

17. See Sir Isaac Newton, *The Chronology of Ancient Kingdoms Amended, to which is Prefix'd, A Short Chronicle from the First Memory of Things in Europe, to the Conquest of Persia by Alexander the Great* (London, 1728).

18. In general, this passage follows Moses Maimonides' *The Guide of the Perplexed,* part 3, chapter 29. Maimonides refers to the Sabians, a reference Shlomo Pines takes to apply generally to pagans. (See *The Guide of the Perplexed,* translated and with an introduction and notes by Shlomo Pines [Chicago: University of Chicago Press, 1963], 514.) It is more probable that both Maimonides and Fordyce are, like Job, referring to the ancient people of Sheba.

manners in forming his Laws. Their Magi were of long Continuance & vaunt themselves to be Noachides or followers of Noah, however they worship the Sun, Moon & Native Genii or Daemones. Job seems to allude hereto when he vindicates himself from the worship of the Sun & Moon, Chap 31. Vers 26. 27. He & his friends were genuine Noachides; but the Zabians & other Arabs were degenerate ones. Both sorts however retain some of the Doctrines of the Noachides which were the Roots of Oriental learning. Pythagoras & Democritus visited them. We have little account of them for the first Ages after Christ, till in the Sixth Century with the rise of Ishmaelism or the Law of Mahomet learning began also to revive among them. For the Arabians or the Sarracens penetrating into the West & making Conquests in Europe with their Arms raised a new Empire to themselves, & by degrees imbibed the Greecian & European Philosophy. As the Aristotelian or Peripatetick Philosophy prevailed chiefly at that time, they embraced it, & propagated it afterwards with great industry & noise. Their learned men, particularly Avicenna & Averroes[19] translated the works of Aristotle & gathered all the Greecian Authors they could find, insomuch that they alone seemed to possess them. As to the Sarracens at the taking of Alexandria, the great & celebrated Library, that vast collection of Ancient learning which had been collected by the Kings of Egypt for many Ages, was, by their barbarous & brutal Emperour at the instigation of his Chief Priest, ordered to be burned, & used as fewel to warm the hot baths. After the times of Mahomet the Arabian learning degenerated into Fable & Allegory.

28. When the Romans extended their Empire over Greece they became acquainted with the learning & Philosophy of that Country. They had indeed got some taste of Greecian workmanship & politeness before, by the taking of Syracuse, which was originally a Greecian City, & therefore Old Cato complains that hostile statues had been introduced

---

19. Avicenna (Ibn Sina) (980–1037) and Averroes (Ibn Rushd) (1126–98) were the two most important Islamic philosophers of the medieval period, the former a Neoplatonist, the latter an Aristotelian intent upon correcting the Neoplatonic readings of Aristotle, such as those of Avicenna.

into the Town from Syracuse. But those Greecian pieces of Virtuoso-ship were rather laid up as rarities to be gazed at, or as piles to adorn their Temples. But the Greecian learning & politic Arts scarce made any Advances till the Thousand Achaian Exiles arrived at Rome & were dispersed up & down the Country.[20] They scattered the first seeds of Philosophy in that Soil which had been formerly possessed by Arms & overrun with the din of War. That Soil however being strong & fertile did, by a happy Culture & greater intercourse with Greecian Wits, bring forth a rich crop of Philosophers, Historians, Poets & Orators. As Philosophers of all Sects began to teach there, the young Romans commenced Partizans of this or the other Sect as best suited their taste & Genius. So that Among the Romans we find the learned Men widely differing in their Philosophy. Cicero the Orator, who con-tributed more than any other to make his countrymen acquainted with the Greek Philosophy, as is evident from his Philosophical works, was a New Academic, & in some things an Eclectic. Cato of Utica & Brutus who killed Caesar were Stoics; Lucullus was an Old Academic; Atticus & Velleius were Epicureans; Seneca the praeceptor of Nero was a strict Stoic, as was also the famous philosophical Emperor Marcus Antoni-nus, who was both the highest pattern of virtue & the greatest Master as well as Patron of learning. This was the state of Philosophy at Rome till the decline of the Empire when barbarity & ignorance overwhelmed the Remains of Ancient learning, & brought on a night of total and almost universal Darkness.

29. The Platonists became famous in the 3[d] & 4th Centuries among whom were Plotinus, Porphyrius, Iamblichus & Proclus, who spent all their time in explaining & writing Mystical & Jejune Commentaries upon the tenets of the founders of the Sect. Untill the 6th Century Aristotle was but little known in the Western World, when Boethius translated some of his writings. The Arabians, whom we have already mentioned, in the Eleventh Century introduced his Philosophy into

20. Sicily was made a province of Rome in the first Punic war, 264–241 B.C. Un-der suspicion of treachery, Achaeans were resettled in Italy in 168 B.C.

Spain, & from thence sprung the Scholastic Peripatetic Philosophers, who overlooked & in a great measure neglected his most beautiful & usefull works, viz. his Morals, his Politics & Rhetoric & spent all their time & pains in writing huge Commentaries upon his Dialectics or Logics & Physical Works the most lame of all his performances which they employed to furnish out materials for endless debate & to support an unintelligible & monstrous System of Theology.

30. After the fall of the Roman Empire & the irruption of the Barbarous northern nations all Europe continued for many years buried in great ignorance. The small remains of knowledge that were to be found were confined to the Cells of the Monks & other Clergy. In the 8th Century the highest ambition of the Clergy was to Vie with one another in chanting the public service, which yet they hardly understood. The Emperor Charlemagne tho' a warlick Monarch allowed a public School to be opened in the imperial palace under the direction of our famous Country man Alcuine,[21] on whom he chiefly relied for introducing into France some tincture of that Philosophy which was still remaining in Brittain. As to Brittain, tho' Learning had still some footing there in the Eighth Century, it was so totally exterminated from thence in the ninth that throughout the whole kingdom of the west Saxons no man could be found who was Scholar enough to instruct King Alfred, then a Child, in the first Elements of Reading, so that he was in his 12th year before he could name the letters of the Alphabet. When that renowned Prince mounted the Throne[22] he became the great restorer of Arts in his Dominions, & gave all encouragement to learned Men.

But these fair Appearances were soon Succeeded by a night of thicker Darkness which quickly overspread the intellectual world. To Common Sense & piety succeeded Dreams & Fables, visionary Legends & ridiculous pennances. The Clergy, now utter Strangers to all good learning, instead of guiding a rude & vitious Laity by the precepts of the Gospel

21. Alcuin/Alcuine (c. 735–804), born near York, England, was an eminent theologian and scholar who, as abbot of St. Martin's at Tours, developed a model monastic school.

22. Alfred the Great (849–99) ruled over Wessex 871–99.

which they no longer read, amused them with forged Miracles, or overawed them with the Ghostly terrors of Daemons, Spectres & Chimaeras. The See of Rome which should have been a pattern to the rest, was of all Christian Churches the most licentious; & the pontifical Chair often filled with men who, instead of adorning their sacred Character, made human nature itself detestable. It was not till late after the Sack of Constantinople by the Turks in the year 1453 that the writings of Aristotle began again to be universally known & studied. They were then brought away & dispersed through the West part of Europe by certain fugitive Greeks who had escaped the fury of the Ottoman Arms. The latin translations of his Books gave birth as we have said to the Scholastic Philosophy, which was neither that of Aristotle entirely nor altogether differing from his. They left natural knowledge wholly incultivated to hunt after Occult Qualities, Abstract Notions & Questions of impertinent Curiosity: By which they rendered the Logic their labours turned upon, intricate, useless & unintelligible.

31. The Scholastics were divided into two Sorts or Sects, the Nominalists, who owed their Rise to Rucelinus[23] an Englishman; the other was called the Sect of the Realists, who had Duns Scotus[24] for their Champion. The titles with which these scholastic Leaders were honoured by their followers on account of the sublime Reveries they taught are at once magnificent & absurd: such as the profound, the Subtile, the Marvellous, the indefatigable, the irrefragable, the Angelic, the Seraphic &c. But these titles prove rather the superlative ignorance of those times than any transcendent merit in the man to whom they were applied. Friar Bacon[25] however was a great Philosopher even in these ignorant times, & made many new discoveries in Astronomy &

23. Roscelin/Roscellinus Compendiensis/Ruscelinus (1050–1125) denied the existence of universals, arguing that items denominated by the same term share no deeper metaphysical reality than their name.

24. John Duns Scotus (John Duns, the Scot) (c. 1266–1308) was a Franciscan philosopher and theologian who, as a realist, maintained that things denominated by the same term share some metaphysical property or relation.

25. Roger Bacon (1214–92), an English philosopher and a Franciscan, was known as *Doctor Mirabilis,* i.e., marvelous doctor.

perspective, in Mechanics & Chymistry: The Construction of Spectacles, of Telescopes, of all sort of Glasses that either magnify or diminish objects, the Composition of Gun powder (Which Bartholinus Swartz is thought to have first hit upon almost a Century later) are some of the many inventions ascribed to him. For all which he was in his lifetime Calumniated, imprisoned & opprest & after his Death called a Magician who dealt in the Black or informal Arts.

The writings of Aristotle ⟨during the medieval period⟩ were both reckoned the fountains of all knowledge & afforded materials for infinite Debate & mutual Animosities. Sometimes they were proscribed as Heretical, & sometimes they were triumphant & acknowledged the great Bulwark of Orthodoxy. In the 16th Century they were not only read with impunity but every where taught with applause; & whoever disputed their Orthodoxy—I had almost said their infallibility—was persecuted as an Infidel & Miscreant. After the Scholastic Philosophy had been adopted into the Christian Theology, far from being of use to explain & ascertain Mysteries it served only to darken & render doubtful the most necessary truths by the Chicanery of Argumentation with which it supplied each Sect in defence of their peculiar and favourite illusions.

32. When knowledge began to dawn & the reformation diffused a new light over Europe, Universities were founded, and Professors were appointed to teach the several Sciences. Nevertheless all Ranks & parties blindly following the Aristotelian Philosophy then in fashion, they made no new advances in Learning, but contented themselves with explaining & defending the Systems of the times; Protestants as well as Papists intrenching themselves behind the Authority of Aristotle, & defending their several tenets by the Weapons with which he furnished them. This unnatural Alliance between Theology & the Peripatetic Doctrine rendered the Opinions of Aristotle sacred so that to dispute them was to pull up & remove the land marks of Faith & Orthodoxy: So that any one who attempted to remove the Awful Veil of Obscurity with which the face of nature was covered, & to strick out new lights in Science, run the hazard of Church Censure, which commonly ended in Tortures & Death. The great end of Philosophy, which is to make

men wiser & better, was wholly neglected, & ones reputation as a learned Man depended upon his being able to maintain a dispute right or wrong, with a Variety of subtile sophistical Arguments. If the Disputant happened to bear hard on the System he was immediately & infallibly refuted with a metaphysical distinction, or with the Authority of Aristotle or some of the Scholastic Doctors. All this while the nature & relations of things were not observed, Philosophy then consisting not of Observations made on the Laws of Motions & properties of Bodies, but of a set of Opinions borrowed at Second hand & received without examination. If any one set about explaining the Phaenomena of nature by second Causes or the powers of Matter & Mechanism, he was immediately supposed to have removed the First Cause, or the All sustaining & all governing Providence, & consequently was condemned as an Atheist; As if it had been less honourable to the Supreme Artist to have the Symmetry & perfect Mechanism of his works thoroughly Understood than to have all the operations of nature in which He is the prime mover resolved into Occult Qualities, substantial & (I know not what) mysterious nothings. Happy is it for us that we live in an age, when people are allowed to see with their own Eyes, when the Authority of fallible men bear no weight in Philosophy & when we are directed to realities as the sole object of true knowledge.

33. Such were the dispositions of men & things when Sir Francis Bacon,[26] Lord Verulam & Chancellor of England in the reign of James the Sixth, appeared upon the Stage. He was the first who saw thro' the Cloud in which Philosophy had for many ages been wrapped up. His vast & penetrating mind soon discovered the Absurdity & fruitless insignificancy of the Philosophy then in fashion, & the impossibility of ever arriving at true knowledge in the beaten tract of Disputation & of composing Theories & Systems without a proper induction of Facts; And therefore he laboured all he could to open again, (as he expresses it) the Commerce between the Mind & things, which had

26. Francis Bacon (1561–1626) was an English statesman, philosopher, and educational reformer.

been for so long time interrupted. He understood well that the Business of Philosophy was not to support Systems, but to observe & explain Nature; & thence in two words he gave a more clear & satisfying Account of Philosophy than others had done in hundreds of Volumes calling it (Interpretatio Natura) The Interpreter of Nature.

My Lord's extensive Genius led him to peruse the registers of learning in all Ages, & to consider the state of all the Sciences, their Origin, the progress & advances they had made & the things in which they were still defective. This put him upon composing that extraordinary work (*De dignitate* & *Augmentis Scientiarum*) Of the dignity & improvement of the Sciences, in which he shews us a Map of the intellectual world, what regions of it have been already discovered & cultivated, what parts remain still Terra incognita (or unknown) by what means, & with what instruments these are to be explored & consequently the great (desiderata or) blank of Science supplied & filled up; A Book which must be admired and valued, while there remains any taste for true Learning among the sons of Men. In his Book called his *Novum Organum* he has traced out the proper Road of experience & observation, by which alone we can obtain the true knowledge of things, & consequently a proper dominion over nature. The first Aphorism of this admirable Treatise contains more good Sense & real learning, than all the books that had been wrote on Philosophy for a Dozen of Centuries before him. It is this; "Homo, Naturae minister et interpres, tantum facil et intelligit quantum de Natura ordine, re vel mente observaverit, nec amplius scit au potest." Literally thus, "Man, the minister & interpreter of nature can act & understand just in proportion to his experience & observation of the order of nature nor can he know or do any thing further." Here the foundation both of our knowledge & power is laid in the observation of things & their mutual connexions.

Lord Verulam is not to be considered so much the founder of a new Sect as the great Assertor of human Liberty; As one who rescued Reason & Truth from the Slavery in which all Sects alike had till then held them. He was not however the first among the Moderns who ventured to dissent from Aristotle; Ramus Patricius, Bruno, Severinus[27] had already attacked the Authority of that Tyrant in learning, who had long reigned as absolutely over the opinions, as his restless Pupil had of old affected to do over the persons of men; But these Writers being of the Scholastic Tribe, invented but little that was valuable themselves. And as to the real improvements made in some parts of natural knowledge before this great man appeared by Gilbert, Harvy, Copernicus, Father Paul[28] & some few others, they are well known, & have been deservedly Celebrated.

We shall afterwards have an Occasion frequently to mention some other Aphorisms of this great but unhappy man, whose writings richly deserve the perusal of all such as wish to be instructed by what they read, & to know things & not words.

34. Towards the end of the 16th Century Renates de Cartes[29] was the Author of a new Sect of Philosophers called Cartesians; He said that in order to find out truth we must first doubt of every thing but our own existence. Accordingly (Cogito ergo Sum) I think, therefore I am, was the only first principle or self evident truth according to his System. He maintained the Doctrine of innate Ideas & established the proof of the existence of God on the Idea of a perfect Being, which he said was natural to the human mind: alledging it was presumptuous for man to attempt to discover final causes in the works of God. Brutes,

---

27. Ramus Patricius, or Peter Ramus (1515–72), was professor of philosophy at the University of Paris, a critic of Aristotle, and a university reformer. Giordano Bruno (1548–1600) was an Italian philosopher of nature and a Neoplatonist. Petrus Severinus (1542–1602) was a Danish physician and follower of Paracelsus.

28. William Gilbert (1544–1603) was an English scientist and physician noted for his studies of magnetism and electricity. William Harvey (1578–1657), an English physician, is credited with the earliest explanation of the circulation of blood. The Polish astronomer Nicholas Copernicus (1473–1543) developed the heliocentric theory of planetary motion. Father Paul (Pietro Sarpi) (1552–1623), a Venetian and a monk, was trained in philosophy, theology, and mathematics. He was a friend and benefactor of Galileo, and is said to have discovered and explained the valves of veins.

29. René Descartes (1596–1650), a French mathematician and philosopher, developed his theories in the *Discours de la Méthod* (Discourse on Method) (1637) and the *Meditationes de Prima Philosophia* (Meditations on First Philosophy) (1641).

according to him, were (mera Automata or) pieces of machinery &
clock work; & by the motion of their animal Spirits he solved all their
actions. His physics were meerly Chimerical, not being founded on
experiments, but upon Data or principles which he took for granted;
Yet he was no mean Mathematician; & had he applied his geometrical
knowledge to facts & the phaenomena of nature, he might have considerably improved Philosophy. The Cartesian Philosophy was for
some time taught in a great many Universities, & it was heresy in
Religion, as well as Philosophy, to Doubt any of his Doctrines; But his
Philosophy is now quite out of fashion, & has been justly exploded by
a more genuin & august Philosophy introduced & cultivated by Sir
Isaac Newton, & other great Philosophers, who following the plan
traced out to them by Lord Bacon have erected a noble structure of
Science beautiful in itself & highly beneficial to mankind.

35. The reformation & the gradual progress of liberty especially in
Great Brittain tended considerably to the improvement of the Arts &
Sciences; & the great plan of Science which Ld Bacon had projected
put men upon a more genuine & successful method of enquiry. Accordingly a whole train of Philosophers & enquirers into nature arose
up from time to time, who following the tract pointed out to them by
the aforesaid great man built up different parts of the great pile of
science. In the year 1663 Charles the 2^d King of England erected, soon
after the Restauration, the Royal Society for promoting all kinds of
natural knowledge: Their Charter bears date the 22^d of April of that
year. A little after that in the year 1666, Lewis the 14th King of France,
did, by means of the famous M^r. Colbert our Countryman, establish
the Royal Academy of Sciences at Paris, & provided Salaries for some
of the members of it. In imitation of these the Emperor Leopol[30] did
also found his (Accademia Natura Curiosorum or) Accademy of the
curiosities of nature & the King of Prussia, one of the same kind at
Berlin. And the late Czar of Muscovy Peter Alexowitz commonly &

---

30. Leopold I (1640–1705) was king of Hungary (1655–1705) and of Bohemia
(1656–1705) and emperor of the Holy Roman Empire (1658–1705).

very justly called the great, who excelled all other Princes in his endeavours to improve his own Country, to instruct & polish a rude & barbarous people by Arts, Sciences & Trade, erected a Society for natural Philosophy in his new built City Petersburgh, by the name of Accademia Petropolitana. These Societies have contributed not a little to the advancement of natural knowledge, that being the professed design of their institution.

Accordingly the last age & this have produced a great many particular men who have enriched all the Branches of Philosophy with noble discoveries. It may perhaps look like partiality in favour of our own Country to say that Brittain may boast of the greatest Philosophers in every kind of Science that ever appeared in the world. It were endless to name them all, Let it suffice to say that some of those who shone in the foremost Rank & made the most distinguishing figure were, The honourable M[r] Rob[t]. Boyl[31] that eminent Ornament in the learned World remarkable no less for his singular Piety, than for his extensive Learning & indefatigable application to the several branches of Natural knowledge; M[r]. Wallis[32] who improved the Doctrine of motion in all its parts so as to render it a compleat Science; But above all Sir Isaac Newton that great name in Philosophy who carried it to a higher pitch of perfection than any had done before him. We may add to these D[r]. Gregory[33] that celebrated Civilian professor of Astronomy at Oxford, M[r]. James Gregory[34] of S[t]. Andrews, D[r]. Halley,[35] the famous brothers

31. Robert Boyle (1627–92), born in Ireland, was a physicist and chemist and prominent member of the "Royal Society of London, for Improving of Natural Knowledge."

32. John Wallis (1616–1708), an English mathematician, authored *Arithmetica Infinitorum* (Oxford, 1655).

33. David Gregory (1661–1708) was the first professor to lecture publicly on Newtonian philosophy and author of *Astronomiae Physicae et Geometricae Elementa* (Oxford, 1702).

34. James Gregory (1638–75), uncle of David Gregory and author of *Optica Promota* (1663).

35. Edmund Halley (1656–1742) employed Newton's gravitational theory in order to predict the return of a comet (now known as Halley's comet). He was elected to the Royal Society at the age of 22 and was appointed astronomer royal in 1720.

The Keils, John & James,[36] M^r. Derham[37] who wrote those ingenious
pieces, the physics & Astrotheology, Hawksby,[38] Desaguliers,[39] to name
no more, that excellent Experimentor M^r. Hailes[40] the Author of the
vegetable Statics. There were other noble Philosophers who have shone
in different parts of Philosophy, viz. M^r. Lock[41] the celebrated Author
of the Essay on the human Understanding, who contributed more than
any other to banish from the schools that unintelligible Jargon, those
insignificant Subtilties & perplext Logomachies which had prevailed
hitherto, & who gave us a simple but elegant history of the progress
& operation of the human Mind; Cumberland[42] who gave us a beautiful detail of the laws of nature in the moral world. D^r. Samuel Clark[43]
& many others whom it would be endless to name.

36. It may appear a Difficulty to account for the prodigious Variety
of Sentiments & Sects among Philosophers, seeing Truth is one un-
variable thing. But in order to explain this appearance, we need only con-

36. John Keil (1671–1721) and James Keil (1673–1719), native Scots, were, respectively, students of David Gregory and, later, professor of Astronomy at Oxford, and
physician and anatomist.

37. William Derham (1657–1735) was an Anglican clergyman who wrote on natural history and mechanics. His *Physico-Theology* (1713) and his *Astro-Theology* (1715)
were the Boyle lectures of 1711–12.

38. Francis Hawksbee (d. c. 1713) was a noted British experimentalist and member of the Royal Society.

39. John Theophilus Desaguliers (1683–1744) succeeded John Keil as lecturer in
experimental philosophy at Oxford.

40. Stephen Hales (1677–1761), a physiologist and inventor, was a member of the
Royal Society. His *Vegetable Staticks* was first published in 1727. He was also the author of *A Friendly Admonition to Drinkers of Brandy and Other Distilled Spirits*
(1734).

41. John Locke (1632–1704) published his *Essay Concerning Human Understanding* in 1689.

42. Richard Cumberland (1631–1718), of Cambridge, was the author of *De Legibus Naturae* (1672), an attack upon Hobbesian political thought.

43. Samuel Clarke (1675–1729) was rector of St. James Church, Westminster,
most noted for his Boyle lectures, *A Discourse Concerning the Being and Attributes of
God* (London, 1705), vol. 1, and *A Discourse Concerning the Unchangeable Obligations
of Natural Religion and the Truth and Certainty of the Christian Revelation* (London,
1706), vol. 2.

sider, that to the Attainment of every End, certain means are to be applied, & that if the means be either not used at all or misapplied, success can never be expected. Now there is a natural & proper method of attaining to true knowledge as well as any other accomplishment, which if neglected must occasion error & contradiction. It cannot be too often repeated,

> that there is no real knowledge, nor any that can answer a valuable End, but what is gathered or Copyed from nature or from things themselves.
> That the knowledge of Nature is nothing else than the knowledge of facts or realities & their established connections. That no Rules or Precepts of life Can be given or any Scheme of Conduct prescribed, but what must suppose a settled Course of things conducted in a regular uniform manner.
> That in order to denominate those Rules just, & to render those Schemes successful, the Course of things must be understood & observed.
> & that all Philosophy, even the most didactic & practical parts of it, must be drawn from the Observation of things or at least resolved into it; Or which is the same thing, that the knowledge of truth is the knowledge of Fact, & whatever Speculations are not reduceable to the one or the other of these are Chimerical, Vague & uncertain.

We may therefore ascribe the various errors of Philosophers either to the Ambition they had of becoming the founders of Sects, or the Authors of Systems, Or to a prevailing Opinion that Philosophy was good for nothing if it left any thing in the Dark; which mistake would lead people to proceed farther than they were warranted by Observation & experience; Or their mistakes may be owing to the fixing too much upon one part of Nature considered as detached from the rest, taking a particular View of one kind of Objects & Strenuously asserting them to be none other than they represented them. Whereas the true Philosopher who has got a view of the Vast extent of things, & is conscious within how narrow a Circle the faculties of the human mind are confined, & how little the wisest of Men can fully comprehend in the works of nature, will be far from entertaining high notions of the Extent or infallibility of his knowledge, but will proceed cautiously in his enquiries, & having an Attachment to truth alone, without regard to Sect or parties, & their Systems, will embrace truth wherever he finds it, how opposite so ever to his former prepossessions or his future interests.

37. From what has been already advanced in the progress of this short sketch, it appears that Philosophy is a very extensive thing, comprehending all knowledge of whatever kind. But according to the common acceptation of the words it extends only to those Branches of knowledge which are called the Sciences; such are Logic, Metaphysics, Pneumatics, Ethics & Physics. Logic is that Science, which from the observation of the nature of the Understanding & the other speculative powers of the mind, & the Laws of our Perception, & the origin of our knowledge directs us in our enquiries after truth. Metaphysics explains the general properties & relations of all Beings whatsoever, or of things as they have existence; & therefore it may be considered as an introduction to the other Sciences, explaining those general principles which are common to all. Pneumatic or Pneumatology considers the nature & properties of thinking Beings or Spirits, & under this head is comprehended natural Theology. Ethics Enquires into the active & moral part of mans constitution & thence deduces the Rule of Life & Conduct, & explains the several offices or Duties to which he is obliged by the Laws of Nature; To this Head likewise belongs the science of Politics, which treats of the nature of Society, of the foundation of Government & of the reciprocal duties of Governors & Subjects. Physics comprehends all the knowledge we have of material things, & is branched out into Mechanics, or the doctrine of Motion, Hydrostatics, or the Nature & Laws of Fluids; Pneumatics, which treats of the properties of the Air; Optics, which considers vision, light or Colours; Astronomy or the knowledge of the motions & Laws of the heavenly Bodies; Anatomy, or the knowledge of the structure of organized Bodies; & in a word, to this head are reduced all the Sciences that relate in any respect to material things. Mathematics whose Object is Quantity make likewise a part of Philosophy.

This is a general View of the Sciences, their Origin, Progress & several Revolutions, By whom they were chiefly cultivated & to what pitch they are now arrived. They are all referable to one great & universal source, the System or Whole of things originally made & subjected to the government of the most simple, most perfect & most glorious of all beings, the God & Father of all, who is the original Fountain of all knowledge as well as of every other perfection, to whom we are to apply for that Light & wisdom which will conduct us in all our enquiries & crown all our Studies with Success.

The several parts of these different Sciences will afford ample matter for our future Course of Philosophical Exercises.

A Few advices of the late M^r Da. Fordyce to his Scholars
at the end of the Session Concerning Reading

Remember that the end of all reading & learning is, To be Wise, good & useful Creatures.

That no man can be a good Creature who is not Religious, or a lover of God, as well as a friend to men.

In all your reading search for truth & seek knowledge, not for shew or mere talk, but for use; the improvement of your own mind, & the advantage of Others.

Be concerned not to read much but to understand & digest well what you read: And do not think you understand unless you have clear & distinct Ideas, & comprehend the coherence & scope of what you read.

Consider nature or the World as the Volume or Book of God in the meanest page of which his perfections are legible; & Consider Books as Copies of one or more leaves of that Stupendous Volume.

Γνωθι σεαυτον (i.e. Know thyself) Remember this as the most useful maxim of wisdom, without which knowledge will breed Vanity, & learning become matter of Ostentation only.

After Reading Ask yourself what you have learned from it, & often revise what you have Read.

Seek rather to be master of one good Book than to glance over a Score in a Cursory manner. Timeo hominem unius Libri. ⟨I fear men who know a single book.⟩

Do not desire to hasten too fast in the pursuit of knowledge; Advance slowly, & your progress will be sure & lasting.

When you have read much on any subject, set down your own Reflections upon it; this will ascertain & range your Ideas & improve your stile.

In reading history, particularly the lives of great men, Study & imitate their most eminent & useful virtues; & examine your own Character & Disposition by observing what you admire most about them.

Remember that without Diligence & the Influence of heaven, no man ever became great or good. Sine afflatu divino, nimo unguam Viz magnus extitit.[44]

44. In *De Natura Deorum,* book 2, 167, Cicero writes, "Nemo igitur vir magnus sine aliquo adflatu divino umquam fuit," or "No great man ever existed who did not enjoy some portion of divine inspiration."

INDEX

Note: Page numbers followed by *n.* and a number indicate material in footnotes.

This book is set in Adobe Garamond, a modern adaptation by Robert Slimbach of the typeface originally cut around 1540 by the French typographer and printer Claude Garamond. The Garamond face, with its small lowercase height and restrained contrast between thick and thin strokes, is a classic "old-style" face and has long been one of the most influential and widely used typefaces.

Printed on paper that is acid free and meets the requirements of the American National Standard for Permanence of Paper for Printed Library Materials, z39.48-1992. ⊗

Book design by Louise OFarrell, Gainesville, Florida
Typography by Impressions Book and Journal Services, Inc., Madison, Wisconsin
Books printed and bound by Worzalla Publishing Company, Stevens Point, Wisconsin